HUNGER, WHITENESS AND RELIGION IN NEOLIBERAL BRITAIN
An Inequality of Power

Maddy Power

With a foreword by
Kate Pickett

T0366667

First published in Great Britain in 2023 by

Policy Press, an imprint of
Bristol University Press
University of Bristol
1-9 Old Park Hill
Bristol
BS2 8BB
UK
t: +44 (0)117 374 6645
e: bup-info@bristol.ac.uk

Details of international sales and distribution partners are available at
policy.bristoluniversitypress.co.uk

British Library Cataloguing in Publication Data
A catalogue record for this book is available from the British Library

ISBN 978-1-4473-5854-1 hardcover
ISBN 978-1-4473-5855-8 paperback
ISBN 978-1-4473-5856-5 ePub
ISBN 978-1-4473-5857-2 ePdf

Cover design: Liam Roberts

For Sky

Contents

Acknowledgements

Thanks, first and foremost, go to the participants who gave up their time to speak to me about often difficult and immensely personal topics. This book would not have been possible without their openness and generosity. Thank you to all members of the York Food Justice Alliance who threw themselves into research and advocacy on food poverty in York, putting their trust, time and energy into a new and untested project when they all had so much else to do.

I would like to thank the National Institute of Health Research, the Economic and Social Research Council, and Food Power for funding various stages of this project. The statements and opinions in this book are, of course, mine alone and not those of the funders.

I have been privileged to learn from many people, too numerous to name, but particular thanks must go to Kate Pickett and Richard Wilkinson, who have hugely influenced my thinking on poverty and inequality, and who encouraged me to write this book and then provided (much needed) support, detailed feedback and food along the way.

I am grateful to friends and colleagues who have commented on the text. Neil Small for his comments on Chapters 2, 4 and 5; Hilary Graham for her feedback on Chapters 6 and 7; and Allison, Lorrie, Suzanne, Natalie and Amy for their thoughts on parts of Chapter 8. I am also very grateful to an anonymous reviewer, whose insightful and thoughtful comments on the first draft much improved the text.

This has not been an easy year for any of us, and it certainly wasn't the easiest year to write a book, but the process has been made possible by the support, advice and inspiration of friends and colleagues. Special thanks to: Ruth Patrick, Kayleigh Garthwaite, Katie Pybus and Sabine Goodwin.

The team at Policy Press, especially Alison Shaw, Laura Vickers and Caroline Astley, were supportive of the book from the start, pushing me to sharpen and fine tune my ideas. I would like to thank them for their patience and kindness throughout the writing process.

Lastly, thanks to my parents – Suzy and Patrick – for your love, encouragement and seemingly limitless support, and to my sisters. To baby Astrid who arrived in the final stages of this book and kept me constant and very sweet company while working on the proofs. At every stage in the writing and editing of this book, I relied on Sky Duthie for guidance, advice and support. Thanks for the countless conversations about research, for reading the manuscript multiple times and providing brilliant comments, for introducing me to mutual aid and Kropotkin, and for uncomplainingly taking on (all) the housework so that I could write this book. Without Sky, there would be no book.

Foreword

Kate Pickett

Living in the US for a number of years, I used to feel – I'm now ashamed to say – quite smug about coming from the UK, a country with a proper social security system. I used to view the very public provision of food aid – in soup kitchens and food banks – as a powerful signal of something rotten at the heart of America. The US's refusal, by the state and by its citizens, to protect the health and wellbeing of all its citizens, particularly the most vulnerable, felt uncivilised, almost Victorian, as if its democracy had not yet grown up enough to recognise its responsibilities. It was all of a piece with the US's non-provision of universal access to health care or of paid maternity leave, its refusal to sign the international Convention on the Rights of the Child (putting it in the same camp as Somalia and South Sudan, the only other countries not to have signed). It looked like the unpleasant underbelly of American exceptionalism.

I was, therefore, shocked to come home to the UK in the 2000s and find a very different society from the one I had left in the 1980s. I returned in the time of New Labour, having missed many of the Thatcher and all of the Major years, and the changes to British life were glaringly obvious. America no longer seemed exceptional: the UK was beginning to resemble the US in myriad unpleasant ways. Inequality had risen dramatically; whole regions had been devastated and left behind after the loss of manufacturing and the decline of trade unions. Council housing and other public assets had been sold off, utilities and transport companies privatised. Public services and local government had been marketised, managerialised and underfunded. Although public spending boomed for a while under New Labour, and pensioner and child poverty were reduced, there was never a serious reversal of the Thatcherite legacy; the Britain I came home to was still firmly astride the neoliberal bandwagon.

The contemporary public discourse around hunger in the UK is often focused on its being a new problem, a post-2010 problem, an austerity problem. And it is, of course, true that dramatic rises in the use of food banks and other forms of food aid have accompanied the draconian restructuring and punitive character of the UK's welfare system since the implementation of austerity by the Conservative–Liberal Democrat Coalition Government in 2010. But food aid in the UK has deeper roots and the ways in which it is structured and the forces that have shaped it are more complex. In this book, Maddy Power digs beneath the simple story to uncover a more complicated narrative, one in which neoliberalism has not only driven austerity and the rise of food aid but has also shaped the very nature of that provision, and even the ways that we, and its recipients, look at it. Woven into that narrative are the warp and weft of religion and race – of Whiteness – and she disentangles them for us adeptly, giving powerful insight into the shameful state the UK is in, as the sixth-largest economy in the world.

This is an academic book, of impressive rigour, that asks how we came to this. But it concerns an emotive, real-world human need – to be able to feed oneself, and feed one's family, with dignity and autonomy. Importantly, Maddy Power's scholarship is grounded in making connections with people experiencing food insecurity and food aid that give expression to their lived experiences and expertise. Her research is underpinned by her responsiveness to them, her listening skills and her practical application of values and ethics of community, cooperation and co-production. And her research, in return, supports their autonomy to act collectively to make changes, directly challenging the inequality and poverty, the power and the privilege that create hunger and food insecurity in 21st-century Britain. So, this is a timely book, not only for its important subject matter, but also as an example of the kind of research, advocacy and collaboration that the academy needs to help us co-create the conditions required for social change.

1

Introduction

'My first visit to a food bank, I was given some pasta and some chopped tomatoes; I was given some passata, and I was basically given tomato puree and then loads of beans and things. And I went home and I cried! I cried! I thought, how am I meant to feed my family on that? What, what, what are we gonna do!? So I thought, right, I'll have a look on the internet and I started scouring the internet but every recipe needed either meat or fresh veg, and I thought well, this is just, you know, ludicrous, what am I gonna do?'

Tina

Tina, a disabled lone parent, laughs in despair as she describes to me the tinned, dried and unappetising rations she was given by the local food bank. Like many of those living in poverty, Tina had been reluctant to use the local food bank, in this case run by the Trussell Trust.[1] The additional costs of fuel, food and clothes in the winter months had battered the carefully managed small household budget and, faced with hungry children, she had capitulated and sought out referral to the food bank.

The food she received was inadequate, based on 'ludicrous' assumptions that people would be content with meals consisting of dried pasta, jarred sauce and tinned beans. Tina was poor but she was, after all, not living in a war zone or in the midst of a climate disaster. The experience of seeking help from the food bank was demoralising, if not insulting, and Tina was adamant that whatever the food shortages in their household she would not return.

Tina's experience is, nevertheless, not one of those heard in the vignettes of food bank users carefully curated by powerful organisations like the Trussell Trust and FareShare,[2] vignettes which present a grateful food aid 'client',[3] failed by the social security system but saved from hunger by food charity. These accounts may acknowledge the shame and stigma associated with food charity, but they do not admit the role which food aid may play in creating stigma, upholding inequalities, and maintaining the very status quo which food charities claim, in public statements and campaigns, to reject.

Scratch beneath the surface of these good Samaritan narratives of food aid and food insecurity and there is a complex and murky scene. In this new and critical reading, food aid is not only a consequence of neoliberal[4] policies but is itself an industry riddled with neoliberal governmentality,[5] governing and controlling people by maintaining a pretence of freedom – of choice and agency – despite obvious power inequalities (see also Möller, 2021); an industry which upholds neoliberal ideas and maintains inequalities of class, race, religion and gender via the distribution of food. In this reading, food aid sustains White privilege[6] and, in so doing, exacerbates racial inequities and racial precarity (see also de Souza, 2019). Embedded within a neoliberal system in which there appears to be no alternative, people in poverty and with experience of food insecurity demonise and stigmatise female and racialised Others for their poverty (Power et al, 2020c), while struggling themselves to maintain an image of economic success and self-reliance in the face of insecure, low-wage employment and a punitive social security system (see also Garthwaite, 2017; Wright et al, 2020).

Scratch beneath the surface even further, however, and there is an alternative and nuanced narrative: one in which the food aid sector is immensely varied, embodying neoliberal individualistic ideologies; radical grassroots organisations, which reject notions of self-reliance and seek to subvert the contemporary corporatised, commodified food system (see also Goodman et al, 2011; Nyman, 2019); and organisations which straddle this binary, incorporating both individualistic and radical ethics. In this narrative, the lived experience of food insecurity, like that of food aid, is shaped not only by neoliberal norms but by gendered, racial[7] and religious identities (and the intersections between them). These personalised and localised identities foster shared experiences and solidarities, giving rise to alternative modes of food redistribution outside the purview of formal food aid.

The analysis in this book is based upon fieldwork conducted between 2014 and 2020 in two cities in the North of England: Bradford and York. As I explain below, York is a fairly ethnically homogeneous city with a predominantly White British and large Christian population; Bradford, by contrast, is a multi-ethnic, multi-faith city with a large Pakistani British and Muslim population and a sizeable Christian population. Within the context of broader socio-political change, the book hence focuses in detail on White British and Pakistani British people, and on Islam and Christianity.

The book draws on and develops existing published work on the prevalence, causes, health consequences and lived experience of food insecurity and food aid (Power et al, 2017a; 2017d; 2018a; 2018b; 2021a; Pybus et al, 2021); the interplay of ethnicity, religion and food aid (Power et al, 2017b; 2017c); and the politics of food aid and food insecurity (Power et al, 2020c; Power and Small, 2021). The book brings together for the first time and goes beyond this body of work to develop new theoretical and empirical insights – not limited to but including: the manifestation of Whiteness and racism in food banks and other food projects; the theological underpinnings and expression of faith in food charity; the ideological foundations of mutual aid in food charity; and food-based social solidarity among minority ethnic and working-class women.

Some essential terminology

Food insecurity

The Food and Agriculture Organization of the United Nations (FAO) defines food insecurity as a 'lack of regular access to enough safe and nutritious food for normal growth and development and an active and healthy life' (FAO, 2019). The FAO measures the prevalence of moderate or severe food insecurity across more than 140 countries via the Food Insecurity Experience Scale. According to the FAO's categorisation, the – highly emotive – concept of hunger is defined as 'severe food insecurity'. People experiencing 'moderate food insecurity' may not, in the FAO's definition, necessarily experience hunger, but they may face uncertainties about their ability to obtain food and may be forced to compromise on the quality and/or quantity of food due to a lack of resources (FAO et al, 2019).

In 2019, an estimated 750 million people worldwide were considered to be severely food insecure, according to the FAO definition, equating to roughly one in every ten people (FAO et al, 2020). Hunger and food insecurity have historically been associated with the Global South (Mayer and Anderson, 2020), and today cases of moderate and severe food insecurity (roughly 2 billion people) are primarily concentrated in low- and middle-income countries (FAO et al, 2017). Since the 1980s, however, food insecurity has increasingly also been a conspicuous feature of the Global North, affecting an estimated 8 per cent of the population in North America and northern Europe in 2017–19 (FAO et al, 2020).

This widely adopted FAO definition of food insecurity arguably reduces food to its nutritional components and physiological benefits, neglecting the social and cultural components of food and food experiences.[8] Sue Anderson's (1990) highly cited definition of food insecurity, adopted in this book, encapsulates not only the nutritional role of food but the critical importance of socially acceptable access to food; in this definition, food aid is antithetical to food security. According to Anderson, food security is:

> Access by all people at all times to enough food for an active, healthy life and includes at a minimum a) the ready availability of nutritionally adequate and safe foods, and b) the assured ability to acquire acceptable foods in socially acceptable ways … food insecurity exists whenever the availability of nutritionally adequate and safe foods or the ability to acquire safe foods in socially acceptable ways is limited or uncertain. (Anderson, 1990: 1560)

In the United Kingdom (UK), the concept of food insecurity can be used interchangeably with food poverty, with the former more commonly found in academic analyses (see, for example, Dowler and O'Connor, 2012; Garthwaite et al, 2015; Loopstra et al, 2016; Purdam et al, 2019), and the latter encountered in third sector publications and advocacy (see Cooper et al, 2014; Tait, 2015; Kellogg's/CEBR, 2017).

Food aid

The dominant media profile of the Trussell Trust food bank network and their related tendency to, not only dominate (Wells and Caraher, 2014), but also control discourse around food charity can foster the impression that food aid in the UK is one-dimensional: a question of food banks distributing food parcels to 'clients' vetted by a referral system (Trussell Trust, 2021a). However, food aid in the UK and internationally is notably multi-faceted:

> [Food aid is an] umbrella term encompassing a range of large-scale and small local activities aiming to help people meet food needs, often on a short-term basis during crisis or immediate difficulty … relieving symptoms of household or individual level food insecurity and poverty. (Lambie-Mumford et al, 2014: 15)

Food aid can also be called 'food charity' (Riches and Silvasti, 2014a), 'community food assistance' (Nnakwe, 2008; Kurtz et al, 2019) or 'community food assets' (Graven et al, 2021). Some types of food aid are commonly described as 'emergency' provision (Salvation Army, 2021; Trussell Trust, 2021c). Emergency food systems, including food banks and soup kitchens, aim to supply food to people in urgent need on a temporary and supplemental basis at no cost (Caruso, 2019). The institutionalisation of emergency food systems in much of the Global North (see Riches and Silvasti, 2014a), particularly in North America, has rendered the notion of 'emergency' food aid spurious, if not meaningless. Indeed, what were once sources of temporary or emergency food have become regular and sometimes primary food sources for people on a low income (Caruso, 2019). 'Non-emergency' food aid encompasses a heterogeneous set of organisations providing food in some form, ranging from community cafes and community supermarkets to urban agriculture (Sustain, 2021). In these organisations, food may be provided alongside other services, or food provision may be part of a broader set of aims. As the food aid sector has expanded, so too has the terminology used to define the organisations working within it. Table 1.1 sets out basic definitions, to hopefully bring clarity to a large, expanding and unwieldy field.

Table 1.1: Terminology associated with food aid

Terminology	Description
Food bank	Provides free emergency food parcels, often, but not always, requiring referral from a third party.
'Independent' food bank	Food bank which is an independent organisation, unaffiliated with a wider network such as the Trussell Trust or the Salvation Army.
Soup kitchen	Provides onsite emergency free food provision.
Soup run	Provides mobile emergency free food provision.
Day centre and drop-in centre	Offers various forms of food provision, free or subsidised, as part of wider support, which can be targeted at particular demographic groups.
Community cafe	Provides low cost or subsidised food, often with very low overhead and staff costs.
Social food charity	Offers food prepared from surplus and locally grown ingredients, to be eaten communally, for very low cost or on a pay-as-you-feel basis.
Pay-as-you-feel (PAYF)	A participative pricing mechanism which delegates the price determination to each customer and requires the seller to accept any price. Also known as 'pay-what-you-want' (Kim et al, 2009: 44).
Food recovery organisations	A blanket term capturing organisations that supply food from corporate donations, including manufacturers and retailers, farms and other sources, to frontline charities and community groups.
Surplus food	Food distributed to and used by charities that would otherwise be thrown away by wholesalers, manufacturers and retailers.
Community kitchen	Community-focused cooking-type programme providing an opportunity for a small group of people to meet regularly to communally prepare and possibly also eat a meal.
Community supermarket	Supermarket where food is sold as groceries at below market prices, also known as a Social Solidarity Store or food pantry; often restricted to people on a low income.

(continued)

Table 1.1: Terminology associated with food aid (continued)

Terminology	Description
Food co-operative	Community-owned and -operated food distributor selling low-cost, sometimes organic, food.
Community gardens and growing initiatives	Plots of urban land on which community members can grow flowers or foodstuffs for personal or collective benefit. Community gardeners share certain resources, such as space, tools, and water. Though sometimes facilitated by social service agencies, charities, housing authorities, or grassroots associations, community gardens nevertheless tend to remain under the control of the gardeners themselves (Glover, 2003).
Food desert	An area where cheap and varied food is only accessible to those who have private transport or are able to pay the costs of public transport if this is available. Access to a cheaper and wider range of healthy food for some of the groups who need it most is extremely restricted (see Cummins and MacIntyre, 2002).

What is hunger? Food insecurity, food poverty and how we got here

In 2010, the terms 'food insecurity' and 'food poverty' were little known in the UK. Poverty was endemic but food poverty, denoting a situation in which household income is too low to enable access to adequate food, did not receive much attention and food banks were barely known. Today, food banks have been incorporated at a local and national level as a vital front-line response to poverty; food aid organisations have received multimillion-pound funding from national government (Gov.uk, 2020a); and, amid the COVID-19 pandemic, food bank staff were re-categorised as 'key workers' 'caring for the vulnerable' (Trussell Trust, 2021d).

Reflecting the creeping normalisation and institutionalisation of food banks (discussed in Chapter 2), since the early 2010s research on food poverty and food insecurity in the UK has grown from a minor topic in social policy to a rapidly expanding interdisciplinary field. Food poverty, or food insecurity, has been successfully constituted as an object of study across disciplines, predominantly shaped by an empiricist paradigm (Loopstra et al, 2015; Prayogo et al, 2017; Sosenko et al, 2019; Loopstra, 2020). Poverty, meanwhile, has been presented as an object of scientific study – it has been medicalised – through a focus on, often behavioural, 'risk' factors – on whether people can cook and what people know about 'healthy' food (Begley et al, 2019). The key concerns are precisely defining (O'Connor et al, 2016) and measuring (Smith et al, 2018) food poverty. Critique and advocacy are sidelined in favour of scientific understanding, and policy impact is presented as a corollary of a more accurate characterisation of this new phenomenon. While food insecurity and food poverty may have the advantage of capturing broader and chronic anxieties about access to food, the terms arguably sanitise and medicalise older concepts of hunger, starvation and destitution (Vernon, 2007), treating hunger as an individual medical rather than a social problem, one which can be solved through targeted food-based interventions with specific populations (see also Möller, 2021). In this framing, poverty, a problem of inadequate income, is presented as *food* poverty, a question of nutrition, cooking and eating.

It is perfectly reasonable to ask whether this book on food insecurity and food aid is also part of this new and burgeoning field of research on a medicalised version of poverty, and in many ways it is. Yet, unlike much research in this area, the book adopts a critical approach, problematising food insecurity and food aid, and asking whether poverty can indeed be disaggregated into distinct types, such as food poverty (see Crossley et al, 2019 for a critical discussion of the disaggregation of poverty). Chapters 3, 4 and 5 question the rise of food aid and interrogate the processes and purposes – political, religious and racial – that this particular form of charity may serve. Chapters 6 and 7 consider the notion of food insecurity, exploring whether it is in fact a symptom of poverty and, as such, requires an income-based response. The terms 'food insecurity' and 'food poverty' are employed with keen awareness that they are social constructions, moderately new to the UK context, and must be scrutinised and problematised rather than accepted as fact.

The setting

A brief history of Bradford: 1850 to the present day

> The England admired throughout the world is the England that keeps open house. … History shows us that the countries that have opened their doors have gained.
>
> JB Priestley, *English Journey*

Writing in 1934, JB Priestly, English novelist, playwright, screenwriter, broadcaster and social commentator, once described as 'the old rhinoceros of English letters' (CP Snow in Day, 1969), describes the Bradford of his childhood, a prosperous, cosmopolitan and evolving city; a city in which migrants augmented the character and success of the place immeasurably. Describing the German-Jews of early 20th century Bradford, Priestly writes: 'A dash of the Rhine and the Oder found its way into our grim runnel – "t'mucky beck." Bradford was determinedly Yorkshire and provincial, yet some of its suburbs reached as far as Frankfurt and Leipzig' (p 161). Today, the suburbs of Bradford reach much further than Germany, to Eastern Europe and beyond, to South Asia. Indeed, Bradford, a city and metropolitan area in West Yorkshire, has attracted substantial numbers of migrants since the industrial revolution (Small, 2012). In 1851, there were roughly 9,850 Irish-born inhabitants in Bradford, around 10 per cent of the population. Their immigration was motivated by the demise of the native Irish textile industry and the continued subdivision of land, as well as by economic expansion in Bradford itself (Bradford Heritage Recording Unit, 1987). Largely confined to the inner-city area, the Irish constituted the poorest group in Bradford, concentrated in jobs such as labouring, peddling, washing and hand textiles. Although the major movement of the Irish into Bradford was over by the mid-1850s, there was steady migration of Irish people throughout the latter half of the 19th and across the entirety of the 20th century, reflected in contemporary Irish cultural, recreational and social facilities and in the location of long-standing Roman Catholic churches. As with other ethnic groups, religious institutions have acted as crucial centres of support and solidarity among Irish migrants (Bradford Heritage Recording Unit, 1987).

The second major group of migrants, European merchants, differed significantly from the Irish, tending to be wealthy, well educated and cosmopolitan. Drawn to Bradford by its thriving textile industry and opportunities for global exchange, they provided a vital impetus to the growth of Bradford's trading power with the development of an efficient international marketing system. Unlike the Irish, their religious principles tended to be muted and their religious institutions only partially embodied the other social functions associated with the Catholic Church.

Immigration between the late 19th century and the Second World War – a period of relative economic decline – was notably slower and slimmer. The interval saw the arrival of Italians, Belgians and Russians, and Polish, German and Austrian Jews. In the immediate post-war period, substantial numbers of Central and Eastern Europeans migrated to Bradford, the majority of whom worked, at least initially, in textiles. As with the Irish, ethnicity, nationalism and religious sentiment, combined with independent social, cultural, recreational, retailing and religious organisations, created a distinctive ethnic community.

The largest migrant group to Bradford – New Commonwealth and Pakistani migrants – was the most recent. Changes to the local textile industry in the mid-1950s precipitated a sharp increase in South Asian migration into

Bradford. South Asian, predominantly Pakistani, migration consisted of a first wave of male workers, recruited by the owners of mills to counteract staff shortages at a time of expansion in demand, followed by migration of workers' families (Bradford Heritage Recording Unit, 1987). There has been continuing immigration since the 1950s, linked to employment opportunities and the reconstitution of families (Small, 2012). The considerable majority of Bradford's South Asians are of Pakistani origin and are Muslim. Of these, the largest single group originates from the predominantly rural Mirpur region, part of the province of Azad Jammu and Kashmir. Today, the South Asian population has matured into a three-generational community (Kalra, 2000). As with the Irish, religious institutions have often acted as crucial ethnic support agencies, a role facilitated by the geographical distribution of Bradford's Muslim population, the majority of whom live within five square miles of the city centre – an area containing roughly 44 mosques (McLoughlin, 2005). Bradford's Pakistani community retains close links with their homeland, through marriage, connections between mosques, frequent travel, the retention of traditional Pakistani practices, financial support of family members in Pakistan and 'second' homes (Small, 2012).

Bradford has a population of over half a million (ONS, 2011) rendering it the sixth-largest city in the UK (in terms of population) (Gill, 2015). Population growth in the Metropolitan District is among the highest in England: in 2020, the fertility rate in Bradford was 1.95 children per woman, higher than the total fertility rate for England as a whole, which was 1.59 children per woman (ONS, 2020). At the time of the 2011 census (at the time of writing the latest for which data is available), 64 per cent of the population of Bradford classified themselves as White British. At 20 per cent, Bradford had the largest proportion of people of Pakistani ethnic origin in England, an increase of nearly 6 per cent since the 2001 Census, contributing to its large Muslim population (24 per cent). Bangladeshi, 'Mixed or Multiple ethnic groups', 'Other Asian', 'Black/African/Caribbean/Black British', and 'Other' ethnic groups, inclusive of Eastern European and Roma populations, also saw an increase in their numbers between the 2001 and 2011 censuses (ONS, 2011).

Bradford is the 19th most deprived local authority (out of 326) in England as measured by the Index of Multiple Deprivation (Gill, 2015), which covers aspects such as area-level income, employment, education, health and crime. Bradford scores substantially below country averages on most health indicators, even in comparison with other English cities marked by social and ethnic inequalities such as London, Birmingham and Manchester. For instance, infant mortality was 7.9 per 1,000 for the period January 2008 to December 2010, compared with a national average of 4.6 per 1,000, and life expectancy is lower than the national average for both men and women (Choudhury et al, 2012).

A brief history of York: AD 71 to the present day

The City of York, situated in North Yorkshire, differs markedly from Bradford in both its long history and contemporary demography. Founded as a city by the Romans in AD 71, York was a pivotal military centre throughout the Roman occupation of Britain. David Olusoga, the British-Nigerian historian and broadcaster, writes of an ethnically and racially diverse Roman York, revealed by the discovery, in 1901, of the now famous Ivory Bangle Lady, a woman of high social status, from the upper strata of Roman York. In 2009, 16 centuries after her death, the remains of this woman were subjected to radioisotope analysis illuminating, for the first time, that she was likely to have been a mixed race woman of North African descent, and either she, her parents or her grandparents had come from Mediterranean North Africa. Such relocation from provinces in North Africa to those of Northern England was not unknown in Roman Britain; Olusoga writes, 'the mobility that was a feature of the late Roman Empire may well have meant that parts of third-century Eboracum [York] may have been more ethnically and racially diverse than parts of York today in the twenty-first century' (Olusoga, 2016: 32).

An important trading post and powerful ecclesiastical province throughout the Middle Ages, by the 18th century, York had become a social and cultural centre for the wealthy of the region. The arrival of large numbers of Irish immigrants in the 1840s contributed to rapid population growth in the 19th century, a period in which York's prosperity was largely a consequence of its position as a major hub of the railway network and its success as a confectionery manufacturing centre, an identity which it maintains today despite the closure of many of the city's main confectionery manufacturers. Population growth in the 20th century was slow and at times stagnant – presenting a sharp contrast with the burgeoning industrial Yorkshire cities of Bradford, Leeds and Sheffield – and arguably contributes to York's contemporary character as a walking city with a large and vibrant tourist industry (Feinstein, 1981).

As of 2019, the City of York housed a population of 210,000 people (ONS, 2019), a growth of 9 per cent on 2001. The population of York has become increasingly ethnically diverse since the late 20th century; however, the city remains relatively ethnically homogeneous compared with the surrounding cities of Leeds, Bradford and Newcastle. In 2011, a large majority of York residents identified themselves as 'White British' (90 per cent), a decrease of 5 per cent since 2001; the categories 'Other White', 'Mixed/Multiple ethnic group', 'Asian' and 'Black/African Caribbean' all saw small increases in their numbers between the 2001 and 2011 censuses (City of York Council, 2011). In the 2011 Census, roughly 60 per cent of York residents described their religion as Christian, and York had a lower proportion of people identifying as Muslim (1 per cent) than regionally (6 per cent) and nationally (5 per cent). Almost one third of York residents

(30 per cent) considered themselves to have 'no religion', higher than the national average (25 per cent) (City of York Council, 2011).

At first blush, York appears to be a relatively affluent city. It has a lower percentage of workless households, and higher than average earnings compared with other parts of Yorkshire and the Humber (ONS, 2019), alongside a buoyant local economy due in part to tourism. Wages, for both those working in York and those living in the city but working elsewhere, saw an overall increase of 16 per cent between 2015 and 2019 (City of York Council, 2019). There are, nevertheless, considerable inequalities in York. The city is, on the one hand, a thriving northern centre. Its economy is strong; its population are well educated, relatively affluent and healthy; and it enjoys a rich built and natural environment. Two fifths of the population live in places that are in the best 20 per cent of areas in England. At the same time, the city has eight areas – home to roughly 13,000 people – in the 20 per cent most deprived areas nationally and one in the 10 per cent most deprived (Newby and Denison, 2012). In these areas, and for those with low incomes elsewhere in the city, the symptoms of deprivation are palpable: shorter life expectancy, lower educational attainment, unemployment, and child poverty. High living costs and severe housing shortages in the city compound disadvantage. There is insufficient housing in the city across tenure types, driving up prices and rents beyond the reach of those on even average incomes. Indeed, only 12 per cent of two-bedroomed properties in the city are classed as affordable within 2018/19 Local Housing Allowance rates (Crisis, 2019).

The study

The two interlinked studies in the cities of Bradford and York that constitute the study as a whole had very different origins and rationales. Disillusioned with the introspective and individualistic world of London's think tanks, I left my post in a small third sector organisation to pursue a PhD at the University of York. At the time, understanding of food insecurity and rapidly growing food bank use in Britain was in its infancy; quantitative survey data was scarce and most studies tended to focus on one or two food banks providing in-depth localised accounts of food bank characteristics and the lived experience of their use. Possibly reflecting the quantitative data available and the interests and geographical location of food bank researchers, there was no published work and seemingly no ongoing research into how ethnicity and religion may shape the provision of food aid and the prevalence and lived experience of food insecurity.

The choice of Bradford was motivated by the availability of quantitative data on food insecurity, as well as the religious and ethnic demography of the city, providing an opportunity to explore in detail the interplay of ethnicity, religion, food insecurity and food aid. The pivot of the project was a pre-existing dataset on food insecurity among mothers in Bradford, collected between 2009 and 2010. The information in this dataset, known as the Born in Bradford 1000 study (BiB1000) (Bryant et al, 2013), could be linked with demographic information from a wider survey incorporating the same women (the Born in Bradford Cohort Study; Wright et al, 2012). This would provide a new, unique and detailed dataset on food insecurity among mothers, at a time of rising food bank use but limited knowledge about both food bank use and food insecurity.

Exploring Bradford, I found an engaging and endlessly interesting city; 19th-century mills, a remnant of the city's thriving industrial past, rose up out of rows of back-to-back terraced houses, mosques, churches and high streets. I encountered a lively voluntary sector, steadfastly committed to the wellbeing of Bradford's diverse population. The study quickly expanded from analysis of the nature of food insecurity among women in the Born in Bradford quantitative datasets to a broader exploration of the character and diversity of voluntary sector responses to food insecurity in the city. Over one year (2014–15), I interviewed public health professionals and food aid providers across Bradford, asking how they distributed food and who used their services; exploring their religious and secular motivations for food charity; and unpicking the relationship between local food charities, government and business. Keen to avoid the objectification that can come from quantitative analysis of survey data alone, in 2016 I held small discussion groups with mothers living in low-income areas of Bradford. Over a couple of hours, we talked about experiences of food shortages, how they maintained sufficient food for themselves and their family, and their opinions on and experiences of food banks and other forms of food aid. I spoke with White British and Pakistani British women, on occasion working with an interpreter to translate dialogue from Urdu to English.

Despite some engagement with community groups in Bradford to identify suitable food aid providers to interview and arrange discussion groups with women living on a low income, the research in the city always felt extractive: information was extracted from a range of participants who had little say in the research process itself. As a result of this, the work in York – motivated in part by an intention to explore food insecurity and food aid in a demographically different city – adopted an alternative approach. As a recent immigrant to the city, I was aware of my position as an outsider, a southerner in the medieval Capital of the North. Disheartened by the aloof world of academia, often detached from the concerns of its immediate (geographical) community, I got on my bike and cycled across the city, talking to community groups, citizens, health and social care professionals, local authority employees, and community activists about food, poverty and growing food aid use in York. I ate and chatted with fellow diners in numerous community and pay-as-you-feel cafes, talking about why they were there, how often they visited, what they thought of the food, and about life in York more generally. These conversations illuminated community commitment to tackling seemingly growing food insecurity in the city, but also revealed a lack of information on the nature and extent of food insecurity and food aid use in York, and limited collaboration surrounding efforts to address it.

These conversations led to an advocacy and research collaboration between community stakeholders and the University of York: the York Food Justice Alliance (York Food Justice Alliance, 2021). Between 2018 and 2019, I worked in partnership with alliance members to understand the extent and experience of food insecurity in York, and to co-develop a 'food poverty action plan' (see Power, 2019). Together, we designed and administered a survey exploring food insecurity and food bank use among parents with children aged 4 to 11 years in York; mapped and assessed the range and inclusivity of community food aid in the city; and conducted focus groups with parents living on a low income to explore lived experiences of food and food aid use in contexts of poverty and low income. This co-produced research underpinned meaningful policy impact, precipitating the establishment of a Food Poverty Scrutiny Group within the local authority, a key demand of the York Food Justice Alliance.

Positionality in the research process

There are valid questions to be asked about why a White British researcher with no experience of poverty, racism or transnational migration, and with no religion, should write a book on the interplay of food aid, food insecurity, ethnicity and religion. One, perfectly reasonable answer, is that I shouldn't; that I should leave this field to other researchers with direct experience of poverty, racism and faith. Another answer proposes that, like White researchers working on the intersection of race and gender, or men leading projects on maternal health, for example, it is possible to study issues of which I have no direct experience. However, doing so requires frank reflection on my positionality, on how my identity may shape my engagement with the topic and influence my interactions with the communities and participants in the study. As a White, middle-class scholar I am a consequence of, embedded within, and benefit from many of the oppressive and unequal systems that I seek to critique. My own narrow life experience may compromise my ability to empathise with the individuals and groups who feature in this book, without humility and considerable effort on my part. The analysis here seeks to reflect on, rather than to interpret, the experiences of participants in the light of their narratives, in the context of the relevant literature, and with keen awareness of my own inevitably limiting epistemological frameworks and points of reference (see Crotty, 1998).

It is highly likely that interactions between myself and participants were influenced by my professional background; by my own assumptions and those of participants; and by my ethnicity (White British), my gender (female) and my age (under 30 at the time of the fieldwork). In interviews and focus groups, participants were aware that the interviewer (myself) was a researcher from an academic, non-clinical background; however, unless asked explicitly by participants, I did not disclose my (non-)religious beliefs. It is impossible to know with any certainty the extent to which participants' knowledge about my professional background and consideration of my White British ethnicity (as discussed in Chapter 2, an identity intimately associated with power and privilege) impacted on their willingness to talk openly about experiences, or how this knowledge may have shaped the dialogue. In particular, it is possible that a perceived religious and ethnic difference between myself and Pakistani British and Muslim representatives of food aid – coupled with potential fear of racist response – motivated them to downplay the importance of religion in the provision of food aid – a feature of my conversations with some service providers, addressed in Chapter 4.

The manner in which my ethnic and religious identity may have influenced interactions with participants is, however, not straightforward.[9] Pakistani British women spoke more openly and at greater length about the impact of their faith on their experiences of food and poverty than White British women. While a potential reason for this may be the relative importance of religion to Pakistani British Muslim women compared to the White British Christian and secular women interviewed, it is also possible that my perceived no/different religion and simultaneous interest in Islam led participants to explain the role of religion at greater length than may have been the case if I myself had been Pakistani British and/or Muslim and knowledge of the issues at hand was assumed. Participants disclosed intimate details about their domestic and familial circumstances, often discussing the inclinations and behaviours of their male partners. It is possible that my gender influenced participants' responsiveness on traditionally gendered issues, such as family life and marital conflict.

I was motivated above all to conduct the studies in Bradford and York by a commitment to social justice, to illuminate stark food inequalities and inequities. Moving from think tanks to academia, I brought policy expertise and a political science background into what began as an epidemiological inquiry, so introducing a fresh synthesis of perspectives, ideas and methods to the study of food insecurity. As the work progressed, I shifted towards collaborative research, creating a space for voices and experiences that may not otherwise enter this arena to shape debates. Am I the best person to undertake this research? Possibly not, but I hope at least to have opened up a conversation that others can take forward.

Finally, it is worth noting that as both a researcher and a participant, I have been immersed in food poverty networks for several years, as Co-Chair of Trustees of the Independent Food Aid Network (2019–21) and Chair of the

York Food Justice Alliance (2018–20). This experience informs my analysis and is the basis for some of the observations in this book, supplementing the empirics. Notable observations drawn from my experience as part of these networks include the Whiteness of the UK food activism scene; possibilities for participatory justice in food aid; and histories of food aid networks among Black and Asian communities in the UK and the United States (US).

Chapter summary

The chapters progress from analysis of the socio–political, religious and racial context and characteristics of food aid to consideration of the gendered, racial and religious lived experience of food. Chapter 2 sets out the theoretical framework that underpins analysis throughout the book. It introduces the idea of neoliberal governmentality, explaining how through this particularly insidious form of neoliberalism, state oversight and control embeds itself beyond centres and institutions of power into all corners of society – into communities, food aid and family life. The chapter shows how religious actors and organisations collude – perhaps unintentionally – with the ruling power to uphold the status quo, and describes how the state, in the form of racial neoliberalism, creates and exploits racial divisions and inequalities to maintain elite power and White privilege.

Informed by these ideas of neoliberal governmentality, religious neoliberalism and racial neoliberalism, the following chapters, 3, 4 and 5, explore the ideological, sociological and cultural underpinnings of food aid in the UK. Chapter 3 elucidates the fusion of neoliberal governmentality and food charity, showing how surveillance and neoliberal ethics are woven into practice and discourse within some food aid. The chapter also, however, disputes the neoliberal genesis of 21st-century food charity, revealing the 19th-century liberal roots of what is often thought to be a modern phenomenon. Chapter 4 explores the interplay of food aid, neoliberalism and religion in the UK; it questions whether religious food charity is a consequence of neoliberal state retrenchment or motivated by longstanding religious traditions of service, worship and communion. Drawing on narratives of service providers, the chapter scrutinises the exclusionary implications of religious food aid and argues that power inequalities, inherent to faith-based food charity, fatally undermine possibilities for participation and solidarity advocated by some service providers. Chapter 5 continues this analysis of exclusionary food aid, explaining how a particular construct of 'Whiteness' – or White privilege – predominates in some food aid, successfully erasing the needs and even the existence of minority ethnic groups.

Chapter 6 moves outside the food aid arena to explore the lives of those who exist in poverty but who do not necessarily access food aid. Drawing on quantitative survey data and extensive conversations with people in and at risk of food insecurity, the chapter unpicks how neoliberal policies and narratives manifest in people's lives. It highlights the systemic factors – income, social security, housing, living costs and transport – which create food insecurity and determine lived experiences of food, and shows how state power and the power of capital manipulates and coerces people living in poverty at every level of society, including within food charities.

Continuing discussions in Chapter 5 on the influence of particular social constructs of race – of Whiteness – on the character of some food aid, Chapter 7 considers the broader impact of ethno-religious identities on the likelihood and the lived experience of food insecurity. It explicates the varying political and ethical frameworks that may underpin lived experiences of food in contexts of poverty – neoliberal ethics of independence, hospitality and mutual aid – arguing that, in some marginalised communities *and* in some food aid providers, mutual aid is the predominant ethical system. Chapter 8 concludes with key reflections on the ideological, socio–political and cultural context and characteristics of contemporary food aid and food insecurity. The book closes with three short – and I hope enlightening – stories from radical and progressive organisations addressing food insecurity in the US.

Notes

[1] The Trussell Trust is a UK charity founded on Christian principles that supports a network of over 1,200 food bank centres providing 'emergency' food to people in need. It was founded in 1997 and created the UK Foodbank Network in 2004. Local churches play a vital part in its work, with around 12,000 churches actively involved in donating food and providing venues, volunteers and financial support for food banks. In the financial year, 2019/20, the Trussell Trust included over 120 employees and reported an income of £21.33 million (Trussell Trust, 2020b).

[2] Founded in 1994, FareShare is a charity network which redistributes food from producers, manufacturers and retailers to front-line charity and community groups across the UK. In the financial year 2019/20, FareShare had 176 employees and reported a total income of £16.1 million (FareShare, 2020).

[3] The Trussell Trust describes those using its services as 'clients', a word more commonly associated with commercial transactions than community initiatives. See Massey et al (2015) for a discussion of the influence of neoliberalism on language.

[4] 'Neoliberalism' broadly means the project of economic and social transformation under the sign of the free market. It also means the institutional arrangements to implement this project that have been installed, step by step, in every society under neoliberal control (Connell et al, 2009: 331). Neoliberalism is defined in detail in Chapter 2. See also Birch (2017) for a detailed overview of the contours of existing discussions of neoliberalism.

[5] 'Neoliberal governmentality' refers to a distinctive rationality of government that Foucault discussed in his lectures on 'The Birth of Biopolitics'. Neoliberal governmentality seeks to multiply the enterprise form within markets and the social fabric, and to encourage individuals to think of themselves and work on their lives as 'enterprise-units' and 'enterprises for themselves'. Governmentality, like neoliberalism, is defined in detail in Chapter 2. See Moisander et al (2018). See also Foucault (2008); McNay (2009).

6 'White privilege' refers to the notion that White subjects accrue advantages by virtue of being constructed as Whites (Leonardo, 2004: 137). 'Whiteness' and 'White privilege' are described in detail in Chapter 2.

7 This book defines racial or ethnic identities as inherently socially constructed, the product of actions undertaken by ethnic groups as they shape and reshape their self-definition and culture, and the consequence of external social, economic and political processes and actors as they construct and manipulate ethnic categories and definitions. Race and ethnicity are therefore seen as dynamic social, historical and variable categories which are constantly recreated and modified through human interaction. Some have felt that it is necessary to put the word race into inverted commas ('race') in order to make it clear that these are social distinctions being described rather than biological ones and in order to distance themselves from the original, pejorative meaning of the term. The history and definition of 'race' is discussed in depth in Chapter 7. See also: Nagel (1994).

8 The FAO's definition of food insecurity has also been critiqued as reflecting and responding to wider trends in political economy. Patel (2009) writes that the expansion of the definition of food security in 2001, to enlarge the community of authors the statement includes, was both cause and consequence of its increasing irrelevance as a guiding concept in the shaping of international food production and consumption priorities. He argues that the terms on which food is, or is not, made available by the international community has, with the pre-eminence of neoliberalism in the 1990s, been taken away from institutions that might be oriented by concerns of 'food security', and given to the market, which is guided by an altogether different calculus. It is, then, possible to tell a coherent story of the evolution of 'food security' by using the term as a mirror of international political economy.

9 Some scholars have pointed out that race and gender may have a negative impact on research interactions if perceptions of such factors differ between cultures (Bhopal, 2000; Shah 2004). Others, however, suggest that, if the researcher is prepared to allow participants to explore the researcher's own personal identity, the research relationship becomes more balanced and differences of status, cultural background, gender and so on may be an advantage rather than a barrier (Sime, 2008).

2

Revising perspectives on neoliberalism, hunger and food insecurity

Introduction: what is the need for theory?

In a study of a topic such as food insecurity – or hunger – it is justifiable to ask why a theoretical framework is needed at all. What difference can theory make to those reluctantly visiting food banks or parents skipping meals to ensure enough food for their children? This is an important and worthwhile question which should be asked of all research – theoretical and empirical. But, however abstract, theory has a purpose: while we may be unaware of it, theoretical frameworks shape how we think, how we act, and what questions we ask. Interrogating existing theoretical paradigms – such as neoliberalism – shines a light on why the status quo is as it is, and how behaviours and systems that seem normal and taken for granted are in fact creations, first of individuals and ultimately of society collectively. Scrutinising the theoretical frameworks that underpin and are used to explain food insecurity and food aid illuminates not only the nature of these phenomena but why they exist at all, and why they are increasingly accepted as everyday parts of society. Constructing a new theoretical framework for analyses of food insecurity and food aid may, therefore, enable fresh understanding, elicit different questions and inspire new challenges to the status quo. This chapter sets out to do just that. It critiques key conceptual frameworks surrounding food insecurity and food aid – neoliberal political economy, rights-based frameworks, and mutual aid – and explicates concepts that inform the empirical analysis in subsequent chapters: religious neoliberalism, racial neoliberalism and the post-racial, and Whiteness. In so doing, the chapter attempts to construct a 'new' theoretical framework, one which is reflective of multi-ethnic, multi-faith Britain.

Political economy of food charity

In *First World Hunger Revisited*, Riches and Silvasti (2014a) document the advance of neoliberalism in rich, food-secure, post-industrial nations, showing how it has been accompanied by the institutionalisation, corporatisation and globalisation of charitable food banking – phenomena documented in detail by Poppendieck in the US (Poppendieck, 1999) and Lambie-Mumford in the UK (Lambie-Mumford, 2017). The growth of food charity in countries such as Canada, Australia, the UK, New Zealand, the Nordic welfare states of Finland and Denmark and, especially, the US is symbiotic with socio-political change from post-war Keynesian social democracy to neoliberalism. From the late 1970s, across Europe and North America, the state abandoned policies aiming for full employment, privatised many public services, reduced the value and the accessibility of social security, and tolerated poverty and unemployment as inevitable and necessary features of a competitive and efficient market economy (Harvey, 2005). This new neoliberal system, which conceived of the state as the enabler of the market rather than the protector of its citizens (Dean, 2014), portrayed 'poor people', rather than the policies and systems which created unemployment and poverty, as the 'problem', demonising anyone who failed to achieve wealth, success and independence from the state in this new compassionless system (Lister, 2011). In Europe, North America and Australasia, as the state withdrew as a provider of welfare services, charities, including food charities, stepped into the vacuum to assist people in need (see Tarasuk and Eakin, 2003; Lambie-Mumford, 2017; May et al, 2019), becoming steadily institutionalised across the Global North from the 1990s (see Dowler, 2014; Poppendiecke, 2014; Riches and Tarasuk, 2014; Silvasti and Karjalainen, 2014).

Liberalism and neoliberalism

This apparently new, individualising system, was, nevertheless, not historically unique but – and as its name implies – closely aligned with its forbear, classical liberalism:

> Neoliberalism reinforces many of the central axioms of classical liberalism. It reinforces those pertaining to the relations between the individual and society, the conception of freedom, the view of the self as a rational public utility maximiser, the view of the distinction between public and private spheres as separate, and the rejection of any conception of public good over and above the aggregate sum of individual ends. (Olssen, 2000: 482)

Neoliberalism can be understood in at least three ways: as political economic doctrine, governmentality and subjectivities (Larner, 2000).

Political economic doctrine

As a political economic doctrine, neoliberalism bears many similarities to its forbear, liberalism, including its enthusiasm for the unfettered market and commitment to the privatisation of public resources and spaces, minimisation of labour costs, reductions in public expenditures, elimination of regulations for private corporations, and devolution of responsibility from the state to private actors and entities (Rose, 1992). Where neoliberalism differs from liberalism, however, is in its tendency not only to roll back the state, exemplified by the anti-statist privatisation of state assets and deregulation of the economy, but to roll out the state to consolidate and extend the supremacy of government and the market in all spheres of social life (Peck and Tickell, 2002). 'Roll-out' neoliberalism, associated with 'Third Way' doctrines of the mid- to late-1990s in the US, the UK and Germany, involves new economic management systems and repressive social agendas rolling out all-pervasive forms of surveillance, immigration control and authoritarian policing, while simultaneously further privatising and marketising public services and assets (Peck and Tickell, 2002).

Governmentality

The idea of neoliberalism as governmentality is primarily attributable to the late French philosopher and historian, Michel Foucault. Neoliberal governmentality implies 'a set of practices that facilitate the governing of individuals from a distance' (Larner, 2000: 6). Under neoliberalism, social control is exerted not necessarily by direct coercion but through the creation of docile bodies – individuals who comprehend and obey the parameters of self-regulation. Instrumental to the production of docile bodies is a particular architecture of control and power distinctive to the modern era: panopticism (Foucault, 1977). The idea of the panopticon, attributable to 18th-century English social theorist and political philosopher Jeremy Bentham, is to allow all inmates of an institution (for instance, a factory, prison or workhouse) to be observed by a single manager or security guard, without the workers or prisoners being able to tell if they are being watched (Brunon-Ernst, 2012). This distinctive and limitless architecture of power, described by Foucault as 'a state of consciousness and permanent visibility' (Foucault, 1997: 201), secures obedience because it normalises the conduct of its inhabitants who act as if they are being watched.

The neoliberal state is responsible for promoting the freedom and scope of the market via this particular form of surveillance (Gane, 2012). Historically expressed in the workhouse, prison and hospital, today disciplinary techniques operate through both a 'culture of surveillance', taking shape in the proliferation of an audit culture and performance indicators in private, public and third sector organisations, and via more direct strategies of government that have the function of 'introducing additional freedoms through additional control and intervention' (Foucault, 2008: 67) – for instance welfare policies. According to Foucault, therefore, neoliberalism does not signify the absence of government or the state; instead, it is an argument for the state to be marketised to its core and for market principles of competition and audit to infiltrate all spheres of social and cultural life (Gane, 2012).

Foucault describes the relational practices through which obedient and self-governing citizens are constituted as a form of 'pastoral power' or pastorship. The concept of pastorship originates in early Christianity, where it was characterised as both a beneficent power, according to which the duty of the pastor (to the point of self-sacrifice) was the salvation of the flock, and as an individualising power, in that the pastor must care for each and every member of the flock singly and in so doing requires detailed knowledge of their mental and physical attributes (Golder, 2007: 165). Pastorship is therefore based on a complex and thoroughly affective relationship between the pastor and her flock. The pastor exercises a careful jurisdiction over the bodily actions and the souls of her flock in order to assure their salvation, and the members of the flock each owe her 'a kind of exhaustive, total, and permanent relationship of individual obedience' (Foucault, 2008: 183). Although the importance of Christian pastorship diminished over time, the contemporary state arguably continues as a site of pastoral power. In this new configuration, the officials of pastoral power are disseminated throughout the 'whole social body', finding support in a 'multitude of institutions' including the family, social security and employers (Foucault, 1982) – and, possibly, also within food banks.

Subjectivities

As subjectivities, neoliberalism infiltrates personal identity and relationships through practices of neoliberal self-government. Embedded within systems of seemingly limitless state surveillance, we act as though we are being watched, maintaining standards, beliefs and behaviours condoned by the state (Rose, 1992) – Foucault writes:

> The subject constitutes himself in an active fashion, by the practices of the self, these practices are not something that the individual invents himself. They are patterns that he finds in his culture and which are proposed, suggested and imposed on him by his culture, his society and his social group. (Foucault, 1988: 11)

The 'patterns' to be emulated within the modern era are informed by the priorities of the market. Achievement of the neoliberal ethical self – the autonomous, competitive, free individual, fulfilled by economic activity and engagement in civil society: 'homo economicus' (Foucault, 2008) – is contingent upon certain behaviours, including industriousness and obedience to authority. Ideals traditionally associated with the market economy – individualism, competition, profit, efficiency and self-help – shape how we see and judge ourselves, to the exclusion of other determinants of wellbeing and care. 'Vocabularies of the economy' alter ourselves and our everyday relationships: 'this vocabulary of customer, consumer, choice, markets and self-interest moulds both our conception of ourselves and our understanding of our relationship to the world' (Massey, 2015: 26).

Individuals attain the neoliberal ethical self not only by relentless self-improvement and assertive independence but also by demarcating themselves from stigmatised 'Others' (Lister, 2004). This concept of 'Othering' refers to the ways in which dominant groups define themselves in opposition to less powerful Others 'by attributing negative properties to them in contrast to which their own identity is defined as normal and good' (Sayer, 2005: 28). As explained by Ruth Lister (2020: 90), the notion of 'Othering' conveys how this is 'not an inherent state but an ongoing process of differentiation and demarcation, by which the line is drawn between "us" and "them" – between the more and less powerful – and through which social distance is established and maintained' (see also Riggins, 1997). Lister notes that this line is not neutral but imbued with negative value judgements that diminish and construct people living in poverty as a 'source of moral contamination, an object of pity, an exotic species or even less than human' (2020: 90). Othering is a process via which the 'non-poor' condemn 'the poor' and, by so doing, further social stratifications according to income, class, gender, disability, race and religion, undermining solidarity among communities and reinforcing the predominance of government (Tyler, 2013). Othering is also, however, increasingly a process by which 'the poor' condemn their peers, as discussed in Chapter 6.

Neoliberalism and critical approaches to food charity

Critical contributions to UK 'evidence' on food insecurity, which challenge dominant assumptions and reflect on the (neoliberal) socio-political and cultural context of food charity and food insecurity research have, to date, been few in number. Important exceptions include Garthwaite's (2016a) ethnographic observations and interviews inside food banks, documenting how shame among service users does not necessarily arise from their experience of the food bank, but from the wider stigmatising culture of 'Othering' which constructs poverty as personal failure. Informed by ethnographic research with service users and providers, Cloke, Williams and May (Williams et al, 2016; Cloke et al, 2017; May et al, 2019; 2020) critically assess food banking in the UK. They highlight the moral ambiguity of food banking and the potential for politicisation of food bank volunteers; the growing convergence of bureaucratic practices of benefits officials and food bank organisations, and the production of moral distance that characterises both (May et al, 2019); and the notion of 'scarcity' that has become embedded at the level of common sense (May et al, 2020). Strong (2019) takes a similarly critical approach. Drawing on ethnography inside a food bank in South Wales, and using Foucauldian theory, he argues that food banks exercise a power over life that seeks to transform hunger into a technical object through which it can be known and acted on by food banks. In this analysis, Strong draws attention to the limits of this biopolitical and disciplinary system, emphasising the 'everyday power of living' that undermines techniques of power exercised over individuals. Like Strong (2019), Möller (2021) applies a Foucauldian framework to the performance of power in three UK food banks. He argues that localised care for the poor operates through the Foucauldian concept of pastoral power, mentioned earlier, which requires 'confessions of crises and obedience to an expert regime in the diagnosis and treatment of poverty as an individual condition' (Möller, 2021: 853). Situating his findings within a broader critique of neoliberal governance, Möller shows how food banks embody disciplinary and paternalistic attributes, managing poverty at a distance while maintaining neoliberal ideals of personal responsibility and active citizenship. The relationship between the neoliberal state, governmentality and capitalism is addressed by Livingstone's (2015; 2017) distinctive analysis of the wider social and historical context of the contemporary 'crisis' of food insecurity, and the position and response of the capitalist state to this crisis. Informed by Marxist theory, Livingstone outlines how the neoliberal government distances itself from those whom the capitalist economy attacks the most: the dispossessed and impoverished. The government employs discourses on food insecurity which alienate and stigmatise people using food banks, thereby reimposing inequality, hunger and food insecurity, and reinforcing and reproducing unequal economic relations brought about by capitalism (2015: 193). According to Livingstone's analysis it is the capitalist economy, not the neoliberal state, that is predominant. In this framing, food aid becomes part of the restructuring of capital,[1] here manifested through charities, the shifting labour market and the wider machine of the state; food aid 'is charity', she argues, 'but it is also commercialised through the corporate social responsibilities of the supermarkets' (2015: 194).

Religious neoliberalism

Recent scholarship has examined the convergence (and divergence) between faith and neoliberalism in the context of charity. Jason Hackworth (2012) posits the notion of 'religious neoliberalism', a promotion of individualistic, anti-state and pro-religious views, advancing the idea that religiously delivered charity is a rational and efficient alternative to collectivist state welfare. While religious neoliberalism is largely used by Hackworth to refer to recent political coalitions among ostensibly compatible groups of the

American Right – religious conservatives, neoliberals, religious social welfare activists – several precedents and parallel literatures evidence a comparable historical affinity between liberalism and particular forms of Protestantism. The sociology of Max Weber is arguably the most important precedent to this approach. Weber argued that the Calvinist work ethic – particularly as exercised by Puritan sects – conditioned societies in Europe and the US to accept the premises of liberal capitalism (Weber, [1905] 2002). In particular, he highlighted the importance of the theological concept of the divine 'calling' for a particular profession, as well as the inclination to save, work hard and avoid immediate gratification. These features, Weber argued, were central to the development of the particular form of capitalism that originated in 19th-century Europe and diffused throughout much of Western Europe and North America during the 20th and into the 21st century. The Calvinist socio-religious underpinnings of various societies can be used to explain much of the character of their contemporary welfare systems (Kahl, 2005). The Anglo-American system, for instance, is dominated by intense individualism, rooted in the Calvinistic ethic; this not only facilitates a political space for policies of religiously based welfare but also underpins contemporary narratives of the 'deserving' and 'undeserving' poor, a binary with a distinctly Calvinist heritage (Kahl, 2005).

The second precedent draws direct connection between the evangelical community and classical liberalism of the 18th and 19th centuries (Hilton, 1986; Bigelow, 2005). Evangelicals were among the most fervent supporters of the original classical liberals in late 18th-century Scotland and England. While they could not be described as liberal in a classical sense – they saw the brutality of the economic conditions faced by the poor as divine punishment rather than as a 'natural' feature of the market – they ascribed to the same policy prescriptions as classical liberal economists: laissez-faire governance (Hackworth, 2012).

The third, and final, precedent attempts more directly to understand the interaction between evangelical Christianity and neoliberalism, specifically in the US (Brown, 2006). It suggests that neoliberals and evangelicals work in partnership to magnify the intensity of their political critique (Connolly, 2008). In particular, Christian fundamentalist literalism has infused economic discourses in the US, subduing dissent about economic alternatives (Connolly, 2005).

These fragments underscore the reality that the union between neoliberalism – or liberalism – and particular denominations of Protestantism, while historically politically powerful, is rooted in different ideologies: a standpoint highlighted by the apparent incompatibility between neoliberalism as advanced by its original proponents, Friedrich Hayek and Milton Friedman, and as propounded by social conservatives. While social conservatives were inclined towards the endorsement of religiously inspired welfare and the inclusion of Protestant morality in politics, for Hayek and Friedman, neoliberalism was an attempt to bypass Keynesianism and return to the unapologetic classical liberalism that accepted the brutality of markets as a virtue (Hackworth, 2012). Hayek went to great lengths to distance himself from what he saw as the backward thinking of social conservatives, devoting a chapter of *The Constitution of Liberty* (Hayek, 1960) to explaining, 'Why I am not a Conservative'.

American geographer Mona Atia identifies a comparable melding of religiosity and neoliberal economic rationales in Islamic faith-based organisations, described as 'pious neoliberalism' (Atia, 2013). Like Hackworth, Atia refers to an intentional and productive merging of religious and capitalist subjectivity; pious neoliberalism 'represents a new compatibility between business and piety that is not specific to any religion but rather is a result of the ways in which religion and economy interact in the contemporary moment. Pious neoliberalism provides new institutions, systems of knowledge production and subjectivities' (Atia, 2013: xvi). The alliance between Islam and neoliberalism takes the form of pious neoliberalism as policy and pious neoliberalism as governmentality (Atia, 2013). As policy, pious neoliberal practices reconfigure religious practices according to principles of economic rationality, productivity and privatisation. In the case of Islam, this operates at a theological and an institutional level. Theologically, preachers and leaders present economic traits, such as economic rationality, productivity and efficiency, as components of a religious life; economic rationality is applied to religious practices, while characteristics of Islam considered incompatible with neoliberalism are marginalised. Institutionally, pious neoliberalism leads to new institutional forms, including private mosques, private foundations and an 'Islamic lifestyle market' (Atia, 2013).

Pious neoliberalism as governmentality takes root through individual self-regulation and entrepreneurialism; subjects invest in a moral economy that is inextricably linked with the market, self-government and faith. Individuals are motivated to self-regulate by both neoliberal ideas of economic efficiency and growth, and Islamic ideals of *khayr*, the performance of 'good deeds' through charitable acts in order to improve the self and its relationship with God (Atia, 2013). Charity is essential to the productive fusion of Islam, neoliberalism and governmentality: in binding aid to religious lessons, Islamic charities unavoidably fuse personal conduct to the regulation of political or civic conduct, producing pious neoliberal subjects who, in turn, self-regulate according to the principles of an Islamic moral economy. In Atia's reading, religion and economic rationales complement rather than contradict each other; like conservative Christian discourses, Islam and neoliberal economics meld effortlessly together, to the advantage of both.

Racial neoliberalism

Neoliberalism is intimately associated with the creation and legitimation of contemporary racial inequality and racism (Goldberg, 2001), and the state has been instrumental in this process (Skeggs, 2019). Increased movement of capital and people consequent on neoliberal trade liberalisation has been seen to require – or used as a pretence to justify – enhanced security from perceived threats within and outside the state (Goldberg, 2009). Accordingly, the central role of the neoliberal state has been progressively restructured from providing welfare to its citizens to maintaining domestic and international security (Kapoor and Kalra, 2013) – a process exemplified by the simultaneous erosion and securitisation of social welfare arms of the state and the associated reframing of those in need as 'imaginatively' linked with the criminal (Wacquant, 2009).

Today, we find the state continuing to withdraw from all aspects of social provision, heavily disadvantaging already precarious Black and minority ethnic[2] groups, while ring-fencing and bolstering counter-terrorism budgets. The turn of the 21st century marked a significant and conspicuous shift in geopolitical frameworks, namely from communism to Islamism as the targeted enemy of the West (Kapoor and Kalra, 2013). The terms 'terrorist' and 'terrorism' were exploited to incite both the cultural context of fear of the suicide bomber and a notion of pre-modern, uncivilised culture threatening 'Western' cultural norms. This phantasm – the threat imagined – has been employed to legitimise an associated escalation of state militarisation and securitisation for the purposes of retaining 'law and order' (Kapoor and Kalra, 2013). In so doing, it gave rise to a reconstruction of the way in which ethnic and religious minorities, especially British Muslims, are disciplined in Britain as they became the targeted enemy within (Choudhury and Fenwick, 2011). Politically, this has been accompanied by an assertion of the failure of multiculturalism as a state response to governing minority ethnic groups. The replacement approach is a politics of integrationism which re-emphasises the 'problem' of 'cultural difference' (Kundani, 2007), constructing a clash of non-Western – often Islamic – and Western belief systems as an explanation of social unrest (Kapoor and Kalra, 2013). The operations of contemporary state racism echo historical colonial formations of governance of the racial Other's 'religious delinquency', particularly as they were actualised across North Africa and Asia (Valluvan and Kapoor, 2016). Indeed, the intertwined binary discourses of the self-segregation of minority ethnic, particularly Muslim, communities and their perceived commitment to living in parallel cultures provided the creative weft and warp of a policy programme of countering radicalisation, and assimilation of minorities into the mainstream of a – supposed – British way of life (Husband et al, 2014).

The post-racial state

Structural shifts in the packaging and deployment of race (and racisms) under neoliberalism have been paralleled by the ascendancy of claims that race is socially and economically irrelevant – that the contemporary state is 'post-race'. The current neoliberal project espouses a colourblind society where people are abstract individuals, not members of racialised social groups. The discourse of racial neoliberalism suggests that, since the state is supposed to treat everyone equally, it cannot act on the category of race because that would favour people of colour (Sbicca and Myers, 2017). The post-racial neoliberal state, then, is committed to individualising responsibility; it renders individuals accountable for their own actions and expressions, not that of their group, and, correspondingly, does not ascribe responsibility to one's racial group for the actions of the supposed group's individual members. In so doing, the post-racial state attempts to deny the agency of social groups, eroding racial connectivity and solidarity (Goldberg, 2013).

In keeping with the neoliberal thrusts of individualisation and self-production, however, the post-racial condition 'doubles racial response' (Goldberg, 2013). Racism is explained as individualised prejudices, refusing responsibility for structural conditions. At the same time, the denial of formal racial barriers in society – and even of the possibility of racism itself – paradoxically serves as a licence for the expression of explicit racism: in the post-racial state, the values and social conditions to be emulated are those of the racial dominant, of Whiteness; resistance to or rejection of such values leads to institutionally mandated violence (Goldberg, 2013). Sbicca and Myers (2017) outline how, motivated by neoconservative[3] ideals, the practice of racial neoliberalism intentionally uses the discourses of equal opportunity and personal responsibility to build a White working-class and middle-class voting bloc that supports a political project to defund the welfare state, enforce austerity on low-income communities, and pursue mass incarceration in order to criminalise the poor (see also Feagin, 2006; Bonilla-Silva, 2013; Omi and Winant, 2014). Despite the move towards colour-blindness, racial neoliberalism has utilised explicitly racist discourse during moments of social and economic crisis in order to reassert the power of the capitalist class over labour, the working class and communities of colour (see, for example, the scapegoating of immigrants to explain low wages and unemployment rather than employers who adopt exploitative employment practices [Paret and Gleeson, 2016; Bryson and White, 2019]). Tacit acceptance of the idea of the post-racial was upended among some members of the political and economic establishment by the murder of an African American man, George Floyd, by a White police officer, and subsequent global protests against racism and racial inequality under the banner of the Black Lives Matter[4] movement. Since the death of Floyd in May 2020, the credibility of the post-racial state has been firmly interrogated; however, the idea itself, embedded within the structures and discourse of neoliberalism, has arguably not (yet) been repudiated at an institutional and political level.

Whiteness

In discussions of race and racisms we primarily focus on those at the sharp end of discrimination – for instance, Muslim children singled out under the government's PREVENT[5] programme, and the under-representation of people of colour in positions of influence. Progressives argue for the 'inclusion' of minority ethnic groups via positive discrimination and call for unconscious bias training. The focus is on the subjects of victimisation rather than the (White-majority) system that perpetuates racism. And yet challenging a hierarchical racial order requires critique of the racial ideology that maintains the dominant system; as Toni Morrison (1992) wrote, it requires us to 'avert the critical gaze from the racial object to the racial subject; from the described and imagined to the describers and imaginers', which brings the focus firmly onto 'Whiteness'.

Whiteness is not a biological category but rather a set of ideas and practices about race that has emerged from historical and social processes of racialisation, themselves based upon ideals of White supremacy (see Frankenberg, 1993; Bonnett, 1996; Kobayashi and Peake, 2000). A foundational marker of Whiteness is its own invisibility, allowing Whites to deny White privilege by not seeing Whiteness as a racialised category (Guthman, 2008). As a consequence, Whiteness comes to represents a standpoint of normalcy, one which entrenches the dominance and privilege of White people (Frankenberg, 1993). Discourses and spaces of power interpolate a White subject, upholding Whiteness as the standard against which Others are assessed and coding social practices and spaces as White, while Whiteness as a racial category remains unmarked and invisible (Bonnett, 1996). Cognizant of the critique that the prominence given to Whiteness scholarship has effectively re-centred Whiteness, I follow those who use Whiteness to de-centre White as 'normal,' unmarked, and therefore universal, and to make Whites accountable for their effects on others (see Frankenberg, 1993; Lipsitz, 1998; Kobayashi and Peake, 2000; McKinney, 2005, among many).

Whiteness can, however, also represent a different – and stigmatised – political identity. As Chris Haylett (2001) showed in her study of abject Whiteness, Whiteness has in recent years been substantially sullied; it now has 'dirty' White manifestations, as did the Irish in the early forms of colonialism (Ignatiev, 1995). Terms such as 'chav', 'white underclass' and 'white trash' (Jones, 2011) are deployed to describe a certain White, largely poor, population. This discourse serves a similar symbolic function to the types of pathologies ascribed to Black and 'non-White' populations of the 'underclass'[6] in the US (Murray, 1994; 1996), where the idea of a highly racialised 'culture of poverty' (Lewis, 1966)[7] has been construed to represent the pathologies of the urban Black family (see Wilson, 2009): the absent Black father and the single-headed Black female household (Aponte, 1990: 132–3). Like the racialised 'underclass' in the US, the derogatory terms 'chav' and 'underclass' are used in the UK to name and stigmatise a group of poor Whites who fail to adhere to dominant norms and practices, while simultaneously negating structural explanations of poverty and focusing instead on individual accounts of cultural and moral degeneracy. The economic and social impacts of government policy – for instance, 'austerity' – are thereby reframed as cultural problems (Rhodes, 2013).

In his ground-breaking book *Race and the Undeserving Poor*, Robert Shilliam (2018) explores the lineage of repeated political attempts from the 18th century onwards to demarcate the 'deserving poor' from the broader category of 'the poor' in general. Some marker of difference was required to distinguish those who merit political sympathy and state support from those who do not; behavioural traits could be the means of differentiation but, more often than not, skin colour formed the basis of deservingness. Shilliam argues that 'elite actors, motivated by concerns for the integrity of Britain's imperial – and then postcolonial – order, have racialised and re-racialised the historical distinction between the deserving and the undeserving poor through ever more expansive terms that have incorporated working classes, colonial "natives" and nationalities' (Shilliam, 2018: 6). A moral relationship has been constructed between Whiteness and deserved-ness; Blackness and undeserved-ness (Shilliam, 2018: 7). Although Whiteness has historically inferred respectability, by the 2000s poor residents of council estates were explicitly racialised as White at a time when Whiteness normatively inferred middle-class respectability. 'This white "underclass"', Shilliam argues, was 'thereby imbued with a hyper-visible social dysfunctionality and a moral character undeserving of welfare' (Shilliam, 2018: 4) (see also Lawler, 2012). In other words, poor Whites were 'Blackened' in the process of also being made to carry undeserving characteristics (Shilliam, 2018: 7).

Rights-based approaches to food insecurity

The second key conceptual approach to food insecurity and food aid is founded in rights-based moral and legal frameworks. This rights-based approach to food insecurity pivots on the concept of the 'right to food' – food as a human right rather than a charitable responsibility (Dowler, 2002; Riches, 2011). This idea, outlined in Article 25 of the 1948 Universal Declaration of Human Rights (UN General Assembly, 1974), and the International Covenant on Economic, Social and Cultural Rights, obligates government not to feed its public but to create the conditions by which individuals can feed themselves (Fisher, 2017); the existence – and success – of a charitable food system is antithetical to the right to food (Dowler and O'Connor, 2012). In focusing on rights and equity, the right to adequate food provides a vital counterfoil to charitable approaches to hunger. As such, the framework is considered a powerful legislative tool to hold national and local governments to account, as well as an effective device to facilitate 'joined-up' transnational food policy (Riches and Silvasti, 2014b).

The right to adequate food is complemented by food sovereignty, food justice and community food security perspectives. Food sovereignty is 'the right of peoples and governments to choose the way food is produced and consumed in order to respect our livelihoods, as well as the policies that support this choice' (La Via Campesina, 2009: 57). The idea of food sovereignty arose in the 1970s when a group of Guatemalan Mayan peasant farmers – or campesinos – worked to establish agro-ecological alternatives to industrial farming practices. In contrast to a corporate food regime characterised by monopolistic control of production; global governance by multilateral organisations and nation-states in the Global North; vast reliance on chemical inputs; and increasing disparities in food access (McMichael, 2005; Holt-Gimenez, 2011), the food sovereignty approach prioritises production for local and domestic markets, demands fair prices for food producers, and emphasises community control over productive resources such as land, water and seeds (Desmarais, 2007; Bello, 2008). Food sovereignty moves beyond a focus on food security – access to sufficient food – to advocate for communities' rights to produce for themselves rather than remain dependent on international commodities markets (Alkon and Mares, 2012).

Food justice represents 'a transformation of the current food system, including but not limited to eliminating disparities and inequities' (Gottlieb and Joshi, 2010: ix). Like food sovereignty, food justice advocates greater control over food production and consumption by people who have been marginalised by mainstream agri-food regimes (Cadieux and Slocum, 2015). Early examples of food justice praxis in the US include the work of Food not Bombs (Wilson, 2013), the Black Panthers Breakfast Program of the 1960s, the Delano Grape Strike and Boycott led by César Chavez in the mid-1960s, policy analysis from the NGO Food First in the mid-1970s, and farmer organising against foreclosure in the 1980s (Cadiuex and Slocum, 2015).

In the US, contemporary efforts to make the food system more socially just have cohered under the banners of community food security and food justice. Community food security combines an emphasis on sustainable, local production with an anti-hunger perspective. It argues that all communities should have access to safe, culturally acceptable, nutritionally adequate and sustainably produced diets (Community Food Security Coalition, no date), emphasising the community rather than the individual level and encouraging structural analyses and efforts to reform the industrial food system and food movements.[8] The concept of food justice speaks to the multiple ways that racial and economic inequalities are embedded within production, distribution and consumption of food (Sbicca and Myers, 2017). Activists working from a food justice and community food security perspective often develop alternatives to the local conventional food system, such as farmers markets, urban farms and cooperatively owned grocery stores in low-income and minority ethnic communities (Alkon and Mares, 2012). While food justice activists tend to emphasise the need for these projects to be created not only for but by these communities, the lack of attention to questions of agency and privilege within the alternative food movement has given rise to sharp scholarly critiques. A particular criticism is that alternative food institutions, such as farmers markets and Community Supported Agriculture (CSA),[9] are largely 'White' spaces, as evidenced not only by the people who frequent them but also by the cultural codings – symbols and systems of meaning relevant to members of a particular culture that can be utilised to facilitate communication within the 'inside group' and also to obscure the meaning to 'outside groups' (see Hyatt and Simons, 1999) – that are performed. These projects appear to lack resonance in the low-income and minority ethnic communities in which they are located; a lack of resonance possibly explained by a set of discourses and practices that reflect White desires and missionary practices (Guthman, 2008). Despite commitments to racial and economic justice, community food movements have been slow to address White privilege, attributable to both the persistent invisibility of Whiteness as a racial category and to the tendency for White bodies to stick together, thereby excluding others in the alternative food space (Saldanha, 2006; Slocum, 2006; 2007). The power inequalities embedded within what may at first blush appear to be more progressive forms of food aid underscore the reality that transitioning beyond food banks towards alternative food networks may not necessarily escape the socio-political and racial inequalities that characterise the former (as set out in Chapters 3, 4 and 5). Chapters 7 and 8 explore the complexities, ambiguities and progressive possibilities of varying forms of food aid, detailing the relational dimensions which may underpin fellowship and resistance to racial and economic injustice.

Food aid and mutual aid

So far, I have described two interrelated theoretical frameworks through which food banking and food insecurity have been assessed in the UK and internationally: neoliberal political economy and rights-based approaches. There is, however, a third theoretical framework, which has emerged from recent UK scholarship. This framework, 'economies of care' (Williams et al, 2016; Cloke et al, 2017), suggests that food charity represents an embodiment and performance not of governmentality but of morality, with provision underpinned by moral imperatives, both secular and religious (Lambie-Mumford, 2017). In this framing, food banks may function as 'ambivalent spaces of care' (Cloke et al, 2017), in which people of different classes, ethnicities, genders and histories share a single encounter. In the performance of care within the food bank exists the potential for collectively formed new political and ethical beliefs that challenge neoliberal austerity (Cloke et al, 2017).

Ideas of 'care'[10] and associated notions of 'mutual aid' have become salient in the context of COVID-19 (see, for example, Spade, 2020; The Care Collective, 2020; Sitrin and Sembrar, 2020). The pandemic exposed the ongoing carelessness in many countries, in particular but by no means limited to the US, the UK and Brazil – countries with hollowed-out care and health systems, a consequence of harsh and prolonged austerity, which dismissed early warnings about the imminent threat of the pandemic (The Care Collective, 2020). COVID-19 highlighted our shared vulnerabilities, our need for care and our interconnectedness; it was the basis for countless acts of mutuality and solidarity (see Sitrin and Sembrar, 2020); and it gave rise to thousands of mutual aid groups across the UK, set up to assist local communities according to need and motivated by ideas of human nature as sociable and cooperative, and of society as interdependent. These ideas, bound up with recent constructions of 'care' and embodied by COVID-19 mutual aid groups, may seem contemporaneous to the present moment but they have long historical roots. Propagated by strains of revolutionary theory, these ideas are historically most evident in work of late 19th- and early 20th-century anarcho-communist Peter Kropotkin (see Kropotkin, 1987a [1902]; 1987b [1927]). In opposition to 19th-century evolutionary theories stemming from the work of Charles Darwin, Kropotkin argued that mutual aid, not competition, is the principal factor in natural and human evolution, and essential to this is our innate moral sense which makes us capable of altruism: 'We maintain that under any circumstances sociability is the greatest advantage in the struggle for life. Those species which willingly or unwillingly abandon it are doomed to decay; while those animals which know how best to combine have the greatest chance of survival and further evolution' (Kropotkin, 1899: 293).

Kropotkin's anarchism is firmly based in a particular view of human nature (Marshall, 2008): that humans are naturally social, cooperative and moral. He writes:

> And finally – whatever its varieties – there is a third system of morality which sees in moral actions – those actions which are most powerful in rendering men best fitted for life in society – a mere necessity of

the individual to enjoy the joys of his brethren, to suffer when some of his brethren are suffering; a habit and a second nature, slowly elaborated and perfected by life in society. That is the morality of mankind and that is also the morality of anarchy. (Kropotkin, 1987b [1927]: 58)

While society is a natural phenomenon, Kropotkin saw the state and its coercive institutions as an 'artificial and malignant growth' (Marshall, 2008), a cause of unbridled, egoistical individualism. Kropotkin's system for organising the economy surpassed Pierre-Joseph Proudhon's mutualism and Mikhail Bakunin's collectivism to present a form of anarcho-communism, politically a society without government, and economically the complete negation of the wage system and the ownership of the means of production in common (Marshall, 2008). Ideas of mutual aid may well inform some contemporary grassroots initiatives established along cooperative principles and eschewing neoliberal ethics, but can food aid, so entwined with neoliberal state restructuring and very possibly incorporating neoliberal ideals of individualism and self-help, also be a place for an alternative and egalitarian politics, rooted in ideas of mutual aid, ideas themselves founded in the revolutionary theory of a 19th-century anarcho-communist?

Conclusion

I asked at the start of this chapter about the need for theory – for ideas – to understand why hunger is rife throughout the UK and why food charity is the predominant response. Does it make a difference to our understanding of food insecurity and food aid; will it change anything? In the UK and the US, scholars have argued for an application of the idea of 'the right to food' to food charity, pointing out that this idea has legislative implications requiring governments to ensure that all their citizens can afford to access food through normal channels – supermarkets, grocers, cafes and restaurants. They have shown how the growth of food banking over the past decade aligns with wider processes of neoliberal state transformation in which public services and welfare provision are 'rolled back' while competition and increasingly aggressive policing is 'rolled out'.

Less prominent in these debates is another interpretation of neoliberalism: neoliberal governmentality. This conception of neoliberalism does not deny state withdrawal from social assistance, but it places greater emphasis on the transformation of public, social and cultural life according to the principles of the market: competition, entrepreneurship, audit and regulation. The state maintains the supremacy of the market through the exercise of both repressive power, marked by an authoritarian approach to welfare and policing, and an insidious and *constructive* form of power – governmentality

– which operates through seemingly limitless surveillance and regulation. The subjects of power – us – are complicit in these processes, through self-regulation according to the expectations of the powerful.

Writing in the 1970s Stuart Hall, the late cultural theorist and political activist, noted that 'racism is always historically specific ... though it may draw on the cultural and ideological traces which are deposited in society by previous historical phases, it always assumes specific forms which arise out of the present – not the past – conditions and organisation of society' (Hall et al, 1978: 26). Today, we live in a multi-ethnic, multi-faith and highly racist society. State withdrawal from public services and welfare provision has heavily disadvantaged Black and minority ethnic groups while the 'roll-out' of an authoritarian state has been at its sharpest and keenest in the 'governance' of minority ethnic communities. This 'racial neoliberalism', however, which stereotypes and stigmatises people by virtue of their 'race', simultaneously individualises responsibility, rendering individuals accountable for their own actions. Fundamental to the continuation of ethnic inequalities and inequities is the dominance of 'Whiteness', which determines the values and social conditions to be emulated.

'Religious neoliberalism', through the productive alliance of religious actors and motifs, and neoliberal policies and programmes, may compound broader processes of neoliberal governmentality. This fusion of religion and neo/-liberal ideologies is, arguably, most commonly associated with the ideas of Max Weber, in particular his notion of the Protestant work ethic. However, the fusion of neoliberalism and religious motifs can also be found in Islam. Neoliberal religious practices reconfigure religious practices – theologically and institutionally – according to principles of economic rationality, productivity and privatisation, while Muslims subscribe to a moral economy that is entwined with the market, self-government and faith.

This configuration of neoliberalism – characterised by neoliberal governmentality, racist oppression, and religious collusion with neoliberal ethics – is not new. It is simply a broader portrayal of neoliberal political economy than is commonly found in existing analyses of food charity and hunger in the UK. Neglect of this broader framework has so far impoverished debate; analysis predominantly focuses on the experiences of White people and fails to acknowledge the significant influence of religious actors and ideas on contemporary food charity. The following chapters explore the extent to which present-day food insecurity and food aid is a consequence and embodiment of this configuration of neoliberalism, asking: does this particular form of neoliberal political economy constitute a meta-narrative to explain contemporary food aid and food insecurity in multi-faith, multi-ethnic Britain, or are there alternative explanations?

Notes

[1] 'Capital' is defined according to Marx as not just wealth but wealth in a specific historically developed form: wealth that grows through the process of circulation. Capital is the accumulation of money, the sole purpose of which is to buy something only in order to sell it again. Capital, thus, only exists within the process of buying and selling, as money advanced solely in order to see its return. Critically, money is only capital if it buys a good whose consumption brings about an increase in the value of the commodity, realised in selling it for a profit. See: 'Capitalism' in Marxists Internet Archive Encyclopedia, available at: www.marxists.org/glossary/terms/c/a.htm

[2] I use the term 'Black and minority ethnic' throughout the book to refer to those from Black British, Black African, British Indian, Pakistani British, Bangladeshi British and Chinese British backgrounds, as well as those from other non-White backgrounds. I recognise the considerable limitations of the term, but I use it because it is the term used in the UK's Census and the one most commonly used in UK policy documents (see also Bhopal, 2018).

[3] Sbicca and Myers (2017) describe the reactionary work of new right and neoconservative projects in the 1960s and 1970s (see also Omi and Winant, 2014), racial projects which whipped up 'racial resentment by using code words and the idea of reverse racism to tap into the class-based anxieties of working class and middle-class whites and pit them against people of colour' (Sbicca and Myers, 2017: 32).

[4] The hashtag #BLM emerged in 2013, when George Zimmerman was acquitted for the murder of Trayvon Martin, which then grew as a movement in 2014 following the murder of Michael Brown in Ferguson, Missouri.

[5] PREVENT is a counter-terrorism programme, used to promote 'British values' which has disproportionately targeted Muslim residents in its surveillance measures; the programme used schools as a frontline of national defence (see Back et al, 2002; Wolton, 2006; National Union of Students, 2015).

[6] Murray gained notoriety in the US by making arguments regarding race, the environment and intelligence, mobilising these arguments to make the case that welfare only exacerbated the social pathologies that produced poverty. While in London, Murray disputed the British presumption that 'the underclass was a "Black" problem' (Murray, 1996: 30), since 'Blacks' formed a negligible percentage of the UK population.

[7] Drawing upon anthropological research on the slums of Puerto Rico, as well as previous research in Mexico City, Lewis (1966) identified a 'culture of poverty', its key characteristics being short-term calculations, a fatalistic attitude, sensual decadence and poor family planning. Lewis was keen to point out that these traits were not the product of traditional culture nor of racial affiliation but an effect of a Western-imposed economic system. Lewis's thoughtful and considered thesis was co-opted and misconstrued by politicians, journalists and scholars on the North American mainland, who racialised the culture of poverty, firmly associating the 'underclass' with Black urban families.

[8] 'Food movement' is used to refer to a constellation of individuals, non-government organisations, alliances, initiatives, companies, and government entities arranged in affiliations of different intensities and scales to support food security and sustainable farming (Levkoe, 2006: 89–98).

[9] Community Supported Agriculture is a partnership between farmers and consumers in which consumers buy local, seasonal food directly from the farmer. A farmer offers a certain number of 'shares', 'memberships' or 'subscriptions' to the public, typically consisting of a box of vegetables. Consumers purchase a 'share' and in return receive a box of seasonal produce each week or month throughout the farming season. See: www.permaculture.org.uk/practical-solutions/community-supported-agriculture

[10] Informed by The Care Collective (2020), I use the term 'care' capaciously to 'embrace familial care, the hands-on care that workers carry out in care homes and hospitals and that teachers do in schools, and the everyday services provided by other essential workers. But it means as well the care of activists in constructing libraries of things, co-operative alternatives and solidarity economies, and the political policies that keep housing costs down, slash fossil fuel use and expand green spaces. Care is our individual and common ability to provide the political, social, material, and emotional conditions that allow the vast majority of people and living creatures on this planet to thrive – along with the planet itself' (The Care Collective, 2020: 6).

3

Food aid and neoliberalism: an alliance built on shared interests?

Introduction: the rise of food charity?

In 2010, George Osborne, the privately educated, fresh-faced Chancellor of the Exchequer, gave his first speech to the Conservative party conference, promising a radical overhaul of the benefits system. He proclaimed to Conservative party politicians and members, affiliate groups and donors: 'If someone believes that living on benefits is a lifestyle choice, then we need to make them think again. And we need to change completely the system that has allowed and encouraged them to make such a mistaken choice' (Osborne, 2010). True to his word, the following decade encompassed eye-watering cuts, freezes to benefit levels, and wave after wave of welfare reform. In parallel with this punitive,[1] albeit populist, programme, food banks expanded from an unknown form of charity, started by Paddy and Carol Henderson in their garden shed in Salisbury, to a major voluntary sector service provider.[2] Today, thousands of food banks as well as thousands of other food aid providers – soup kitchens, pay-as-you-feel cafes, community kitchens, community supermarkets, community gardens, and many more – distribute food on a daily and weekly basis to desperate and hungry people.

This 'contemporary' phenomena is, however, perhaps more complex than it first appears. Community-based responses to poverty and hunger have long-existed in the UK, including the distribution of poor relief from monasteries prior to the Reformation; relief for those too ill or old to work in the form of the 'parish loaf' in the 15th century; basic provision of food in the workhouses of the 19th century; and the vastly more progressive British Restaurants, or communal kitchens, established in 1940 to help people who had been bombed out of their homes or had run out of ration coupons, and to equalise consumption across class lines (Vernon, 2007). The rising activity, expanding scope and sharp growth in the media and political profile of the Trussell Trust food bank network since 2010 has, however, created the impression that the provision of food assistance to help people in need is new (Wells and Caraher, 2014).

It is clear that today there are a multitude of organisations providing free or low-cost food that did not exist – or at least not in their present form – in 2010, with a notable expansion of provision initiated from March 2020 in response to the COVID-19 pandemic (see Barker and Russell, 2020; Lambie-Mumford et al, 2020; Graven et al, 2021). It is also evident, however, that many food aid organisations were founded prior to 2010 and, of the provision in existence today, there is considerable variety – projects vary markedly in their activities and size, in their funding, staffing and commercial arrangements, as well as in their aims (Dowler and Lambie-Mumford, 2015). Against this background, the chapter examines the socio-political context, ethical frameworks and historical antecedents of UK food aid, considering whether food charity is indeed an attribute of the present neoliberal moment.

"Whose responsibility is it to feed the poor?"

The austerity programme of deficit contraction, initiated by the Conservative–Liberal Democrat coalition government from 2010, was by no means new; it represented a continuation of longer processes of state transformation since the 1970s. The electoral victory of Margaret Thatcher in 1979 led to a profound transformation in the nature of the state, the design and purpose of the welfare system, the role of the voluntary sector, and the flexibility and scope of the economy (Glennerster, 2020).[3] State assets were privatised, public services marketised and the economy deregulated; models of welfare, established in 1945 and premised on ideas of universalism, were replaced with limited and punitive means-tested welfare assistance, informed by an ideology of free-market fundamentalism (Harvey, 2005). The withdrawal of the state from the provision of social assistance saw the voluntary sector increasingly adopting responsibility for welfare services – indeed, it was encouraged to do so – becoming embedded within the structures, institutions and expectations of the state. In so doing, it expanded its remit and became increasingly embroiled in state funding contracts, becoming institutionalised[4] and professionalised in the process (Peck, 2008). Underpinning these abrupt and far-reaching processes, in which the state was 'rolled back' as a provider of services and welfare but also 'rolled out' as an authoritarian state in the domains of punitive welfare and aggressive policing (Peck, 2010), was the advancement of a spirit of enterprise, embodied by the entrepreneur.

Thatcher's transformation of the nature and responsibilities of the state was continued by her successors – despite the impression, at least, under New Labour (1997–2010) of policy change. Tony Blair's humanisation of Thatcherism, by means of increased public investment and the introduction of a minimum wage and tax credits,[5] obscured what was in reality a highly neoliberal administration, privatising public services, reducing corporate taxes, extolling personal responsibility and further expanding the scope and responsibilities of the voluntary sector. New Labour's public services agenda exerted pressure on voluntary sector organisations to deliver services while, as part of a broader emphasis on organisational collaboration and 'new localism',

British public agencies were increasingly required to collaborate with private and voluntary sector providers to deliver welfare services (Milbourne and Cushman, 2015).

Unlike New Labour, David Cameron's Conservatism was marked by a distinctive moralism and 'libertarian paternalism', in which policy makers would act as 'choice architects', 'nudging' local publics towards those decisions that would have been taken in accordance with the desires of the state (see Corbett and Walker, 2013; Shilliam, 2018). At the Hugo Young Lecture in 2009, Cameron laid out his plan to alleviate social exclusion through the inclusivity of a 'big society' (Cameron, 2009). His address signalled a partial reorientation of the party's moral compass away from individual freedom towards the normative ground of New Labour with its emphasis on redistribution and equality of opportunity (Shilliam, 2018). Cameron's key criticism targeted New Labour's perversion of the self-improvement principle. At present, he claimed, Britain's so-called meritocratic system kept 'millions of people at the bottom locked out of the successes enjoyed by the mainstream'. Cameron argued that New Labour had embraced the worst of Fabianism and its 'mechanistic view of the state', thereby 'ignoring the social consequences of economic reforms'. By 'undermining personal and social responsibility' New Labour had ended up 'perpetuating poverty instead of solving it'; 'state control' had become substituted for 'moral choice'. Alternatively, Cameron advocated both a focus on equality of opportunity (largely through education) and on a 'stronger, more responsible society,' one that was 'aggressively pro-family, pro-commitment, pro-responsibility'. Cameron's 'big society' committed to a rebirth of moral agency along social conservative lines (Kisby, 2010) and, to this effect, Cameron proposed further significant decentralisation of the provision of (and responsibility for providing) public services, as well as the continued opening up of service delivery to local private (for profit) and voluntary organisations. Most of the principles behind the 'big society' arguably resonated with those espoused by New Labour: social conservatism ran through both parties. However, in reality, Cameron's conservatism was neither compassionate nor paternalistic; it was, in fact, more punitive than the Fabianism of New Labour, as illustrated by heavy-handed responses to Muslim communities who were seen to threaten 'national cohesion' – and thereby jeopardise 'big society' politics – and by ideologically driven austerity measures (discussed in detail later), motivated primarily by a demand for unprecedented cost-cutting (Shilliam, 2018: 129).

This wider historical trajectory is essential to the study of food aid in the UK, 'particularly the ways in which shifts in interpretations around the causes of and responses to poverty are manifest in the phenomenon of rising food bank use' (see Lambie-Mumford, 2018: 9).[6] The rise and contemporary prominence of food aid is the embodiment of this longer political–economic trajectory of social policy change away from collectivism and towards increasingly individualised notions of risk and care (Dean, 2008). While this 40-year context provides the foundations of contemporary reforms, social policy changes have intensified significantly since 2010. Analysts have drawn attention to the sheer scale of change introduced in the last ten years through policies of austerity and welfare reform, reporting the largest cuts in public finance ever seen and some of the most extensive welfare reforms since the introduction of the welfare state in the 1940s (Taylor-Gooby and Stoker, 2011; Beatty and Fothergill, 2013).

These themes of state withdrawal from social assistance, evolving responsibility for poverty, and new localism were manifest in food aid in Bradford and York. Charities in both cities had adapted strategically to unmet need, identifying new funding sources and cultivating public sector and corporate partnerships. While diverse local welfare systems, combining state and voluntary provision, are not new in the UK (Buckingham, 2012), the funding policies of food charities in the two sites, as well as the broader collaborative ways in which local food distribution was realised, provided insight into state retrenchment and the contemporary manifestation of public–private partnerships (see also Lambie-Mumford, 2018).

Food charity in Bradford relied on a combination of in-kind and monetary resources from private, public and third sector sources. Only one organisation – a homeless shelter providing cooked meals – was fully funded by the state, through local authority grants. A minority were part-funded by the state – for instance through free or subsidised use of local authority buildings or small grants for specific elements of their food work. This minority included soup kitchens, food banks and community cafes, none of which were governed by or accountable to the local authority. The majority of food aid in Bradford was funded primarily by churches or mosques (discussed in Chapter 4), and a further minority either were supported by donations from religious or non-religious sources (or both) or received in-kind and monetary resources from the broader public.

In York, like Bradford, only a small number of organisations – for instance, well-established homeless hostels providing food as part of other services – were fully funded by the state through local government grants. However, the relationship between local government and food aid did appear to be closer and deeper than in Bradford – possibly reflecting the time difference between the fieldwork in Bradford (2014–15) and York (2018–19). The local authority provided land at no cost for community growing initiatives; at ward level it distributed grants to local food projects; and it contributed to the establishment of a local-level alliance of organisations addressing food insecurity through small grants and linked oversight.

In an attempt to expand the scope and inclusivity of its services, local government in York collaborated with well-established and nascent food provision to develop community centres, providing food alongside other services. Community food providers were keen to partner with local government personnel within these centres in order to collectively address food insecurity. The local authority, schools and primary care services were also key referral partners to Trussell Trust food banks in York, while primary schools were adapting to apparently rising hunger among their pupils by providing free or low-cost food in school-based food banks.

For all types of food aid in Bradford, alliances with local government were, unlike in York, limited and, where they did occur, operated predominantly through the provision of buildings, subsidised or gifted by local government. Talking with a local community leader, Andy, I found there to be hostility to – not support for – public sector involvement in food aid: "Any partnerships have to be down at the bottom. There is no point those councillors sitting up there in their ivory towers because they don't know how it is going to work. What do people want, what do people need?" The local authority was perceived as a hindrance to the effective provision of food aid. Low levels of knowledge among those at leadership level about the nature of food insecurity in Bradford was thought to underpin their unrealistic demands, which inhibited the day-to-day distribution of food. Andy told me:

'Some of the people at leadership level are not well informed so immediately they want to go to quantities, "How much is being distributed? How many are receiving it?" We could spend time on that but I'm not sure what it would tell us, because even if we know how many people, it doesn't actually inform us because there are different levels of stuff.'

By contrast, food charities in both Bradford and York were enthusiastic about corporate partnerships with national retailers and local businesses. Surplus – or waste – food from retailers and manufacturers was integral to food sourcing and many newer food charities would have been unable to operate without it. Unlike for the national organisations FareShare and the Trussell Trust documented by Lambie-Mumford (2018), there was little evidence that the cultivation of corporate partnerships among grassroots food aid was particularly strategic or critical. Like larger and more powerful food charities, local providers capitalised on opportunities presented to them as a consequence of the high-profile issue of food insecurity; however, there was limited discernment as to the types of partnership into which they entered and there was considerable (although not total) patience with inedible food and unpredictable food deliveries.

A critical approach was, nevertheless, applied to welfare state retrenchment and ongoing local-level shifts in responsibility for poverty. Concern was expressed by a vocal minority of public health professionals and food charities that community initiatives should not replace the welfare state. Staff in food aid questioned where responsibility for food insecurity should lie – the individual, civil society or the state. David ran a busy Salvation Army food bank; the church in which the food bank was situated had distributed food on an ad hoc basis for decades, but David decided to establish a more formal system of food distribution in 2012 when the number of those seeking help increased. David expressed unease about the role of food banks in facilitating state retrenchment, "I am aware of criticisms of food banks, that they let the government have a lot more breathing room. Whose responsibility is it to feed the poor?" His discomfort was, however, subordinated to his sense of responsibility towards desperate people seeking food. Confronted by rising need he put his ethical unease about the wider consequences of the food bank to one side and fed the people in front of him.

Grant funding from local authorities, food bank referral systems, and partnerships between local government and food charities in the administration of welfare highlight how increasingly interlocked food charities are becoming in local welfare landscapes. At times facilitated by local government, these charities are taking responsibility for food insecurity as the state continues to retreat from the direct provision of social security and social care support. The differential experiences of food charities in Bradford and York, most likely reflecting the time difference between fieldwork in the two sites, does imply that food aid is becoming ever more embedded in local welfare. However, in both cities there was resistance from some food charities to collaborative forms of food distribution and, more fundamentally, moral objection to the ongoing transfer of responsibility for poverty from the state to charities. The institutionalisation of food aid, while steadily advancing, was by no means an inevitability at the time of my fieldwork in these two northern cities. In contrast, however, enthusiasm for corporate partnerships among many food charities, alongside the absence of critical thinking, suggested that the corporatisation of food aid in the UK is quickly becoming the norm.

"Universal Credit has wrecked us"

Rapid growth in food bank use in the 21st century occurred in parallel with the Coalition Government's programme of austerity, encompassing a large reduction in funding for local government accompanied by extensive 'reform' to UK welfare policy. Between 2010 and 2021, £37 billion was cut from working-age social security (Butler, 2018b). This includes the abolition of the Health in Pregnancy Grant;[7] the localisation of the Social Fund;[8] and the abolition of the Educational Maintenance Allowance in England.[9] The value of working-age benefits, for people in and out of work, has been steadily eroded by uprating changes and, in 2016, working-age benefits and tax credits[10] – including some for people who are too unwell to work – were frozen for four years. The imposition of local rent limits has reduced the value of Housing Benefit, forcing some tenants to pay a proportion of their rent out of their food budget, while the 'bedroom tax' – whereby tenants in social housing have their benefit reduced by 14 per cent if they have one spare bedroom or 25 per cent if they have two or more – has had a similar effect. The localisation of Council Tax support has, in effect, forced those in receipt of working-age social security to pay some or all of their Council Tax – an abrupt and sharp increase in outgoings for households who were previously exempt. The introduction of the benefit cap (a limit on the total amount of income from certain benefits a household can receive) and the two-child limit (in families where there are already two or more children, the child element in Universal Credit and tax credits – worth £2,780 per child per year – is restricted to the first two children) have similarly resulted in huge losses for larger families. Most detrimentally, the roll-out of the Universal Credit system[11] from April 2013 has caused sudden and severe financial losses for many households. Excessive waiting times, delays in receiving payments, debt and loan repayments, and an enhanced benefit sanction regime have rendered many people destitute (Cheetham et al, 2019).

These changes to working-age social security are directly reflected in rising food bank use. In 2019/20, the Trussell Trust attributed 17 per cent of its referrals to 'benefit delays' and 16 per cent to 'benefit changes' (Trussell Trust, 2020a). In 2019, it found that Trussell Trust food banks in local authorities where Universal Credit had been rolled out for at least a year had seen a 30 per cent increase in emergency food parcels provided over the 12 months from when Universal Credit went live (Thompson et al, 2019). This increase exists after accounting for seasonal and other variations, suggesting Universal Credit is a causal factor.

Between 2014 and 2015, I spoke with representatives of many different types of food aid in Bradford – food banks, soup kitchens and soup runs, community cafes, community kitchens and community supermarkets. Staff and volunteers described those using their service and spoke of welfare reform in driving the growing and changing need for food aid. In food banks, the majority of service users were in receipt of, largely inadequate, social security. Many were experiencing an acute financial crisis – predominantly induced by social security sanctions, errors and delays, all of which were set against a backdrop of chronic low income – and required immediate assistance with food.

In soup kitchens and soup runs, those using the service were largely single men, who unlike food banks users, were often homeless or vulnerably housed. Many members of this group were longstanding users of food aid and had a history of addictions and mental ill health. Some staff explained that the demography of those accessing their services was becoming more diverse as austerity progressed and demand for food assistance from the wider community increased. Providers reported that they were increasingly seeing people in part-time, low-income work, as well as people with children.

Chris, soup kitchen manager:	It is more to do with the increase in the number of people, they may be a little bit different kind of service user than we were used to but we are adapting pretty well.
Interviewer:	Different service user in what way?
Chris:	It is a younger group and people who are working part-time and some sort of employment. I don't think we had very many people like that, even a few years ago.

The service users of community cafes and community kitchens, as well as other forms of 'non-emergency' food aid, were more varied than those of food banks and soup kitchens. This included people who were homeless or vulnerably housed as well as those who were financially secure. Accommodating service users with different needs and varied demography – but all in need of some form of support – could prove challenging for staff, many of whom had no formal training in supporting vulnerable adults and children:

> 'We have one particular Polish lady who comes down with her two-year-old little boy in a pram and we try and sort of serve her first and get her off the street because it is not exactly the best atmosphere for the child to be in and, as somebody pointed out, there could be a safeguarding issue with having the child on the site, but if they are hungry you got to feed them. Damned if you do, damned if you don't.' (Thomas, community cafe manager)

Interviews with food charities in Bradford were conducted between 2014 and 2015,[12] prior to the full roll-out of Universal Credit. While benefits sanctions and the benefit cap featured significantly in discussions of food bank use – though not the use of all types of food aid – Universal Credit was less prominent. Fieldwork in York, which took place between 2018 and 2019, found Universal Credit to be a decisive factor in the use of food aid.[13] The statutory delay of five weeks on payment of a first Universal Credit claim rendered people, like Theresa, a lone parent of one child, suddenly destitute, forcing them to use food banks: "Universal Credit has wrecked us. We have just gone on it and I have been told that me and my five-year-old will have to go at least seven weeks with no income at all. We will have to go to food banks and try to get food." Theresa's experience of a punitive social security system causing sudden and extreme destitution is increasingly reflected in literature on food banks. There is now a robust body of evidence showing that welfare reform from 2010, and the roll-out of Universal Credit in particular, has caused rising food bank use (Lambie-Mumford and Green, 2017; Thompson et al, 2019; Reeves and Loopstra, 2020; Jenkins et al, 2021). Conversations with service providers in Bradford and York would certainly support this contention: in Bradford, sanctions, delays and inadequate benefit levels drove people to food banks, while in York, moving on to Universal Credit tipped some households into destitution, forcing them to seek food charity. The research in Bradford and York suggested that welfare reform caused people to use multiple types of food aid, not just food banks. However, it also showed that the users of other types of food aid, such as soup kitchens and community cafes, varied from the 'typical' food bank user; their use of food charity was not only a consequence of recent welfare reforms but also associated with wider and longer state retrenchment. Examples of this include the closure of children's centres, requiring families to seek support and company in community cafes, and reduced funding for drug and alcohol services, contributing to the increased importance of charitable soup kitchens in assisting homeless people with addictions. Again, this wider historical trajectory was essential to understanding contemporary manifestations of food insecurity and food charity.

COVID-19 and the institutionalisation of food charity in the UK

At the time of the fieldwork in York (2018–19) and, to a significantly lesser extent, in Bradford (2014–15), there was some evidence that food charity was becoming institutionalised as part of local welfare systems. Community food organisations received small grants from local government; public sector institutions were key food bank referral partners; and there was evidence of growing collaboration around service provision in community centres. The COVID-19 pandemic compounded pre-existing trends in charitable food aid. Sharp and sudden rises in unemployment, increased living costs for low-income households coupled with the absence of everyday forms of support, and poor access to food among people required to shield or self-isolate increased the need for food assistance significantly (IFAN, 2020; Power et al, 2020b).

Notwithstanding temporary financial assistance for households announced by the Chancellor, Rishi Sunak, in March 2020 – including the COVID-19 Job Retention Scheme ('furlough') and the temporary £20 weekly increase to Universal Credit and the basic element in Working Tax Credit – the Westminster Government largely adopted a food- rather than cash-oriented approach to rising poverty and hunger resulting from COVID-19. The devolved governments, by contrast, adopted more localised responses, including cash-based approaches. In Northern Ireland, Scotland and Wales, nationally funded and managed emergency payment schemes were in operation during the first COVID-19 national lockdown (March–June 2020) to provide money for people in financial hardship to buy essentials. In England, there was no national emergency payment scheme, although central government provided local authorities with additional funding to support people to meet essential needs (Lambie-Mumford et al, 2020).

There was a substantial reliance on charitable emergency food providers by government throughout the pandemic. When the first UK national COVID-19 lockdown was announced in March 2020, the UK Government designated food banks as essential services and permitted them to continue their operations. Each of the governments of the four constituent countries provided funding to FareShare (a food redistribution organisation), including £10.5 million from the Department for Environment, Food and Rural Affairs (Defra) to purchase and redistribute ambient food[14] through their network in England and £2.1 million from the Scottish Government. This funding enabled FareShare to scale up their operations significantly with 6,100 tonnes of food redistributed through their network a month – four times the pre-COVID-19 amount – and allowed them to purchase food, a major shift in their operations having previously distributed surplus food only. In addition to this, Defra funded a £3.5 million grant scheme for individual food charities.

Neither the Trussell Trust nor the Independent Food Aid Network (IFAN) accepted government funding to purchase food for distribution through their networks.[15] However, as each food bank in the Trussell Trust and IFAN is an independent charity, some did apply for Defra grants in their own right. The Defra funding structure (grants of £30,000–£100,000 to be spent within 12 weeks) was not well suited to smaller charities and, therefore, organisations benefiting from the scheme tended to be bigger charities, further embedding the dominance of large, corporatised charities as providers of welfare.

In November 2020, the Westminster Government introduced the COVID-19 Winter Grant Scheme, making available £16 million to fund local charities (all of which went to FareShare to distribute ambient food to front-line charities) and £170 million to support those in need across England with the costs of food, utilities and other essentials between December 2020 and March 2021. The scheme was administered by county councils and unitary authorities, which were granted autonomy over delivery through a variety of routes, including issuing grants to third parties, providing vouchers to households or making direct provision of food. While some local authorities circumvented food charities, providing food or money direct to households, others used the COVID-19 Winter Grant Scheme to further embed partnerships between local government and food aid, calcifying the place and importance of food charity within local welfare systems.[16]

Despite the calls of many food and anti-poverty charities for cash-first approaches and enhanced investment in social security during COVID-19 over increased funding for ad hoc charitable food provision, national and local government favoured the latter. The Trussell Trust and IFAN's rejection of government funding was an important step in resisting the institutionalisation of food aid; however, FareShare's acceptance of £28.6 million,[17] facilitating widespread distribution of ambient food to front-line food charities, many of which were set up in response to COVID-19, undeniably expanded and entrenched charitable food aid as essential welfare provision.

The manifestation of neoliberal ethics in food charity

The fieldwork in Bradford and York thus suggested that food charity is bound up with broader socio-political processes of state retrenchment. However, it also indicated that food aid may itself embody and entrench neoliberal ethical frameworks (see also May et al, 2019; Strong, 2019; Möller, 2021); through systems of food distribution and via the discourse of staff, food aid in Bradford and York maintained artificial divisions based on neoliberal notions of the ideal citizen: hardworking, active, entrepreneurial.

Food charity, neoliberalism and exclusion

Organisational policies manufactured exclusion in some food charities, particularly in food banks. Exclusion was most explicit through the food bank referral system. All Trussell Trust and 'independent' food banks in Bradford, but only Trussell Trust food banks in York, provided a food parcel and associated support – care, advice and signposting – exclusively on receipt of a food bank voucher. This was accessed via a third-party referral agent – for instance, a social worker, GP, welfare professional or local charity. As noted by May et al (2019), referral vouchers are a useful tool for managing stock and monitoring food bank use and have been 'instrumental in collecting evidence to inform public debate on UK food insecurity' (May et al, 2019:1262; see also Williams et al, 2016); however, the system poses significant difficulties for people in need of food. The process through which a voucher can be accessed by someone desperately needing food is complicated, bureaucratic and, at times, opaque: "They have to go to the doctor and get a doctor's appointment, and then the doctor has to agree to issue a voucher because each of the agencies will have this batch of vouchers, but they have our criteria, which is they have to live within our catchment"(John, food bank manager). The difficulties posed by the referral system do not end when a person arrives at the food bank. 'People must also hope that their voucher has not expired, that it has been completed properly by the referral agent, or that by the time they navigate the referral system the food bank will still have food to offer' (May et al, 2019: 1263).

Despite the obvious obstacles to accessing the food bank created by the referral system, some of the volunteers I spoke with did not consider it to be a barrier. For Denise, the manager of a recently opened Trussell Trust food bank, the voucher was a vehicle for inclusivity, a passport to the food bank. What mattered to Denise was that another person, not her, had made the decision about whether someone received that passport, so distancing herself from the moral responsibility of deciding who received food and who did not. The voucher was essential to producing this perception of distance between service users and volunteers:

'It is not that we haven't fed them and there is nothing to stop them coming, in the sense there is no barrier that we put in. Everybody and anybody, as long as they have a food voucher, that is all we want, some other organisation has made that assessment that they are the people that need food because we haven't got that expertise, or the training to check paperwork.'

Commenting on the technology of the voucher in food banks, May et al (2019) describe this separation of those assessing and processing food vouchers as a form of 'moral outsourcing, in which ethical dilemmas relating to those who should and should not have food are displaced from food bank volunteers to referral agents' (May et al, 2019: 1264). The implication, evident in May et al's (2019) ethnographic work and Denise's remark, is that professionally trained staff are less likely to 'succumb to the prejudices that can hinder the judgement of volunteers and more likely to embody a proper "bureaucratic ethic"' (May et al, 2019: 1264). Nevertheless, the criteria according to which an individual was eligible for referral to a food bank from a third-party welfare provider were ambiguous and, as such, decisions about access to food were open to being influenced by the prejudices of 'professionally trained staff'. Where criteria did exist, they appeared to be informed by neoliberal constructs of the 'deserving' – enterprising and independent – and 'undeserving' poor. The influence of these ideological constructs in shaping who received food was most conspicuous in the flexible spaces surrounding the referral system. People seeking support from the Trussell Trust and certain independent food banks were ostensibly allowed to redeem a maximum of three vouchers in six months – a policy intended to discourage 'dependency' on food banks;[18] however, in practice, some food banks would redeem a fourth voucher or assist people who turned up without a voucher, according to perceived need. In John's description, the components of this need are opaque and, on a day-to-day basis, dependent on the subjectivities of staff members: "After they have been three times, we then get much more stringent and it is on a discretionary basis thereafter according to what we judge their needs to be or not to be." For Shahid, while the food bank in which he volunteered did not officially ascribe to a set criterion of need, his conception of who was entitled to a food parcel appeared to be informed by neoliberal constructs of legitimate and illegitimate dependency – constructs inherent to the administration of social security in the UK.[19] Each case was "treated individually" and while "young girls" were given a food parcel, men from Poland, whom Shahid perceived to be drinking, were not:

'That [voucher] you saw is to be sent to us by the latest Wednesday. By Wednesday evening we prepare the food parcels; Thursday they collect. However, yesterday, these two young girls had no food at all so obviously we treat each case individually. ... We had this agency sending us people from Poland, and then we had to say, "enough is enough" because they used to come up here totally pissed out of their brains and collect a food parcel. So I put a stop to it, I said, "hang on a minute, if the guy can afford to drink then does he deserve a food parcel?"'

None of the soup kitchens interviewed excluded service users from receiving food according to subjectivities of deservingness. However, service user inclusion could be contingent on their behaviour in the venue, their acquiescence to religious preaching or their responsiveness to staff questions about their circumstances. Chapters 4 and 5 continue this discussion, revealing the religious and racialised dimensions of exclusion in food aid.

"There are certain people who, kind of by default, are choosing their situation": neoliberal narratives in food aid

Neoliberal definitions of need

The approach of some staff and volunteers providing food aid – especially those running food banks – appeared to be marked by a particular form of rationality, characterised by individualistic ethics of neoliberalism. This manifested in hierarchal definitions of need and dismissive judgements about recipients. Service providers' conceptualisations of the 'food need' in the local population could be ill informed, inconstant and heavily moralised. A perceived absence of data on food insecurity and food poverty, as well as the lack of a clear, accepted conceptualisation of the terms, allowed for discussions based on speculation and subjectivities. Service providers, like Helen, the coordinator of a local food poverty alliance, disputed whether food poverty was a question of scales or absolutes: food quality or food quantity; poverty or food poverty: "I get asked this question a lot and ask it a lot to people in Keighley and Bradford, and people feel there are levels of poverty, not food poverty."

This discussion of need could be situated within a wider neoliberal framework in which poverty was pathologised. Echoing popular neoliberal discourse, some service providers in Bradford and York characterised those using their services as responsible for their food insecurity, emphasising defective behavioural practices – laziness, greed, fraud – and financial mismanagement. The notion that food insecurity is a choice was a key component of this characterisation of the (food) poor. In considering the causes of food insecurity in Bradford, Frank, a local authority employee, said: "I think that skills links to culture, there is a culture of not being bothered. I know there are people in extreme situations, but I think there are certain people who, kind of by default, are choosing their situation." Framing food insecurity as, not an inevitability induced by systemic faults, but a self-inflicted and avoidable phenomenon permitted some service providers to question the authenticity and legitimacy of the 'food need'. A notable minority of service providers suggested fraud was a preoccupation in the provision of food charity. For John, the manager of a food bank, a key "challenge" was determining the authenticity of need: "For the coordinator the biggest challenge is not being abused, not having the wool pulled over our eyes – people who shouldn't be getting food when they are." Such discussions of the authentic, deserving and the illegitimate, undeserving 'food poor' were present in varying types of emergency food aid. Volunteers in food banks and soup kitchens questioned the legitimacy of service users; however, it was only food banks – and especially Trussell Trust food banks – that gave material form to these discursive divisions through the referral system. While these constructs were less present in conversations with representatives of community cafes, community supermarkets and community gardens – types of food aid which were open access and might include a financial transaction in the distribution of food – they were frequently heard in interviews with local authority staff – perhaps reflective of the infiltration of public services by principles and practices of neoliberal capitalism (see Connell et al, 2009).

Approved food choices

I set out to talk to people employed by or volunteering in community food aid and the local authority about food insecurity and their role, as an organisation or an individual, in addressing it. Many of those I spoke with, however, were also keen to talk about the diet and food choices of those who accessed their services. In these conversations, there was broad agreement that a "healthy" or "good" diet includes sufficient fruit and vegetables, is low in salt and sugar, and requires most food to be freshly prepared. This expensive, time-consuming diet was presented by multiple staff members employed by or volunteering in food aid as their own diet, in contrast to that of those using their services who ate "salty", "rubbish" or pre-prepared food. Correspondingly, approved food behaviour involved skilled food preparation and knowledge; service users who were perceived to display ignorance, arrogance or laziness in food choices and food behaviour were condemned. Describing changing food practices, Ayesha, a local authority employee, captured these opinions:

'It's that mindset of thinking, "I don't have to make my own food; I can afford to buy it now because there is a Roti house there". There is that element of turning what we would class as a negative thing, that people couldn't be bothered to make their own Rotis, to someone thinking, "I can buy them professionally made".'

Approved food choices were thus entwined with the reification of select skills associated with household management. Budgeting, planning meals, buying in season and cooking with raw ingredients were valorised. Incompetence in or failure to perform such skills was attributed to laziness and passivity, ignorance and thoughtlessness:

'They don't have a clue. They think they are cooking a decent meal when they buy a jar of sauce. I can't believe one of my clients ... I had loads of those bags of already prepared carrot batons, but the date was that day, so I said, "Do you want to take a load of vegetables home for your family?" She went, "No, I'm not feeding my family vegetables this week. I've been in Farmfoods and I got pizzas and things like that, so I won't be giving them vegetables this week" [laugh]. Not even a bean?' (Emma, community cafe volunteer)

The inherent irony to this discourse – that many food charities and especially (Trussell Trust) food banks distributed tinned and dried foods, often poor in quality, limited in diversity and unsuitable to the nutritional and cultural needs of some service users – was never acknowledged.

Virtue and ambivalence

Underpinning the moralisation of food need and food choices, and the reification of select household management skills was a particular construct of virtue, but notably one which was applied only to service users. Virtue was conceived by service providers as an individual phenomenon associated with a particular type of behaviour and the performance of certain skills. Virtue was not characterised by civic duty to the state or community but by personal responsibility; a virtuous citizen (service user) aligned with the 'ideal neoliberal citizen' (Galvin, 2002): autonomous, active – but not politically active – and responsible. Virtue could be inculcated in service users through teaching "life skills", such as cooking, demanding a certain standard of behaviour (obedience and politeness) in the arena of food aid, and in the immediate act of providing people with food, thereby mitigating other deviant behaviour. John, a food bank manager, used food as a vehicle to manipulate the behaviour of a supposed deviant: "Sometimes we give him food because we think it stops him stealing."

When applied to service providers, however, virtue was conceptualised in an alternative manner. Among those providing food charity, virtue evolved and was solidified through community engagement and the performance of civic duty, primarily via donations of food, and was situated within a paternalistic framework of responsibility for the poor. Antonio, a volunteer in a Catholic soup kitchen, considered members of the congregation to be virtuous because of their monetary donations to the soup kitchen: "Our people [the congregation], rich people, generous people. They give money so we don't ask for money from the public. To do good, we don't need a lot of money, just good will." The views of those I spoke with in community food aid and the local authority, nevertheless, incorporated a tension between stigmatising conceptualisations of service users, largely informed by neoliberal narratives of independence, and the lived experience of assisting people in poverty. There was some acknowledgement that chronic low income and an increasingly punitive social security system were key causes of food insecurity. Nutritious food, in particular, was recognised as unaffordable on a low income, forcing people to consume food that was deemed unhealthy by service providers: "I guess for the person who has a pound and are trying to decide what to do, well, why have they only got a pound? I mean real food is more expensive than actually a low income can afford" (Andrea, community group representative). In addition, there was broad acknowledgement that for many people, not only those on low incomes, the components of a healthy diet could be ambiguous, with competing messages trumpeted by different parties. For a minority of interviewees in Bradford and York, such structural obstacles were situated within a broader system of inequality "between the rich and poor" which maintained the future necessity of food aid. This recognition underscored the reality that, while neoliberal ideas had infiltrated the ethics of certain providers, there was also strong resistance to individualistic narratives of poverty; the reality on the ground was nuanced and variegated.

Diversity and complexity in contemporary food charity

Food charity may be symbiotic with state retrenchment and, in some circumstances, may embody neoliberal ethics; however, it cannot be neatly characterised as neoliberal. Food charity, as it manifested in the two English cities of Bradford and York, was a heterogeneous not a singular phenomenon, incorporating diverse types of organisation and variegated ethical frameworks. At the time of my fieldwork, there were 67 organisations in Bradford and 50 in York working in some way to alleviate food insecurity in these cities. This encompassed organisations distributing 'emergency' food, through structured processes and gatekeeping, and on an open access basis, alongside organisations providing a diverse (non-emergency) food offer interwoven with other services – for instance, community centres offering food on a low cost or pay-as-you-feel basis; community gardens working with local residents to collaboratively grow food; and food co-ops, collectively owned by residents, selling food at wholesale cost to local citizens. While in Bradford soup kitchens and food banks were key providers of food across the city (a total of 28 organisations at the time of the fieldwork), in York – possibly due to the different demography of the city – they were in the minority.

Approaches towards food distribution varied markedly among and within different types of food charity. One approach was formal and professional, emulating the bureaucracy and audit culture characteristic of the market. In these organisations the process of collecting food was controlled and bureaucratic, with the quantity of food a person could receive strictly rationed (see also May et al, 2020), and eligibility defined by ostensibly inflexible rules. This approach was most commonly found in Trussell Trust food banks, themselves constrained by centralised rules, processes and diktats. However, it was also a feature of some independent food banks, many of which employed systems of referral and rationing (Loopstra et al, 2019a). Many soup kitchens, while purportedly open access, also tightly controlled behaviour in the venue and rationed food. These organisational approaches were informed by top-down managerialism and by individualistic neoliberal ethics permeating through the organisational and staff culture.

Alternative approaches rejected gatekeeping and rationing, providing open access, universal provision. A notable example of the diversity within types of provider was evident among independent food banks, some which operated on an "informal" (as described by interviewees) and inclusive basis. This alternative form of food bank provision differed markedly from the dominant provider, the Trussell Trust: they were open access, rejecting any barriers to entry, particularly referral systems; they opposed rationing, permitting users to take as much food as necessary; and they were largely embedded within broader, pre-existing services – for instance, a longstanding community centre providing company and housing support to residents, a community cafe or a community kitchen. In this way, they differed from some more formalised independent food banks, many of which use referral and rationing (Loopstra et al, 2019a). It is worth noting, however, that just as significant diversity was apparent among independent food banks, so too was there variation in the ethics and operations of Trussell Trust food banks, many of which sought to challenge a punitive social security system by offering onsite benefit advice and signposting service users to financial and debt advice services (discussed further in Chapter 7 as part of a broader consideration of mutual aid and food aid).

Other forms of food aid, such as pay-as-you-feel cafes, aimed to reduce the stigma associated with food charity by introducing market-based mechanisms into systems of food distribution: food was sold at very low prices or on a pay-as-you-feel basis. This approach did successfully mitigate the stigma of food charity; however, by introducing forms of purchase, it reiterated the primacy of the market as the only alternative to charity, while simultaneously excluding those whose incomes were too low to afford even the lowest price.

Historical precedents and parallels

Food charity is not only a heterogeneous, it is arguably also a historical, phenomenon. There has long been food assistance in the UK (McGlone et al, 1999). Provision today may appear to be on a scale and embodying a level of professionalism and formalisation that is new (Lambie-Mumford, 2018); however, bureaucratic approaches to contemporary food distribution and a tendency toward moralism echo the practices and (liberal) ideology of food charity in the late 19th century.

Numerous social policy inquiries of the 1880s, 1890s and 1900s uncovered a vast, diverse mass of voluntary, self-governing, parochial and philanthropic provision that, in responding to apparent hunger and poverty, attempted, in a multitude of different ways, to 'assist, elevate, reform or coerce the poor and other persons in need' (Harris, 1992: 116). The attempted shift to a more 'organised' form of charity from 1869, pioneered by the Charity Organisation Society, instrumentalised the already-present distinction between the deserving and the undeserving poor (Humphreys, 1995). Charity was reconfigured as a mechanism to stem the 'widespread moral deterioration of the poor' and, therefore, relief was to be provided only after a case had been rigorously investigated to ascertain the applicant's worthiness (Humphreys, 1995: 5). Such Victorian social welfare provision – largely purveyed through face-to-face relationships within the medium of civil society – was an integral part of the social structure and civic culture of late 19th-century Britain. Indeed, the annual income and expenditure of registered and unregistered charities, friendly societies, benefit-paying trade unions and other benevolent and self-help institutions well exceeded the annual budget of the Poor Law, the main form of government-sponsored social assistance (Prest and Adams, 1954; Mitchell and Dean, 1962).

The monumental structural transformation of welfare provision that occurred in Britain between the 1870s and the 1950s was of central importance, not simply in the history of social policy, but in the wider history of politics, government, social structure and national culture (Harris, 1992). The creation of the British welfare state from 1946 represented a watershed in welfare principles and practice within Britain (Jones and Rodney, 2002). Post-war governments adopted William Beveridge's holistic approach to social welfare by accepting, unlike in the 1930s and, again, in the 1980s, that economic and social policy should be complementary and not antagonistic. Simultaneously, the principle of universalism, underpinned by the National Insurance Act 1946, eradicated the division between first-class and second-class citizens, thereby achieving a measure of social solidarity (Baldwin, 1992). The attack on the welfare state initiated in the 1970s, expanded by Thatcher and furthered by Blair, echoed arguments proposed by the Charity Organisation Society in 1869. Politicians on both sides of the Atlantic asserted that the growth in public transfers not only diminishes the act of charity by crowding out private anti-poverty efforts but is itself culpable for moral degradation (Jones and Rodney, 2002).

The fieldwork in Bradford and York pointed towards a complex picture of old and new provision. In Bradford, a minority of the food charities I spoke with were founded after 2010. Among these organisations, rising food insecurity in their local area was an important motivation for the development of their service, but it was a motivation that coexisted with other concerns, such as reducing isolation or performing corporate social responsibility:

> 'The reason for establishing it was we actually observed people looking in the bins outside for food, outside the office here and, in one day, we saw two people going in the bins for scraps of food. So we spoke with the centre manager, looked at the availability of the hall downstairs and looked at what provision there was in the centre. But also we questioned – because the centre is in the heart of this area which is one of the most deprived wards – we questioned what level of CSR [Corporate Social Responsibility] they were exercising across the District and, when it came to looking at people who were destitute or homeless, very little, so we agreed then that we would pilot something.' (Samia, soup kitchen manager)

Newer organisations were more likely to be food banks and social food charities, offering meals on a pay-as-you-feel basis; some older organisations had recently expanded their food activities into emergency food provision, while some longstanding emergency food providers discussed serving a new type of in-work service user (albeit also often in receipt of tax credits). Nevertheless, community food assistance for people in need was long-established in the area, and even organisations that appeared new tended to be affiliated to older organisations, often churches, with a long history of charitable work – as described by David, the manager of a busy food bank: "In an ad hoc form the provision has been going for decades – giving people food from a cupboard. We now have formalised provision with a voucher system, like the Trussell Trust, and this has only been going for three years or so." In York, roughly half of the organisations supporting community food needs were founded after 2010. This included four Trussell Trust food banks, six independent food banks, and nine community cafes; of the 50 community food organisations in York, 38 per cent responded that rising food insecurity in their local area had encouraged their development. But, as in Bradford, many of the more informal forms of food charity, such as some independent food banks and community cafes, were affiliated to older organisations with a history of charitable work and service provision. Food insecurity was a contemporary manifestation of need among the communities they had served for decades.

In Bradford and York, food aid in its entirety arguably emulated a system of 19th-century charity rather than constituting a new sector: a variegated group of ad hoc, charitable and parochial provision which, in its response to hunger, may both assist and reform people in need. Trussell Trust food banks – professionalised, bureaucratic and moralistic – did appear to be a distinct and new part of localised systems of food provision. Nevertheless, while new within the confines of 20th- and 21st-century food aid, Trussell Trust food banks (and those independent food banks that emulated them) in fact closely echoed many of the characteristics of late 19th-century food charity, pioneered by the Charity Organisation Society – represented by the orchestrated shift towards a more organised form of charity, instrumentalising the already-present distinction between the deserving and the undeserving poor. In Trussell Trust food banks, charity serves as a mechanism to stem the 'widespread moral deterioration of the poor' (Humphreys, 1995: 5) and relief is therefore provided only after a case has been rigorously investigated to ascertain the applicant's worthiness – today, through the referral system.

Conclusion

"Living on benefits is a lifestyle choice", asserted George Osborne in 2010. In changing the system to deter people from making such a "mistaken choice", Osborne and his colleagues in the Conservative Party pushed millions into deep poverty, forcing them to seek food charity. Out of these social policy choices grew food banks, a community response to the sudden and extreme destitution people saw around them. Like others across the UK, charities, community groups and individuals in Bradford and York responded to rising and urgent need created by welfare reform by setting up new food charities and expanding older organisations to provide food aid.

George Osborne's policy choices, while brutal in their scale and depth, continued more than four decades of cuts to public services and social security, accompanied by increased governmental emphasis on the role and responsibility of the voluntary sector in managing poverty. The growth of food aid, and especially Trussell Trust food banks, from 2010 fitted neatly into this longer neoliberal trajectory; food banks, at first willingly and later (at least publicly) begrudgingly, adopted responsibility for hunger in local communities, becoming enmeshed within local welfare systems. In line with this national picture, there was evidence in Bradford and York that food aid, especially food banks, was becoming formalised as part of a denuded welfare system: a minority of organisations received direct funding from local authorities through community grants and buildings; local government collaborated in alliances around food insecurity; and public sector care and welfare professionals distributed food bank vouchers.

George Osborne's spurious and stigmatising claim that some people 'choose a life on benefits' was not only reflected in the growth of charitable responses to the poverty and hunger that his policies created, but it was also built into the structures and practice of some of those charitable responders. Trussell Trust food banks erected a referral system to distinguish those deserving of food from those who, because of their own life choices, were undeserving. Where flexibility in the distribution of food was permitted – as was the case in a majority of organisations, despite the supposed inflexibility of the referral system – it was often accompanied by stigmatising attitudes towards a particular type of service user. Such narratives appeared to be closely aligned with a neoliberal framework which individualised and pathologised poverty, portraying it as self-inflicted, and thereby permitting scrutiny of the authenticity of need.

Food charity, in its entirety, is, however, a more ambiguous phenomenon than the above depiction may suggest. Food charity is heterogeneous and multifaceted, spanning from the bureaucracy and corporatisation of the Trussell Trust to the localism and inclusivity of some independent food banks and community cafes (discussed further in Chapter 7). In Bradford and York, food charity supported service users in receipt of – inadequate and punitive – social security, but it also served those in work, people seeking company and those who were vulnerably housed and not engaged in social security. Arguably, contemporary food aid best emulates 19th-century philanthropy: voluntary, self-determining and unregulated but also, on occasion, moralistic.

The fieldwork underpinning this book was conducted between 2014 and 2019; at the time, growing relationships between local government and community food aid intimated a creeping institutionalisation of food charity at the local level but by no means was food aid fully institutionalised within local welfare systems. The COVID-19 pandemic sharply accelerated collaboration between food aid and government at the local and national level. Despite resistance from the Trussell Trust and IFAN, funding contracts and partnerships have further – and firmly – embedded food charity within national and local welfare systems.

Notes

[1] A defining feature of UK welfare reform since 2010 has been the concerted move towards greater compulsion and sanctioning, which has been interpreted by some social policy scholars as punitive and cruel. Wright et al (2020) document the suffering that unemployed claimants experience because of harsh conditionality and find that punitive welfare conditionality often causes symbolic and material suffering and sometimes has life-threatening effects. They describe the wide range of suffering induced by welfare conditionality as 'social abuse', including the demoralisation of the futile job-search treadwheel and the self-administered surveillance of Universal Jobmatch.

[2] Carol and Paddy Henderson founded the Trussell Trust in 1997 based on a legacy left by Carol's mother, Betty Trussell. In its initial form, the Trussell Trust developed projects in Bulgaria focusing on improving conditions for children sleeping at Bulgaria's Central Railway Station. In 2000, Paddy Henderson received a request from a mother in Salisbury who was struggling to afford food. This was the catalyst for the first Trussell Trust food bank, the 'Salisbury Foodbank', located in Paddy and Carol's garden shed and garage and providing three days' 'emergency' food to people in crisis in the local area. See: www.trusselltrust.org/about/our-story/

[3] The neoliberal political transformation under Thatcher was in fact initiated by the monetarist agenda of Prime Minister Jim Callaghan and his chancellor, Denis Healey in the 1970s.

[4] Institutionalisation is defined as making something (a process, organisation, norm) a permanent part of society or the state system.

[5] Certainly, New Labour initiated very important social reforms, including the minimum wage, shorter waiting times for medical treatment, better health targets, attempts to reduce child poverty, doubling of student numbers and edging – tentatively and reluctantly – towards equal pay and human rights legislation (Hall, 2011).

[6] This point also applies to broader analyses of the political economy of welfare; recent literature on the age of austerity and contemporary welfare reform highlights the dangers of ahistorical social policy analysis and the importance of understanding current shifts within a wider historical context (Farnsworth and Irving, 2015). See Lambie-Mumford (2018) for a discussion of the importance of understanding the growth of food banks within their wider historical context.

[7] The Health in Pregnancy grant was a one-off, tax-free payment. It was paid to expectant mothers from 25 weeks gestation to help them stay well and healthy and to meet extra costs during the later stages of pregnancy. See: HM Revenue and Customs (2009); Stewart and Reader (no date).

[8] The Social Fund was a government scheme to help people with expenses that are difficult to meet on a low income. There are several different types of Social Fund benefits, including budgeting loans, cold weather payments, funeral payments, short-term benefit advances,

and Sure Start maternity grants. Until April 2013, the Social Fund was also responsible for Crisis Loans and Community Care Grants which helped people in an emergency.

9   Education Maintenance Allowance – EMA – was an income-assessed weekly allowance of £30 to help students with the cost of further education. The Conservative–Liberal Democrat coalition government cancelled the scheme for England in 2010. The scheme is still available in Northern Ireland, Scotland and Wales.

10 Tax credits are a form of social security. There are two types of tax credit: Working Tax Credit and Child Tax Credit. Working Tax Credit is paid to people who work and are on a low income. Child Tax Credit is paid to people who have children. It is paid in addition to child benefit. Both types of tax credit are incorporated into Universal Credit.

11 Universal Credit is a means-tested benefit for people of working age who are on a low income. Introduced in April 2013, it is an attempt to simplify the welfare system by rolling six existing means-tested benefits and tax credits – Income Support, Income-based Jobseeker's Allowance (JSA), Income-related Employment and Support Allowance (ESA), Housing Benefit, Child Tax Credit, and Working Tax Credit – into one monthly payment. The benefit has been heavily criticised since its introduction, see: Butler (2018a).

12 The research with women living on a low income and at risk of food insecurity was conducted subsequent to this in 2016–17.

13 This is further explored in Power et al, 2021c and Pybus et al, 2021.

14 Ambient food, also known as shelf-stable food, is food of a type that can be safely stored at room temperature in a sealed container. This includes items such as tinned foods.

15 This response was in line with pre-existing policy in both organisations. The Trussell Trust has historically demarcated the space between their projects and the state to resist the institutionalisation of food banking evident in North America. The organisation has largely done so by refusing to enter into contractual and service-led agreements with local and central government and by maintaining discursive distance from the state via high-profile criticism of welfare reform. The Independent Food Aid Network has similarly (and arguably more assertively) rejected government funding and formal partnerships to withstand the institutionalisation of food aid.

16 In Bradford, the local authority utilised this additional government funding to financially support food banks.

17 The combined value of Defra funding in March/April 2020; Scottish Government funding in March/April 2020; and Defra funding in November 2020, as part of the COVID-19 Winter Grant Scheme.

18 The Trussell Trust standardly limits users to three vouchers for three days' worth of food in six months, which is explained as a strategy to reduce dependency, see: Trussell Trust (2015). A survey of independent food banks found that over 60 per cent require new clients to have a referral from a third-party agency and over 30 per cent restrict access to food parcels to six times or fewer in a 12-month period. See Loopstra et al (2019a).

19 See May at al (2019: 1257): 'The surveillance to which different claimants are subjected varies both within and across different domains (for example, between those claiming state pensions and those on JobSeekers Allowance) and according to welfare officials' moral evaluations of different groups; with those more at risk of 'dependency' subject to more intensive monitoring and stricter penalties if unable to change their behaviour because they are understood as incapable of governing themselves.'

4

Soup and salvation: realising religion through contemporary food charity

'I don't know what is going to happen when I die, but while I am on earth, I will live out the message of Jesus through helping people. This is central to my work in the church and the food bank.'

David, manager of a Salvation Army food bank

Introduction: faith and food charity in the 21st century

On a cold afternoon in November 2015, I sat with David in a small office adjacent to the church hall from which food parcels were distributed and asked him why he chose to set up a food bank. David said that his reason for doing so was religious; charity work through food was integral to his life as a Christian, to serving the poor and God. Thus, his work in the food bank today continued a long tradition of Christian charitable works for the hungry and destitute. He recognised that rapid increases in need in the local area were partly related to harsh austerity and, in this way, the hunger of the people who visited the food bank was the responsibility of government, not the Church, but his faith told him to help people in need, regardless of the cause. The result was a busy and regular food bank, overseen by David and supported by equally committed Christian volunteers.

While David's reasons for giving food were acknowledged to be part of a religious framework, he did not necessarily consider his food bank to be part of a broader movement of food banks run by Christian groups across the UK. His food bank was perceived by him as merely the formalisation of a historic distribution of food from the Church, which became necessary as demand increased. But David's food bank *is* part of a wider movement; of the thousands of food banks that have opened in the past decade, the majority of them are run by or affiliated to Christian groups. Some of this is attributable to the – increasingly and intentionally – hidden Christian ethos of the Trussell Trust, the largest coordinator of food banks in the UK, an ethos which is maintained by its Head of Church Engagement, who holds responsibility for 'strengthening and shaping the relationship between the

Trussell Trust and the Christian community' (Trussell Trust, 2019). It is also, however, attributable to the motivations and praxis of thousands of Christian groups and individuals: the Church of England estimates that 8,000 churches (60 per cent) support food banks in some way – running them directly, providing volunteers or donations, or working in partnership to host and assist them (Church of England, 2019).[1]

Other faith groups in the UK also appear to be increasingly targeting their activities towards hunger among those outside their congregation – a particularly notable feature of the COVID-19 pandemic response. For instance, informed by the concept of *langar*, or shared meal, British Sikhs are delivering food aid within Gurdwaras – with an estimated 5,000 meals served to non-Sikhs each week – as well as in the wider community outside the temple. British Sikhs have established food relief organisations in cities across the UK, including the Midland Langar Seva Society in Birmingham, the Kirpa Food Bank in Wolverhampton, and the Sikh Welfare and Awareness Team in London. Muslim organisations have similarly established food banks, such as Sufra in London, and supported secular and Muslim food charity with food and financial donations. The involvement of other faith groups in the delivery of food charity through emergency food systems is, nevertheless, considerably more limited than the engagement of Christian communities. A survey of independent food banks found that, while over half were run by Christian groups, only one belonged to a Muslim faith organisation and one was run by a multi-faith group (Loopstra et al, 2019a). This single survey is by no means a comprehensive account of the composition of the sector; it does, however, provide insight into the potentially uneven balance of religious food charity in the UK.

In Chapter 3, I argued that the contemporary responsibility of food charity for managing poverty and hunger at the local level is intimately associated with state retrenchment since the 1970s. Religious charities have been subject to similar governmental pressures to their secular counterparts to adopt localised responsibility for poverty (see Cairns et al, 2007; Jarvis et al, 2010); the predominance of faith-based food aid may therefore, in part, be a consequence of wider neoliberal processes of state transformation. To consider religious provision simply as part of broader political processes, however, would be to neglect the obvious: food is fundamental to faith. Across many different religious traditions there are shared commitments to the reception of food as a gift from the divine (or divines) and to its role in defining the boundaries of the community (Pemberton, 2020). Against this context, the chapter seeks to understand how and why religious groups participate in contemporary food charity in the UK. Informed by the demography of the case study areas and the high prevalence of Christian provision nationally, the empirical sections focus on Christianity and Islam. I start, however, by examining the place and function of food, and its relationship with charity, in Sikh, Muslim, Jewish and finally, and at length, Christian traditions.

Theological perspectives on food and charity

Food and charity in Sikhism

Langar, a communal free kitchen in which food is offered to all, is a central tenet of the Sikh tradition. The performance of *langar* constitutes a practical demonstration of the values promoted by Guru Nanak – selfless service (*seva*); hard work; sharing and equality beyond any categorisation of caste, gender, social status, ethnicity or religion – practices undertaken in a faith that is marked by an absence of proselytising (Singh, 2015). Importantly, for Sikhs in diaspora, rather than simply referring to members of a particular ethno-religious group, 'community' refers to anyone with whom they engage at a local, national or international level. In extending the idea of *langar* exponentially, this view allows Sikhs to enact the ideal of '*sarbat da Bhala*', or work 'for the betterment of all' (Singh, 2015).

Charity and food in Islam

Zakat, compulsory charity, constitutes the Third Pillar of Islam. Analogous to Christian conceptions of caritas,[2] Islamic charity purifies the soul from greed and moves the donor closer to the divine (Fisher, 2017). *Amanah*, a form of trusteeship where all things that belong to God are entrusted to humans for their collective wellbeing, is intimately linked to charitable obligations (Atia, 2013). Individuals have the right to possess private property and the right and agency to allocate resources, but they also have a moral and spiritual responsibility to use those resources to benefit society. *Amanah* operates through the institutions of *zakat* and *sadahaq* (Atia, 2013), the latter term used to describe voluntary almsgiving as opposed to the mandatory contributions of *zakat*. Unlike *zakat*, where donations are restricted to certain categories of individuals (the destitute, the indebted, stranded travellers, New Muslims) and purposes (to free slaves, projects that help Muslims, and to pay workers who collect and distribute *zakat*), the uses of *sadahaq* are flexible and unprescribed. Much of the Qur'ānic emphasis is on giving to those in need, whether through tax, alms or charity, as a way of 'creating new relationships [and] a new and more generous social order' (Siddiqui, 2015: 32). Eating, like charity, features as a part of a single, coherent Muslim identity: the production and consumption of food are theological, part of wider practice to sustain how humans receive the abundance of the world as a gift and return the gift to God in worship (Kassam and Robinson, 2014). The Qur'ān describes how food originates, what it signifies, and what foods are allowable or prohibited, which informs

Muslim identities and Islamic theology, law, ethics and aesthetics (Kassam and Robinson, 2014).

Justice and charity in Judaism

The Hebrew word for charity, *tzedakah*, is derived from the Hebrew root *Tzadei-Dalet-Qof*, meaning righteousness, justice or fairness (Ulmer, 2014). In Judaism, charity for the poor is not viewed as a generous or magnanimous gesture, instead it is an act of social justice, of 'giving the poor their due' (Bird, 1982). In correspondence with the concept in Islam, charity in the Judaic tradition becomes increasingly more virtuous the less the giver and the receiver know of each other. The highest level of *tzedakah* is considered to occur when the giver enables the receiver through gift, loan, partnership or employment to be self-reliant so that she no longer depends on charity (Baker, 2003).

Food and charity in the Judeo-Christian tradition

In the Judeo-Christian tradition, both the Old and New Testament contain frequent mentions of hunger, food and a Christian's relationship to the land (Fisher, 2017; Pemberton, 2020). The Book of Isaiah (Chapter 58) in the Old Testament encourages people to be charitable out of their own good will rather than to ingratiate oneself with God or others, while in Leviticus and Deuteronomy, farmers are mandated to resist harvesting the corners of their fields such that the poor may glean them. Hunger, similarly, forms a fundamental component of the New Testament. The accounts found in all four gospels of Jesus feeding multitudes, in addition to both the Last Supper and the Eucharist, in which bread and wine become Jesus's flesh and blood, illustrate the centrality of the self-sacrificial giving of food – of life – of salvation – to others within Christianity.

The Bible does not, however, present a unified approach to social welfare. Instead, biblical parables point to both social justice and charity-based approaches to addressing hunger. While Christianity has motivated many to focus on social justice-oriented solutions to hunger – for instance, multiple Protestant denominations in the US operate anti-poverty and anti-hunger focused initiatives – charity has arguably dominated the contemporary Christian response to hunger in the Global North. In the US, for example, an estimated two thirds of the nation's 61,000 emergency food outlets affiliated with the Feeding America network[3] are linked to a house of worship (Fisher, 2017).

This binary within the Christian tradition between social justice and charity-based approaches is exemplified by the varied representations of Christian thought in the works of the US scholar Rebecca de Souza (2019) in *Feeding the Other: Whiteness, Privilege and Neoliberal Stigma* and the British academic and theologian Charles Roding Pemberton (2020) in *Bread of Life in Broken Britain: Food Banks, Faith and Neoliberalism*. De Souza, concerned with the intersection of racism, neoliberalism and charity, orients her engagement with Christian thought towards the overlap between Calvinism and capitalism, explicated in the early 20th century by Max Weber. As noted in Chapter 2, Weber argued that the Calvinist ethic, to save, work hard and avoid immediate gratification, underpinned the development of industrial capitalism in 19th-century Protestant Europe. Today, the Anglo-American welfare system, dominated by intense individualism, can be explained by the Calvinist socio-religious underpinnings of Anglo-American society. This Calvinist ethic is manifest in US food pantries[4] in which service users are stigmatised and Othered by staff, according to moral frameworks which seek to uphold the ethics of neoliberal capitalism (de Souza, 2019).

Pemberton, by contrast, emphasises the participatory and communistic ethos of Christianity. He outlines recurring values in Christian engagement with food to assess whether food banking is consistent with the commitments of the Christian tradition and, drawing upon the writings of Alexander Schmemann, the Orthodox Christian priest, teacher and writer, sets out core elements of this tradition. The material world, and the food within it, is not secular because the world is not separate from God: participating in the world, for instance through eating, only becomes meaningful via an understanding that 'only in God is found the meaning of everything' (Schmemann, quoted in Pemberton, 2020: 78). The whole world is the site of God's blessing and humans can, by their practices – including preparing, eating and redistributing food, participate in God through living. For Pemberton, therefore, 'because the kind of participation theology advocates is "reciprocal", a circulation of gifts, it includes an affirmation of the existence of the other and a desire that they persist' (Pemberton, 2020: 80). Pemberton goes on to suggest that 'a significant part of the reason why Christians are so involved in food banking is that food is so prominent in Christianity's writings and history'; he argues that 'in continuity with how food practices have featured in the history of the church … food banks give contemporary Christians a way to contribute to a common world outside the boundaries of the church and a means to show the distinctiveness of the Christian identity' (Pemberton, 2020: 80). Pemberton's ethnographic research in a County Durham food bank leads him to conclude that food banks, while partially informed by the economic and political times in which they have occurred, also reproduce principles of participation inherent to Christianity.

Chris Allen, a Liverpool-based theologian and social scientist, offers a sharply differing analysis of the ecological-political consequence of food banks, offering a Marxist account of Christian food charity (Allen, 2016). Allen argues that 'the Christian churches and their leadership have historically occupied privileged social and economic spaces' (Allen, 2016: 365) and 'consequently their message has historically borne the imprint of its privileged origins' (Allen, 2016: 369). For Allen, it should not therefore be a surprise that food banking constitutes the predominant Christian response to poverty in Britain as:

> It is entirely consistent with the historically dominant Christian social tradition that has oriented largely middle-class church organisations and their leadership towards charitable giving activities rather than radical social change. Foodbank theology is merely the product of a church whose privileged being has shaped its theological episteme such that it understands charitable giving, rather than radical social change, lies at the heart of God's message. (Allen, 2016: 365)

Allen is critical of human rights approaches to food insecurity; he argues that by framing food insecurity as an inability to participate in a contemporary consumer society we obfuscate the ecologically destructive nature of modern neoliberal capitalism and further an individualistic understanding of human beings. Allen writes, 'food consumerism appeals to a privileged and individualised life of buying, possessing, and gratification, and is incompatible with a Jesus that used food to emphasise our "communism of being"' (Allen, 2016: 371).

For Allen, Christian charities and social justice campaigners have been insufficiently critical of agribusinesses ('destroying the earth and its inhabitants in food producing regions in order to serve food consumers in countries such as Britain': Allen, 2016: 370) and human rights discourses which assume the primacy of individual consumption in neoliberal capitalism. Allen argues that, instead of food charity, churches should focus on radical hospitality. The Church should restate publicly and act out visibly its radical heritage by transforming its own land to create 'community allotments and encourage collective practices of cultivation' (Allen, 2016: 373). However, it should go further, adopting the role of a 'land activist church' to reclaim land that has been forcibly seized from poor families for prestige development to 'morally reclaim and physically occupy such land in order to create new collective food growing spaces, even though this would involve violating private property rights' (Allen, 2016: 374).

Faith and food charity in Bradford and York

The religious composition of food charity in Bradford, a multi-ethnic, multi-faith city, and York, a largely White British city with a small but growing Black and minority ethnic population, reflected national trends. In Bradford, almost half of food aid organisations (48 per cent) were run by a faith group, the majority of which were Christian. The influence of religion was most pronounced in the case of food banks, 75 per cent of which were managed by a Christian group (only one food bank in Bradford was organised by a Muslim group). Soup kitchens and soup runs in Bradford were also largely run by Christian groups (58 per cent); however, there was a sizeable minority of soup kitchens operated by Muslim groups (26 per cent), as well as a minority by secular organisations (16 per cent). In York, religious groups were less prominent providers of food charity (only 11 out of 51 community food organisations described themselves as faith-based); nevertheless, all four Trussell Trust food banks and one independent food bank were faith-based – Christian – organisations.

Commenting on religious food charity in the US, de Souza (2019) notes that faith-based organisations employ a wide range of theories, ideologies and practices, ranging from 'faith-permeated' organisations in which there are explicit references to faith, to secular or post-secular organisations, in which humanistic values are prioritised (see also Adkins et al, 2012). Salonen (2016a; 2016b; 2016c), informed by an ethnography of food assistance programmes in a Finnish city, similarly highlights diversity of practice and the context-dependent character of faith-based food aid. The role of religion in food assistance, Salonen (2016b) argues, is not only subject to particular contexts, but is socially produced in the practices of food banks and the goals of food providers. This diversity of theology and practice, as well as the importance of context in shaping food assistance, was evident among faith-based organisations in the case study areas.[5] Religious involvement in food aid could materialise in a variety of forms and religion was (re)produced via the practice of food charity.

Religious organisations and groups established and managed food charities, often supported by long-established faith-based networks. Such networks were particularly useful in expediting the development of food banks, as described by Julie, a volunteer in a Christian Trussell Trust food bank:

'Then we had just got to the point of signing up the Trussell Trust, we got loads of churches ... and said, "We are thinking of looking at this, would any of you like to be involved?" And I think it was out of 24 churches in total we got 13 churches who were dead keen on doing it, which was really good. So we got a steering group together and we started investigating how we might do it, whether we would go with the Trussell Trust or not and decided we would.'

Churches and mosques provided large financial donations and offered the use of buildings rent free, while members of their congregations donated food and money, as described by Faysal, a volunteer in a Muslim food bank, "We get more donations here [in the mosque] as well. If I make an announcement to our congregation on Friday I will be inundated. Initially we got huge donations, bags and bags of rice, everything, crates and crates of kidney beans."

People of faith were employed by and volunteered in food charities and some providers drew on pre-existing religious networks and groups for volunteer support:

'Now we have a church college here, which is like a theology college, and we take students from that college who want to get involved in the pastoral side of things. We take those on the street without any qualms, it is part and parcel of our serving ethos.' (Martin, Christian soup run volunteer)

Despite a broader context of limited, short-term third sector funding (Clifford, 2016), faith-based food aid in Bradford and York appeared to be well financed, staffed and resourced, with a steady stream of food donations and volunteers and broadly adequate income to cover any overheads, such as rent: a sharp contrast with a public sector which, at the same time, was administering steep cuts to staffing and public services as central government drastically reduced local authority budgets. The diversity of religious involvement in food provision – from organisational networks, to donations, to staff, to proselytising (to be discussed later) – was echoed in the breadth of motivations among religious groups for charitable food provision.

"Bringing heaven down to earth": motivations for faith-based food charity

In Bradford and York, I asked Muslim, Christian and secular providers about the moral systems which informed their provision of food assistance. However, only interviewees of a Christian faith, in Christian food aid, described the religious frameworks underpinning their work. This response, from Shahid, a (South Asian) volunteer in a food bank located in a mosque, is reflective of the broader presentation of charitable endeavours, apparently unrelated to theology, by the members of Bradford's British South Asian, and predominantly Muslim, community I spoke with:

Interviewer: Is the faith aspect a motivation, does that have a role in what you do?
Shahid: I think faith also tells us to give to charity, see. Now in my case when I joined Lions Club, I was not a practising Muslim, I am now the last few years but that had nothing to do with faith when I started, I wanted to serve the community, give back to the community,

see. Because Lions are all volunteers, we have got
1.4 million members worldwide, in 209 countries.
Now if you donate £100 to Cancer Research you will
find that £60 will go, you know what they pay; with
Lions Club if you give us £100 for a project it is actual
£100 that gets there.

Shahid's broad, unspecific representation of the influence of his faith on his
role in food charity – "faith tells us to give to charity" – was illustrative of a
wider tendency among members of Bradford's South Asian Muslim community
to either describe the influence of Islam in general terms – giving to charity,
helping the community – or not to mention it at all. By contrast, Islam was a key
feature in conversations with low-income Muslim women in Bradford about
lived experiences of food amid poverty. Islam shaped their everyday practices
around food and their relationships with others; it was deeply embedded within
daily life. The apparent difference between Christian and Muslim food charities
in their motivations for providing food may in part be attributable to this identity
of Islam as a lived religion (Jeldtoft, 2011), intimately woven into daily practice,
including sharing food with others. This is further explored in Chapter 7; the
discussion in this chapter focuses largely on Christian motivations for food aid,
which were explicit in conversations with food charities.

Among Christian providers, motivations for food charity were informed
by ideas of caritas, the principles of hospitality and participation described
by Pemberton, as well as the moralising and hierarchal tendencies of the
Christian Church critiqued by de Souza and Allen. David, a member of the
Salvation Army, described the absence of separation between the spiritual life
and the realities of everyday work life in his understanding of Christianity.
The idea of charity work through food was integral to human fulfilment and
to Christian practice. Spirituality was presented as a practice of the everyday,
with all of life becoming re-sacralised. David told me:

'In providing food, support and social services we are bringing heaven
down to earth. Most people think that doing good work when
alive means that they will go to heaven when they die but this is a
misunderstanding of the Lord's Prayer: it is about helping people on
earth so that you bring heaven down to earth.'

He continued:

'You can't compartmentalise who we are as people; you can't separate
the spiritual from the physical being. The spiritual person and the
physical person make a whole. Education over the past century has
taught us to do this, but it is a false separation: you can't divide the

spirituality from the person. We try to help the person and in helping the person we are drawing upon spirituality and helping the spirituality in them. It is just like you can't separate the mental from the physical being, mental illness has physical implications.'

The 19th-century founders of the Salvation Army, William Booth and Catherine Mumford, sought to bring salvation to the hungry, poor and destitute by meeting their 'physical and spiritual needs' (Hill and Larsson, 2017). The food bank in which David volunteered provided an opportunity for him and his colleagues to continue this longstanding tradition, to bring physical and spiritual salvation to users through food and care.

'The Salvation Army has always been an important provider of social services and it remains so today. The training the officers get is lengthy, with a focus on practical and social skills, rather than purely theological. The Salvation Army works nationally and internationally. The type of services provided will be tailored to context, so in the UK it may be homeless shelters or social services. The Salvation Army set up many services which the government later took over.'

David's description of his work in the food bank reflected the participatory, communistic and egalitarian ethos of Christianity, highlighted by Pemberton (2020) – according to David:

'Salvation means being free; it is a physical thing. Through helping people in the food bank, we are helping them achieve salvation. It is a church with its sleeves rolled up. We were started by the poor, for the poor and hence today we are biased towards those on the edge of society. Other churches do help people, but they can often be aloof and may have very few poor people in their congregation. The Salvation Army sees the wholeness in people, as do I.'

Luke, a Franciscan, looked on the performance of charity through food as integral to his religious life. He and his Franciscan brothers existed to live the Gospel: they practised simple living and detachment from material possessions in emulation of Jesus's life and earthly ministry, and to experience solidarity with the poor (Havely, 2004). With the assistance of largely Catholic volunteers, the Franciscans ran a twice-weekly soup kitchen, providing "Christian charity to the poor and destitute":

'It is not so much limiting but our work is always to be focused on those in the lowest places, you know, so the most destitute, so as long as we can continue serving them – hopefully it is not the same people forever, hopefully they will be able to move forward and things, but our main hope is as long as the destitute are in Bradford and in this neighbourhood, we would like to be able to serve them and meet their needs in whatever way we can.'

For Luke, food charity was a form of worship; an opportunity to express his love for God and his neighbour, and to emulate St Francis's spirit through charitable work with the poor:

'It is religious for sure; it is based on our faith. It is certainly not, we don't see it so much as a social work, as much as like a response to a spiritual call and serving the Lord and the poor. Yes, we couldn't do it without our spiritual base really.'

The belief that food charity was an opportunity to express one's love for God was a common theme among staff and volunteers in soup kitchens and food banks. Luigi, a volunteer in a Catholic soup kitchen, described himself as "lucky to have the opportunity to help these people". He went on: "Because when you give you receive. It is the evangelical situation. This is the good situation that God gave us, to serve somebody. We are not one, an island, we are with many others." The "warm hospitality" of the soup kitchen, providing a weekly hot meal, tea and coffee, embodied a shared commitment to the reception of food as a gift from the divine. Luigi enjoyed being able to help the largely homeless population who attended the soup kitchen and was disappointed when numbers were low.

The soup kitchen in which Luigi volunteered was well supported by the local Catholic community through prayer – "many people pray for us on Saturday" – and by donations of food and money. However, the Catholic soup kitchen also received support from Anglicans and people of no religion. Luigi valued the opportunity presented by food charity to engage with other faith communities, as well as the homeless people he served: "One group is English, not Catholic, Anglican – not a problem. This job opens one's mind and there are so many other people who want to help. For that we are open for many men, other opportunities. For me, it's nice." The opportunity for community engagement and participation provided by food charity was similarly expressed by Natasha, a food bank volunteer. The food bank, a partnership between multiple Anglican churches, was an opportunity to address the growing – and broader – disconnect between the Anglican Church and the local, increasingly secular, community.

Interviewer: Do you think faith is a motivation for people to help?
Natasha: Definitely, oh definitely, yes. I think there is quite a
                 strong influence in the church at the moment of living

out your faith in your community. I think people, and
sometimes the churches, have been accused of being in
little huddles and being separate from the rest of society.
I think we are realising now that that is not the way
that it is and it has been really interesting that working
with different churches, we have all got on so well and,
sometimes in the past, different churches don't always
see eye to eye, they have different interpretations of their
faith but I can say that categorically this has been the
best group of people I have ever worked with and I have
spent quite a lot of time working in the voluntary sector.

The convenient coexistence of food insecurity and faith provided
opportunities for collaboration among and between religious groups.
Margaret, a volunteer in an evangelical soup kitchen, considered faith to
be integral to food charity because it provided ready-made networks, while
Faysal described a mutually beneficial partnership between a Christian food
provider and the Muslim food bank in which he volunteered:

'Maria [member of local Christian church congregation] has actually
donated £1,400 this year towards our food bank because Maria, what
they do from now until February is take all the homeless off the street,
put them in churches. What we do in addition to food bank for them,
my wife, myself and there is two other members, we actually provide
a hot meal one evening for them in the church.'

Food charity provided an opportunity to build relationships and community
with those inside, as well as outside, the food aid space. For both David
and Luke, committed to Christianity's egalitarian ethos, the food bank was
"all about building relationships" and caring for those using the service
by providing food but also by addressing the underlying reason for their
hunger: "Often food is the immediate but not the real, underlying reason
they are coming to the food bank, this may be addiction, mental illness,
they may be an EU migrant – effectively just a refugee as they often don't
have access to benefits; they may be in debt" (David).

'Yes, it is very complex. That is why our work, we generally focus
on first level encounter, first level service, it is basically just warm
handshake and a cup of coffee and building relationships with people
because many of them are just not even, most of them are sleeping
rough so you have to kind of get them to the place where they are
looking for the next step in their life, takes a lot of TLC first, and
human, bestowing some human dignity on them.' (Luke)

In the early stages of food bank expansion, their rapid growth was framed as a supply- rather than a demand-led issue; the Trussell Trust in particular were accused by some government ministers of courting publicity as part of their business model to promote their own growth (Shipman, 2014). This claim of food bank expansion underpinning growing food bank use has been rebutted by numerous studies demonstrating a clear link between food bank usage and welfare reform (Perry et al, 2014; Loopstra et al, 2015; Pybus et al, 2021). Nevertheless, previous research indicates that the Trussell Trust food bank franchise model and its faith basis were key factors in the development of the first 148 food banks (Lambie, 2011). Conversations in Bradford and York would suggest that food aid, especially food banks, did partly serve as a device to strengthen relationships between religious – largely Christian – groups and their local communities, as part of a wider programme of living out the Gospel through food charity and against a longer backdrop of declining religious participation and influence over the course of the 20th and into the 21st century (see Sacks, 1991; Inglehart, 2021).[6] In this way, emergency food provision was motivated by a convenient confluence of religious and practical concerns.

"They have tried sex, drugs and alcohol, but they haven't tried God": saving the hungry through food charity

There was a distinct moralising dimension to some emergency food aid. Service users were criticised for turning up "drunk" or "dirty", which could be portrayed as attributable to "bad choices". June, a volunteer in an evangelical soup kitchen, drew on an individualising ethic – of choice rather than need or rights – in her discussion of those accessing the soup kitchen: "Need is a funny word. It's a choice. When it comes to poverty, drugs and addicts, they choose the drugs and alcohol and then have nothing for food." Faith-based food charity introduced the potential for "change" or reform, a message which was communicated by volunteers, including both June and Luigi:

> 'They have tried sex, drugs and alcohol, but they haven't tried God and that way of life, because that way of life can change your life. They step into this world. The more they hear, the more they think, "I can change". They twig. It is warm; they are cared for; they feel a sense of belonging. There is a ripple effect, more people see this and come. The church is something they can belong to every day. It is a choice you can make. We are the people who will help them in the long term, their backup. We constantly reinforce the message that you can change your life, you can have a different plan, but you have got to want it.' (June)

'So, we need good preparation for these people but sometimes we are not prepared. Sometimes they arrive dirty, so we send them to wash their hands; we give them clothes if they need it. We ask, what do you need? We are pedagogues for these people.' (Luigi)

Change was framed as a choice: people had made bad choices which had led them to need food charity, but they could reform their life by choosing God, and a measured, sober (Christian) life. Absent from these dialogues of choice and change was consideration of the systemic factors that had led those using food charity to become homeless, alcoholics or addicts, or recognition of the immense challenges of personal transformation for those who were homeless and destitute within the present unequal socioeconomic structures.

The soup kitchens in which June and Luigi volunteered were, like many faith-based food charities in York and Bradford, run by middle-class volunteers who predominantly adopted a charitable rather than a social justice response to food insecurity. The privileged and unequal socio-economic structures of society were emulated in the charitable activities of the Church; this took the form of transactional food charity delivered by White, affluent people which could, on occasion, reinforce a moralised and individualistic portrayal of poverty and seek to reform its users in line with a Protestant (and especially Calvinist) ethic of self-reliance and self-improvement. A participatory Christian ethos motivated some food aid providers whose commitment to egalitarianism and care was resolute. These religious groups sought to live out Christian principles of egalitarianism and reciprocity through food charity, forging an alternative mutualistic ethics amid the individualism of neoliberal capitalism. As such, they were an example of prefigurative politics, 'the embodiment, within the ongoing political practice of a movement, of those forms of social relations, decision-making, culture and human experience that are the ultimate goal' (Boggs, 1977: 2). However, the power-difference inherent to the charitable relationship could not be overcome through the provision of food and care. Providers may have been motivated by a participatory ethos and ideas of communion, but exchange was one-sided: 'the poor' could not reciprocate. Thus, participation was not between service providers and users but between people of faith and God. The act of seeking and receiving a food parcel or meal remained individualising and innately hierarchical.

"Before the meal, we say a word from the Bible": manifestations of faith in food aid

Faith was not only a motivation for the provision of food charity but, in some organisations, inherent to the process of giving and receiving food. Religion was a visible and performative element of food aid, at its most conspicuous in Christian providers. Food banks, soup kitchens and community cafes were commonly housed in religious buildings, including churches and, to a lesser extent, mosques; in a minority of food banks and soup kitchens, the aesthetics of the space were inseparable from the provision of food. In the evangelical soup kitchen in which June volunteered and the Catholic soup kitchen staffed by Luigi, service users were required to acknowledge or engage with the space from which food was distributed:

> 'They know it is a church; it has a church feel. With council-run places you are just a number and they know that. When they come in, I say to them, "Know that when you step in here it is God's building."' (June)

> 'We say, "This is your house". We show them the chapel. Some of them stay one moment to pray.' (Luigi)

In some faith-based providers, religious ideas were shared through music, Bible classes, prayer circles among staff and service users, and by short sermons delivered before or during food distribution. Faith-based food aid was considered by some providers to be more welcoming, caring and respectful than secular food aid, particularly secular food aid funded or provided by local government. Requests for prayer from some service users and regular attendance at longstanding faith-based providers intimated that service users may benefit from the possibilities – solace, community, friendship and reform – offered by faith-based food charity. This was an observation reflected in the ethnographic research of Salonen (2016c), who found that religious services integrated into food delivery systems in Finland were rarely criticised by users but rather responded to favourably.

The agency of service users in accepting or rejecting religious concepts or practices offered as a component of food charity was, nevertheless, questionable. In food banks – and especially Trussell Trust food banks – prayer was offered frequently on a voluntary basis to service users, in line with the Christian identity of the Trussell Trust; Sally, the manager of an Anglican food bank, described the practice of offering prayer and the perceived agency of services users to decline:

> 'Then the other thing which some people find difficult but which we do offer, we make it clear that we are a group of churches running it and that the Trussell Trust is a Christian organisation. We believe in the power of prayer and we offer to pray with people. We are not hiding behind our faith at all but, on the other hand, we are not ramming it down people's throats either. The priority is that you meet the need that is set before you that is for food or whatever, you listen to the person. If they don't want to talk to you that is absolutely fine, that is their prerogative. And we offer to pray with them but if they don't want it then fair enough, again they are treated no differently.'

Sally was adamant that those visiting the food bank were entirely free to decline prayer and would not be discriminated against for doing so. Yet her analysis obfuscates the power differences of the situation, which contain an intrinsic pressure on service users to participate in any practices that take place in the food bank, including prayer, even if explicitly told it was not obligatory. This power inequality, set within a context in which the service is being provided by an organisation and individuals with their own set of religious ideals regardless of the religious affiliation of those seeking help, exposes an inherent limitation of faith-based food aid: it cannot provide the space where a universal welfare service is provided without that being accompanied by a tacit pressure to engage with the inherent religious ethos of the setting.

In a minority of Christian soup kitchens, service user respect for religion and "good" behaviour was explicitly maintained through the possibility that food and care could be withdrawn. The receipt of food could be conditional on praying with those providing the service or listening to Bible readings, as described by June and Luigi:

'People engage with the faith aspect. We also run Bible classes, a street church and informal prayer circle – people join in. Before the meal we say a word from the Bible and then we say a prayer. People are interested, you could hear a pin drop. We play only Christian music, but it is rocky, they think it is rocky music.' (June)

'There is very warm hospitality by ourselves; they can see this is their house. We see someone outside, we open, we sit down with them. We don't give them food, but tea, no coffee, good tea with sugar. Then we start our prayer. They say this prayer. This is important. We have to say thank you, God.' (Luigi)

In Bradford and York, both faith-based and secular food providers were critical of proselytising in food banks and soup kitchens, which was considered exploitive of vulnerable people and inhibited those in need from accessing support. Samia, a Pakistani British volunteer in a soup kitchen, and Molly, a White British manager of a busy community centre, told me:

'I think that [religion] is a massive thing. I don't know about Bradford but we have heard of a lot of examples up and down the country where people will serve food to poor people but in return they will want to preach to them and indoctrinate them in some way, shape or form and that is just not within the Islamic faith, that is Christianity, every faith you are talking about, so that is one thing we are adamant this is not about that, this is about basic humanity and it is about serving your neighbours and this is what we do.' (Samia)

'People who are already vulnerable and quite often at rock bottom and hungry, trying to keep themselves or their families fed, do not want to have religion pushed in their faces. To be prayed for because they are hungry is not how people should be treated. I have several times complained to the Trussell Trust and was told that, "It is [our] policy and will not be changed". We have several people that have refused to take a food voucher due to this issue and have gone hungry.' (Molly)

A minority of faith-based organisations providing food aid, like those staffed by June and Luigi, proselytised people accessing their services; all organisations doing so were Christian. The motivation to share religion with service users was often borne from a commitment to a shared humanity and a desire to help others escape destitution, rather than an attempt to convert someone from one religion, or none, to another. Nevertheless, the exclusive implications of both proselytising and the less explicit although still powerful manifestations of religion, such as the building and the offer of voluntary prayer, were inescapable. Service providers were adamant that service users were appreciative of – or at least not hostile to – the faith element integrated into their systems of food distribution; the work of Salonen (2016b; 2016c), in Finland, and Sager and Stephens (2005), in the US, would, however, suggest that the case can be otherwise. In Salonen's ethnographic study of Finnish food aid, while religious elements integrated into food aid were rarely openly criticised, criticism was expressed through tacit resistance. Open criticism was inherently undermined by a broader framing of choice: service users were constructed as choosing to use religious food assistance, which impaired the possibility of open criticism of the integration of religious services into the food delivery programmes. In Sager and Stephens' (2005) analysis of client reactions to religious elements at congregation-run feeding establishments, service user hostility to religious elements of the food programme was, in interviews with the researchers, palpable. The authors found that, regardless of their religious beliefs, two thirds of the homeless respondents reacted negatively to the sermons they heard at the congregation-based food programmes, characterising them as coercive, hypocritical, condescending and conflicting with their own beliefs. As in Bradford and York, the sermons preached in the food programmes in Sager and Stephen's study could ignore local knowledge and neglect the experience of service users, while assuming that the homeless individuals were 'responsible for their own troubles'. Open hostility to the religious elements of food provision was less apparent in Bradford and York; however, as will be shown in Chapter 6, service users did on occasion characterise food charity as coercive, condescending and conflicting with their own beliefs.

Conclusion

> It was a queer, rather disgusting scene. Below were the handful of simple, well-meaning people, trying hard to worship; and above were the hundred men they had fed, deliberately making worship impossible. A ring of dirty, hairy faces grinned down from the [church] gallery, openly jeering. What could a few women and old men do against a hundred hostile tramps? They were afraid of us, and we were frankly bullying them. It was our revenge upon them for having humiliated us by feeding us.
>
> George Orwell, *Down and Out in Paris and London*
> (Orwell, [1933] 2001: 145)

George Orwell's description of receiving a free cup of tea and six slices of bread from an evangelical church bears remarkable similarity to some religious food charity today. Hungry and desperate people, humiliated by seeking charity, are entangled in the religion of others through the offer of 'voluntary' prayer or participation in a compulsory service. The key difference with Orwell's account is that, while today the food poor outnumber staff and volunteers, they do not revolt or reject the religion that is pressed on them; instead, they engage with offerings of faith or, alternatively, remain silent.

In Bradford and York, Christianity – but not Islam – motivated food charity and closely shaped the manner in which food was distributed. Food banks and soup kitchens offered Christians a way to live the Gospel: to express one's love for God through charitable work with the poor; to bring physical and spiritual salvation to the poor through the provision of food and care; to share a commitment to food as a gift from the divine; and to live out Christianity's egalitarian ethos through building relationships with and caring for those in need. Christian ideas of hospitality and participation may have been an important motivation for those providing religious food charity, but participation was one-sided. Service providers and users may be purportedly equal in the eyes of God and the law, but they are profoundly socially and economically unequal. The poor, by virtue of their poverty, could not reciprocate, and therefore the relational aspects of religious food charity were confined to reciprocation between staff, volunteers and God through food.

Food charity offered practical benefits to Christian communities, providing a way to participate in the community outside the boundaries of the church. Food banks, in particular, offered churches with diminishing congregations an opportunity to reassert their role in the community and expand the reach of their services beyond prayers and sermons. The well-established infrastructure of religious communities, which long predates the arrival of food banks, was invaluable in expediting the development of and sustaining food aid; it was arguably because of this infrastructure that faith-based food aid was more resilient than some secular provision amid growing need and limited third sector funding. Perhaps unintentionally, therefore, faith groups furthered processes of state transformation in their localised, non-state solution to issues – poverty and hunger – which were, according to the 1945 welfare model, the prerogative of the state (Jones and Rodney, 2002). There was little evidence that, unlike faith-based welfare provision in the US, faith-based food aid in the UK considered itself superior to state welfare, as is consistent with the idea of religious neoliberalism. Faith-based food aid was, outwardly at least, largely apolitical.

Religious food charity could, however, be inwardly political, embodying a Christian communistic ethos but also personifying the ethics of neoliberal capitalism. The Calvinist ethic, a key forbear of neoliberal individualism, which Rebecca de Souza identified in US food pantries, was also manifest in Christian food banks and soup kitchens in Britain. Through moralising structures and discourses, staff attempted to reform service users in accordance with the ethics of capitalism to become independent, sober, economically active and responsible subjects. Resistance to this moral code could result in loss of food or support. Only a minority of religious food charities stigmatised and coerced service users in this explicit way, but coercion could also be subtle, as in the case of Trussell Trust food banks. As faith-based food aid continues to grow amid rising poverty and destitution, exacerbated by the COVID-19 pandemic, it is worth asking who gains from these arrangements: people in poverty, people of faith, or God? The following chapter reveals how race, as well as religion, influences the provision of food charity, exposing how those seeking assistance are reformed not only according to a Calvinist ethic but also in line with ideals of Whiteness.

Notes

[1] Again, UK food charity is echoing the history and development of food charity in the US, where faith-based organisations, and especially Christian organisations, are dominant sources of community engagement and service provision.

[2] Caritas is defined as Christian love of humankind, expressed through charity (Oxford English Dictionary, 2021).

[3] Feeding America is the largest food bank provider in the US.

[4] The US equivalent of UK food banks.

[5] See also: Power et al (2017c).

[6] Writing in 1991, the late Jonathan Sacks (British Orthodox rabbi, philosopher, theologian, author, peer and public figure) asked whether Britain is in fact a post-religious society. He argued that the Enlightenment, and the intellectual and social processes to which it gave rise, had a devastating impact on the traditions which gave meaning and shape to life lived in communities. Enlightenment thinkers focused relentlessly on two entities: the individual, detached from historical context, and the universal political, realised in the secular state. The world that emerges is of individuals as makers of their own meaning,

and of the state as neutral arbiter between conflicting interests; religion becomes a private affair. Despite the appearance of a resurgence of religion as the 21st century began, marked by resurgent religious fundamentalism in the US and the rise of militant Islam, analysis of religious trends from 2007 to 2020 in 49 countries containing 60 per cent of the world's population did not find a global resurgence of religion; an overwhelming majority (43 out of 49) of these countries were becoming less religious. This decline in belief is strongest in high-income countries but it is evident across most of the world (Inglehart, 2021).

5

Whiteness, racism and colourblindness in UK food aid

'But the BNP [British National Party], their main office is in this area. This is an area that is very White, and the local secondary school has got, you know, a handful of ethnic, non-British people at it, simply because it is not in an area where those people are, not because there is any restriction on them coming, just because they are not around.'

Emily, Christian food bank volunteer

Introduction: from religious to racial exclusion

Emily, a White British woman, volunteered in a large Trussell Trust food bank in Bradford. With support from her own church and those in surrounding parishes,[1] she and others started the food bank when another food bank in Bradford restricted its catchment area, excluding many people in a "very deprived" part of her parish. The people who accessed the food bank, in which she volunteered, were almost entirely White. Emily ascribed this to the purported demography of the local area, which she described as "very White". The implication was that food banks located in ethnically diverse areas would have a multi-ethnic population of service users. But this was in fact not the case. The vast majority of food banks in Bradford catered to predominantly White service users.

Emily seemed surprised when I asked her why those using the food bank were almost entirely White; she could see no barrier to anyone accessing the service so their absence must reflect the absence of 'non-White' people in the local area more broadly. There was no reflection on how the food bank could be exclusionary, including via her own role in maintaining its Christian identity. Emily may not have been racist, but she was colourblind: race was immaterial in her consideration of food charity; she met the need that was set before her and that was deemed sufficient to her volunteer role. And yet the food bank itself, shaped by Christianity and by paradigms of Whiteness, was arguably institutionally racist. Emily, steeped in unchallenged ideas of Whiteness, failed to recognise this.

Chapter 4 described the influence of religion on contemporary food aid, drawing attention to religious motivations for food charity but also to the manifestation of religion in the context of the food aid encounter: faith could shape how food was given as well as why it was given. In so doing, it highlighted the potential for exclusion arising from religiously informed structures and discourses. This chapter continues that discussion about exclusion in the context of a broader consideration of how race and ethnicity influence food charity in the UK. The chapter does not seek to criticise those providing food aid; however, informed by US scholar Rebecca de Souza (2019), it argues that, in the absence of critical thinking into the types of food charity that religion and Whiteness brings, food aid may continue rather than challenge structural inequalities and structural racism in the UK. Unlike in the UK, consideration of the influence of Whiteness on the nature and inclusivity of food aid in the US has been a focus of academic and policy debates for well over two decades; I therefore start with brief consideration of the US terrain before turning to the UK context.

Racism and Whiteness in US food aid: colourblindness and universalism

Critique of both the community food movement and the emergency food system as overwhelmingly White and closely shaped by paradigms of Whiteness is well established among US food scholars. In her commentary on the cultural politics of US community food movements, American social scientist Julie Guthman (2011) calls attention to two related manifestations of Whiteness which shape practice and space. The first is 'colourblindness', an ideology in which race is considered immaterial. The ideology of colourblindness is premised upon liberal concepts of citizenship, characterised by civil rather than political or social rights: 'the rights necessary for individual freedom–liberty of the person, freedom of speech, thought and faith … and the right to justice' (Marshall, [1949] 1992: 8). According to Guthman, colourblindness is perceived by members of the community food movement to be non-racist. Guthman argues, however, that the doctrine of colourblindness 'does its own violence' by 'erasing the violence that the social construct of race has wrought in the form of racism' (Guthman, 2011: 267) while simultaneously erasing the privilege that Whiteness creates. In this way, Whiteness may function as a set of expectations and institutional benefits historically derived from White supremacy that in their contemporary invisibility operate to naturalise inequalities.

The second, related manifestation of Whiteness is described by Guthman as 'universalism': the assumption that values held by Whites are normal and widely shared. This may take the form of an aesthetic ideal that is not obviously racialised but is predicated upon Whitened cultural practices

(Kobayashi and Peake, 2000), for instance the idea that a White ethnocentric 'healthy' diet is the only healthy diet that exists. Whiteness as universalism erases difference by refusing to acknowledge the experience, aesthetics and norms of others, with the effect that those who do not conform to White ideals are marginalised – or it is assumed that those for whom these seemingly universal (White) ideals do not resonate must be educated to adopt them. This missionary impulse – most obviously exemplified by Western colonialism and imperialism of the 18th, 19th and 20th centuries and more insidiously upheld through continued White supremacy in the 21st century – reinscribes difference, while denying its existence. Universalism thereby entrenches privilege for the dominant White group.

Racism and Whiteness in US emergency food provision

In *Feeding the Other: Whiteness, Privilege and Neoliberal Stigma in Food Pantries*, Rebecca de Souza (2019) argues that Whiteness is inherent to the US emergency food system. Through ethnography in two food pantries in Duluth, Minnesota, she shows how Whiteness is not just evident in individual people but at organisational and institutional levels: the food pantry 'in its everydayness obscures the racialised poverty that is at the heart of the unjust food system' (de Souza, 2019: 123). De Souza describes the racialised poverty manifesting in US food pantries, where all the volunteers are White and most of the clients are people of colour. She calls attention to the 'discursive erasures' in the dialogue of White volunteers overlooking the 'history of white domination that continues to privilege whites' and framing charity as a 'fruitful way to help people in need – overlooking systemic interconnections and the need for more empowering rights-based approaches' (de Souza, 2019: 98). Volunteers align with the outlook of the food pantry more broadly, adopting a colourblind discourse which reinforces White superiority, virtue and moral goodness – it is the Whites who are performing the charity – while continuing to 'Other' people of colour. Moving towards food justice, de Souza argues, may be achieved, not by problematising brownness, but interrogating Whiteness.

Racial inequality in UK poverty and food insecurity

In the UK, Black and minority ethnic households are over twice as likely to live in poverty as their White counterparts. In 2018/19, nearly half of households of Black/African/Caribbean/Black British origin were in poverty, compared with just under one in five White families, and Black and minority ethnic families as a whole were between two and three times as likely to be in persistent poverty than White households (Social Metrics Commission, 2020). The Social Metrics Commission found that 19 per cent of people in families where the head of the household was White lived in poverty (2018/19), compared with 32 per cent of mixed ethnicity families, 39 per cent of Asian/Asian British families, 42 per cent of families classified as 'Other ethnic' and 46 per cent of Black/African/Caribbean/Black British families (Social Metrics Commission, 2020). Reflecting higher levels of poverty among Black and minority ethnic households, the Family Resource Survey, which in 2021 published data for the first time on household food insecurity, identified significant racial inequalities in food insecurity in the UK. The survey of 19,000 people showed that food insecurity is highest, by a considerable margin, among Black/African/Caribbean/Black British households (19 per cent) and lowest among Indian households (5 per cent), closely followed by White households (7 per cent).[2] Food insecurity was also notably high among 'Other' ethnic groups (14 per cent), which includes 'Gypsy, Traveller and Irish Traveller' households, Mixed/multiple ethnic groups (10 per cent), and Pakistani households (10 per cent) (DWP, 2021).

In *White Privilege: The Myth of the Post-racial Society* Kalwant Bhopal carefully shows, using examples from education, how race operates as a form of disadvantage in contemporary British society. She writes, 'Individuals from black and minority ethnic backgrounds, by virtue of their racial identity, are positioned as outsiders in a society that values whiteness and white privilege' (Bhopal, 2018: 1). In a neoliberal context, policy making (under the guise of being inclusive) has created an image of a post-racial society when, in reality, vast inequalities between White and Black and minority ethnic communities continue to exist. Bhopal argues, 'Policy making has exacerbated rather than addressed the inequalities which result from processes of racism, exclusion and marginalisation in which white identities are prioritised and privileged above all others' (Bhopal, 2018: 1). The programme of public spending cuts – 'austerity' – announced by former Chancellor of the Exchequer, George Osborne, in the 2010 Emergency Budget disproportionately impacted on Black and minority ethnic people. Black British and South Asian origin households in the lowest fifth of incomes experienced the largest average drop in living standards and were disproportionately disadvantaged by cuts to public services as a consequence of their greater use of further and higher education (South Asian households) and social housing (Black British households) compared with White households (Reed and Portes, 2014). These cuts to taxes, benefits and public spending – which were experienced by Black and minority ethnic households against a backdrop of profound, longstanding and persistent structural inequalities in education, employment, health and housing – enhanced and entrenched existing inequalities between ethnic groups (Women's Budget Group, 2017).

The greater likelihood of Black and minority ethnic people to live in poverty prior to 2010 and their relative disadvantage within a broadly punitive post-2010 policy programme, as well as high levels of food insecurity among

Black/African/Caribbean/Black British households, may imply that Black and minority ethnic individuals are likely to be over-represented at emergency food provision in the UK. The Trussell Trust's own data suggest, however, that for some groups the opposite may be the case. According to the Trussell Trust's seminal *State of Hunger* report on the demography and circumstances of the individuals and households accessing Trussell Trust food banks, nine in ten people (89 per cent) referred to food banks in the Trussell Trust network are born in the UK, above the national level (86 per cent) (Sosenko et al, 2019). Of UK-born people referred to food banks, 93 per cent described themselves as 'White', 4 per cent as 'Black' and 1 per cent as 'Asian', indicating an apparent over-representation of White and Black households and an under-representation of Asian households (Sosenko et al, 2019).

Exploring the under-representation of minority ethnic households in emergency food aid

The population of Bradford District is ethnically and religiously diverse. The district has the largest proportion of people of Pakistani ethnic origin (20 per cent) in England – disproportionately represented in Bradford's city centre wards – which contributes to its large Muslim population (25 per cent) (ONS, 2011). The other minority ethnic groups of any size include Indian (2.6 per cent), Bangladeshi (1.9 per cent) and Other Asian (1.5 per cent). Alongside a large Christian population (46 per cent), Bradford houses small Sikh (1 per cent) and Hindu populations (0.9 per cent) (ONS, 2011). Despite Bradford's ethnic and religious diversity, there was limited ethnic and religious diversity among the service users of food aid, especially faith-based food aid. Food banks, in particular, reported serving very few South Asian people, and Christian food banks had a considerably less diverse user base than those that were Muslim or secular. The one Muslim food bank interviewed had a more religiously and ethnically diverse user base than its Christian counterparts, with a large minority of South Asian female service users.[3] The population of service users at soup kitchens was also predominantly White, often including a large minority of service users from Central and Eastern Europe. However, soup kitchens run by members of Bradford's South Asian community tended to report a more ethnically diverse population of service users than those overseen by White British staff – as told by Rasheed, the South Asian manager of a secular soup kitchen:

'What we cook here is very simple, traditional, we don't do fries here and we make, as you have seen today, one is meat dish, one is lentil curry and sweet rice or sometimes boiled rice and sometimes we make brown rice but those are universal, they are edible by anyone, vegetarian, non-vegetarian; so the beauty of our food is that we make only one meat dish. And the other thing, we make fresh chapattis, you see the girls, we make dough here and chapattis here, so they are freshly cooked and freshly eat. And it is a very healthy diet and well liked by our community [South Asian] but there are many people from the host [White British] community. We have open community kitchen, so yeah so people do come, and they can pay £2.50 for a meal, but on Friday it is all free.'

The ethnic demography of service users in York was almost entirely White. However, the contrast between the ethnic demography of the city's population and the characteristics of service users was, while notable, less stark than in Bradford given the relative ethnic homogeneity of the city – in the 2011 Census, 94 per cent of York residents identified themselves as 'White' (ONS, 2011).

The apparent under-representation of Black and minority ethnic people in soup kitchens and, especially, in food banks in Bradford and York was in line with the – very limited body of – British literature providing insight into the ethnic demography of food aid service users, including the Trussell Trust's assessment of their own users, mentioned earlier, and analysis by Prayogo and colleagues (Prayogo et al, 2017). Assessing the demographic characteristics of those seeking help from food banks compared with individuals accessing support from an advice centre, Prayogo et al (2017) found that people of Black, and Mixed, Asian or Other ethnicity were under-represented in food banks in comparison with the advice centre. Until more research is done in this area it will be impossible to conclude for certain whether, on a national scale, Black and minority ethnic people are under-represented in emergency food aid.

Manifestations of Whiteness in the emergency food system

The two interrelated manifestations of Whiteness – colourblindness and universalism – highlighted by Guthman (2011) in her critique of the cultural politics of US community food movements were evident in food aid in Bradford and York. These two manifestations of Whiteness shaped the practice of food charity and, thereby, compounded ethnic and religious inequalities.

Colourblindness

I described earlier the apparent absence of ethnic diversity among service users in food banks and some soup kitchens in Bradford, despite the ethnic heterogeneity of the city. When questioned about this lack of diversity – particularly the apparent absence of Pakistani British service users – interviewees, like Emily above, either did not consider it to be a concern or believed that the service user demographic was reflective of those in need and, concomitantly, there was less need among the local Pakistani British community. There was also a common perception, as voiced by Emily and Anna, White British managers of Christian (Trussell Trust) food banks, that the service user demographic reflected the local demographic, which was perceived to be largely White. In this way, food banks were considered by those running them as representative of the local demography; questions of race, accessibility and exclusion were immaterial. Anna told me, "This area is almost exclusively White; this area and one other area of Bradford are very unusual in their ethnic mix – so no, we haven't had many ethnic minorities at all".

Looking at the geographical distribution of food aid organisations in Bradford, however, Anna's reasoning for the low numbers of minority ethnic individuals at food aid was cast into doubt. Mapping exercises undertaken at the time of my own fieldwork and updated in 2021 by myself and researchers at the University of Leeds (see Power et al, 2017b; Graven et al, 2021) clearly illustrated that the majority of food aid in Bradford (including secular, Muslim and Christian providers) was located in and around the city centre and in the parish of Keighley, areas with high levels of deprivation and a high proportion (often above 60 per cent) of Muslim and Pakistani British residents. The under-representation of Pakistani British and Muslim service users at emergency food aid was, thus, unlikely to be a consequence of their distance from a food bank or soup kitchen and, contrary to the perception of Emily and Anna, the services users of food aid in Bradford tended not to be representative of the local demographic.

Universalism

Universalism – the assumption that values held by Whites are normal and widely shared – was a marked characteristic of food banks and soup kitchens run by White staff members in Bradford and York, and may have contributed to the under-representation of Black and minority ethnic service users. The potential for exclusion arose from the Whiteness of the staff and users, the 'White' character of the food provided and the diets promoted and, on occasion, the expectation of certain behaviour, including respect for Bible readings and prayer, tied to Christianity and largely requested by White Christian volunteers – as described in Chapter 4. Despite Bradford's religious demography (25 per cent Muslim), only Muslim food providers and the one secular food bank in Bradford I spoke with provided halal food. A majority of the non-Muslim soup kitchens provided a vegetarian, but not a halal, option and this was deemed sufficient to accommodate cultural and religious needs. Lisa, a White European manager of a secular soup kitchen, told me:

'No, the food isn't halal because of the price and availability of it, but people do get the choice of an alternative or vegetarian [option]. Because it is a drop-in centre, we don't operate on order. Something, you know, like the day before, if you can order by 11am then we can make sure that there will be an alternative option.'

Food banks provided a strictly defined parcel of food, largely in line with Trussell Trust guidelines, regardless of whether the food bank was affiliated to the Trussell Trust or independent. This food parcel, described as 'nutritionally balanced', did not appear to be informed by religious needs or the cultural preferences of minority groups and best represented a White healthful diet. Patrick, a White British manager of a large Christian food bank, described removing the tinned meat produce from their food parcel to accommodate Muslim service users. The inability to provide a halal option was not considered problematic due to the infrequency of Muslim users:

'I know that when a Muslim person comes in, I'm going to have to change the food in the parcel – none of the meat is halal. I have no halal food, so I just have to replace it with other stuff. But it is so rare to have a Muslim person in the food bank that this just isn't something that's often a problem.'

In organisations in which the food was not prescribed – for instance by Trussell Trust guidelines – White staff provided their conception of 'good' food, which could be inflexible to the needs or preferences of minority groups. Predicated upon Whitened cultural practices, this 'good' food was deemed the most practical – the default – option, as described by Sam, a White British volunteer in a secular community cafe:

'We do a meal once a month for one of the charities that deals with asylum seekers in Bradford, and they have their meeting in the centre of town so we produce food for them and, it's interesting, the woman who sort of leads it had a conversation and said, "Could you produce food like this?" And it's quite difficult because our background, we just cook what we get, you've probably seen, we produce good stuff, we produce a lot of good vegetarian stuff and she said actually that is not what she described as "worthy food". Equally we couldn't use pork, we couldn't use bacon, and there are issues around beef, so the question is what do you use? You got to understand that we got what we got.'

Sam's comment intimates an element of disdain for the requirements of the asylum seekers served by the organisation in which he volunteered. By providing the meal free of charge, Sam and his colleagues sought to be inclusive but when the food he and his colleagues prepared was questioned, he became frustrated. In *White Privilege: The Myth of the Post-racial Society* Bhopal documents the subtle exclusion experienced by a Black working-class female professor in a British university by her White and largely male colleagues (Bhopal, 2018: 59). She describes the episode as an example of a micro aggression, drawing on the work of Sue and colleagues (Sue et al, 2007: 271):

> Racial micro aggressions are brief and commonplace daily verbal, behavioural or environmental indignities, whether intentional or unintentional that communicate hostile, derogatory or negative racial slights and insults towards people of colour. Perpetrators of micro aggressions are often unaware that they engage in such communications when they interact with racial/ethnic minorities.

The Black working-class female professor is treated as an outsider because of her identity as a Black working-class woman, she is quietly sidelined in meetings, ignored by her White, largely male, colleagues. The micro aggressions of the professor's White colleagues perpetuate Whiteness and White privilege, even though at times her colleagues appear unaware of their actions (Bhopal, 2018: 59). Sam's reaction to the requests of the asylum seekers represents an example of micro aggression; there was no suggestion that Sam intended to insult the asylum seekers but his micro aggression towards them perpetuated White norms and White privilege. Whiteness as universalism in food aid, thus, effectively erases difference by refusing to acknowledge or respond to the experience, aesthetics and norms of others, with the effect that those who do not conform to White ideals can be marginalised; educated, through budgetary or cooking classes; or reformed, as described in Chapter 4 and Chapter 6.

Duality of Whiteness in emergency food aid

Staff working in emergency food aid were predominantly White, as were service users, but the constructions of Whiteness applied to each differed. The first construction aligned with the Whiteness of staff and denoted privilege, respectability and acceptability; this construction of Whiteness, influenced by a Christian caritas framework and liberal ideas of independence and individualism, shaped the self-perception of White, largely middle-class volunteers in food aid. The second, relating to some service users, was the stigmatised abject Whiteness of the poor, White 'underclass'. The practices and behaviours of these poor Whites were pathologised: deprivation and poor educational outcomes were constructed as a consequence of low motivation and inadequate commitment to middle-class standards of educational success, rather than attributable to long-standing structural disadvantage and stigma. Talking to Maggie, a White British volunteer in a Christian food bank, I was told:

'I'm a school governor as well, there is stuff on the news that it is the poor White British boys that are the ones who are doing really badly at school and it is because often the families of immigrants are dead keen on education and even though they have come from very poor White areas, they all are absolutely behind the kids going to school and getting on and becoming doctors and becoming lawyers and doing well, and that inspiration and motivation is not coming from the poorer White parents, sadly. It does come from some of them, I don't want to paint a brush and say they are all like that but there are a substantial number of families in this area who couldn't care less about education and schools.'

In Maggie's commentary, the racialised reading of the "families of immigrants" is also applied to the families of "poor White British boys"; while the immigrant families are committed to education, the poor White families reject education and the respectability inherent to it. In this way, the poor White families are 'Blackened', imbued with underserving characteristics of idleness, licentiousness and poor parenting, characteristics which, as Robert Shilliam explains, have historically been racialised as Black – founded in the initial racialisation of deserving and underserving characteristics, with the 'slave' – and thereby the condition of Blackness – exemplifying the latter (Shilliam, 2018: 7). Like many of those before her, Maggie, a member of the White elite, racialises the distinction between the deserving and the underserving poor, drawing upon historically embedded cultural tropes and maintaining an economic and racial hierarchy which upholds her own privilege.

Conclusion

The UK is a racially unequal country, one in which the colour of your skin affects your experience of the labour market, your likelihood of living in poverty and poor housing, and your life expectancy. Racist structures and institutions, which continue and exacerbate inequalities between ethnic groups, are embedded within the UK's long history of racist oppression, of imperialism, colonialism and slavery. Food aid, like the society in which it is situated, can be racist.

The predominance of Whiteness in secular and faith-based food aid, accompanied by the manifestation of religion in Christian food aid, as described in Chapter 4, compromised the inclusiveness of provision in

Bradford and York. The values and social conditions to be emulated in the majority of food aid (which was largely White secular or White Christian) were those of the racial dominant, of Whiteness. These values were represented by the staff and leadership, the food distributed and the diets promoted and, in a minority of Christian providers, the expectation of engagement with Christianity in some form. Slocum (2006; 2007; 2010) calls attention to comparable manifestations of Whiteness in US food aid, where the food distributed and the diets promoted aligned with 'White' notions of healthful food and bodies, thereby erasing the identity and histories of Black and minority ethnic communities.

The widely held presumption by staff that race was irrelevant in the performance of food charity reflected a colourblind approach and echoed arguments of the post-racial (Goldberg, 2013). In keeping with the post-racial, staff denied racial difference as an inhibiting factor thereby obscuring the 'racist, classist and gendered features of the food system' (Slocum, 2006: 330), negating the agency of minority ethnic groups and undermining any 'ontological claim to racial groups more broadly' (Goldberg, 2013: 17). By refusing responsibility for structural conditions and reducing the use of food aid to individualised accounts of poor Whites using food aid and Asian families choosing to stay away, staff in food aid obscured – and so exacerbated – the generalised contemporary circumstance of racially expanding precarity in the aftermath of the 2007–08 economic crisis and the COVID-19 pandemic (Kapoor and Kalra, 2013; Khunti et al, 2020).

Preliminary data from the Trussell Trust suggest that there may have been changes to the demography of food bank use amid COVID-19. Data collected during the pandemic highlight that people from Black and minority ethnic backgrounds and people born outside Europe have been significantly over-represented among those accessing support from food banks in the Trussell Trust network during this period (Bramley et al, 2021).[4] One in 10 (9 per cent) of those referred to food banks in the Trussell Trust network during the pandemic identify as Black or Black British – three times the corresponding rate in the UK population as a whole (3 per cent) – while 10 per cent identify as Asian or Asian British, higher than the corresponding rate in the UK population (7 per cent). In contrast, just seven in 10 (71 per cent) identify as White British, with a further 5 per cent identifying as White Other, while in the UK population as a whole these groups comprise 79 per cent and 8 per cent, respectively. Whether these shifts will continue in the long term is yet to be determined. Without fundamental change to processes and attitudes it is unlikely that the majority of food banks will ever be inclusive and anti-racist spaces, where people from any ethnic and religious group feel respected as equals.

Notes

1   The food bank developed as a partnership between multiple churches and was therefore geographically defined by parish boundaries rather than, for instance, ward areas.

2   It is important to note that food insecurity was 8 per cent among Asian/Asian British households as a whole (incorporating Bangladeshi, Indian and Pakistani households), suggesting considerable variation in food insecurity between Asian/Asian British groups and indicating that, when utilising aggregated categories of ethnic groups, household food insecurity is lowest among the 'White' group.

3   This was in part related to the nature of one of the food bank's main referral partners: a domestic violence refuge located in a majority South Asian area.

4   The Trussell Trust propose that the increase between early and mid-2020 in the proportion of people referred to Trussell Trust food banks who were born outside Europe (an increase from 7 to 18 per cent) could be attributable to the 'no recourse to public funds' (NRPF) status and its impact on destitution. Unless they had British citizenship or 'indefinite leave to remain', many people in the category 'born outside Europe' would have been unable to apply for Universal Credit. Before the pandemic, between 2 and 4 per cent of people referred to food banks were likely subject to the NRPF condition; this rose to 11 per cent in mid-2020. Additionally, people born outside Europe are over-represented in low-paid jobs – resulting in lower-than-average levels of savings – which may have been a further factor contributing to food bank use (see Fernández-Reino and Rienzo, 2019).

6

Lived neoliberalism: food, poverty and power

'I don't know them, but I know *of* them, she's got six kids, she is on Income Support and the baby's dad don't help her at all, but she goes out every weekend and she uses food bank because she ends up spending the money on clothes and beer.'

Gemma

Introduction: individualising and responsibilising food insecurity

Gemma lived in Bradford with her partner and two young children. Her partner worked long days in a local restaurant while she looked after their children. They had struggled for money since the children were small, when she stopped work to care for them, and now they lived payday to payday, eking out their last few pounds until another pay cheque arrived and they could relax, just for a while. She avoided food banks and instead sought support from her husband's mother, who lived close by. Gemma was highly critical of others who received benefits and used food banks. She considered them to be greedy and selfish – they bought clothes, beer and flatscreen televisions, which left them with little money for food. Gemma distanced herself from these people; she was poor, but she saw herself as making good, respectable choices. She wanted a better life for herself and her family but the only route she could see to achieving this was by criticising other people and thereby attaining a form of social status that her poverty prohibited. But Gemma's criticism of other people, in fairly similar situations to herself, could be seen as in fact compounding her own struggles; her criticism individualised the poverty which she and her peers experienced and negated the government's role in ensuring a decent standard of living for its citizens. She strove to be the ideal neoliberal citizen – independent of government support, hardworking and successful – but her own circumstances made this impossible, so instead she denigrated other people.

Gemma's juxtaposition of her own behaviour with that of her peers closely aligns with broader neoliberal narratives individualising and stigmatising poverty and food bank use, narratives which have become sharper and meaner as food bank use has increased. Indeed, political responses to rising destitution have largely characterised individuals as responsible for their poverty (Caraher and Dowler, 2014), with a specific focus on poor financial management and faulty behavioural practices (see discussion in Garthwaite, 2017). Food bank users are accused of consciously opting 'not to pay their rent, their utilities or provide food for their children because they choose alcohol, drugs and their own selfish needs' (Lepoidevin, quoted in Elgot, 2014). Accompanying this rhetoric, and intimately associated with the post-2010 welfare reform agenda, is a distinct deepening of personal responsibility (Patrick, 2012). As responsibility for welfare has shifted from the state to individual citizens, notions of 'dependency' have been denigrated while ideas of 'active citizenship' are extolled (Kisby, 2010).

Framed as a problem of moral and economic contagion, the shifting threat of welfare dependency has proven instrumental to the political crafting of austerity (Jensen and Tyler, 2015). Welfare austerity has been presented as a necessary step towards restoring economic productivity, overturning 'dependency' on the state and reforming the welfare subject's character and decision making (Edmiston, 2017). The welfare reform programme is, accordingly, situated within a justificatory programme of neoliberal paternalism (Whitworth, 2016): neoliberal welfare discourse conceives of those receiving out-of-work social security as self-interested and economically rational whereby they 'choose a life on benefits' (David Cameron, quoted in Edmiston, 2017: 316), while a paternalistic discourse justifies welfare reform on the basis that welfare subjects are either unable or unwilling to exercise 'good choices' or fulfil civic duties (Whitworth, 2016).

Amid this ideological and policy context, those perceived to be more 'at risk' of 'dependency' are subject to intensive and seemingly limitless surveillance, particularly in the domain of welfare (see Bryson and Jacobs, 1992; Wacquant, 2009; Dwyer and Wright, 2014). The UK 'social assistance system has a long history of highly intrusive, detailed and ongoing surveillance of claimants' (Henman and Marston, 2008: 194); however, recent years have seen a marked heightening of these characteristics (May et al, 2019). Today, sustained surveillance is maintained in the social security system through (online) programmes such as Universal Jobmatch (a government online vacancy system that ran from 2012 to 2018 and was mandatory for most jobseekers) and the Universal Credit 'journal' (an area in a claimant's online Universal Credit account in which they communicate with their 'work coach', report on job applications, interviews and work experience or training, and record all job-related activity completed while applying for and claiming Universal Credit) (see also Fletcher and Wright, 2018). Both Universal Jobmatch and the Universal Credit journal can be best understood as calculated tools for 'managing and manipulating human behaviour'

(Henman, 2004: 176) with the aim of engendering self-governing subjects who seek to avoid 'dependency'.

The marked shift towards an individualisation of poverty and distinct deepening of personal responsibility that has occurred in recent years – today embodied in the design of working-age social security – has intensified the stigma and shame of poverty. Chapter 2 discussed the process of 'Othering' through which 'the non-poor' condemn 'the poor' and thereby uphold social stratifications. However, Othering is increasingly also a process through which 'the poor' disparage and demarcate themselves from 'Others' living in poverty in order to distance themselves from the stigma of their own poverty (see Garthwaite, 2017). While this process of demarcation may be a protective response to the ubiquity of poverty-induced shame (Chase and Walker, 2013), its effect is to fragment the social bonds in the immediate milieu and undermine social solidarity more broadly, compounding the atomisation of modern society (Chase and Walker, 2013).

The denigration of the Other may be associated with their purported economic inactivity or apathy; however, it may also be a product of intertwined economic and racist agendas. With the growth of globalisation running alongside an increasingly uncertain Western imperialism, 'race' has come to form an important element of identity-making, feeding into definitions of citizenship, nationality and, more generally, 'Otherness' (Goldberg, 2001) (further discussed in Chapter 7). The literature promoting race as a valid concept (see discussion in Ward, 1978) can be framed as part of a broader political venture validating the entwinement of racist and economic agendas (Alam, 2015). In the 18th century, for instance, Edward Long, the British colonial administrator and slave owner, in his famous and highly racist text *The History of Jamaica* (Long, 1774), claimed that Europeans and Blacks were different species of the human genus and, thus, the Atlantic slave trade was a rational cull of genetically inferior races. Similarly, Robert Knox, the 19th-century advocate of a purportedly biologically grounded hierarchy of races, sustained representations of the Irish Other in which 'behaviour, culture and disposition coalesced and conflated with nation, religion and race' (Knox, 1862: 81).[1] Today, a common representation of the racialised Other in the UK is the Muslim Other. The linkage of British Muslim culture with the marginalised structural position of British Muslims within the majority society underpins a racialised perspective on their identity which 'rather than addressing the forces that reproduce the exclusion and denigration of minority communities, instead produces an analysis that focuses upon the dysfunctional adaptation of minority individuals to their circumstances' (Husband et al, 2014: 210).

Chapter 3 explored how neoliberalism manifests in contemporary food aid; this chapter seeks to unpick how racialised and stigmatising neoliberal policies and narratives manifest in the lives of those, like Gemma above, in or at risk of food insecurity but not necessarily accessing food aid. It starts by assessing the structural factors surrounding food insecurity, drawing on quantitative and qualitative data from Bradford and York to show how low income, social security and housing underpin and shape lived experiences of food and poverty.

Low income, social security and food insecurity in Bradford and York

Survey data collected between 2007 and 2010 among mothers in Bradford and between 2018 and 2019 among parents in York evidenced a clear relationship between household income, social security and food insecurity (see statistical analysis in Power et al, 2017d; Pybus et al, 2021; and Power et al, 2021a). In Bradford, there was a strong[2] association between food insecurity and multiple markers of low socioeconomic status, including unemployment, low education and a respondent's perception of moderate or high financial insecurity. Of these socioeconomic measures, a woman's perception of her financial security had by far the strongest association with food insecurity, even when adjusted for other demographic characteristics such as ethnicity, age and cohabitation status. Receipt of means-tested benefits[3] was also highly associated with food insecurity, independent of other sociodemographic characteristics, such as whether the woman lived with a partner, and her age. A mother in receipt of means-tested benefits had an estimated 18 per cent probability of reporting food insecurity, compared with a 10 per cent probability for a mother not in receipt of benefits.

The survey data in York identified a similarly strong relationship between food insecurity and low income, showing a clear association between lower annual household income and increased risk of food insecurity. Those in the middle household income bracket in the sample (£21,250–£27,999 per annum), for example, were four times less likely to be food insecure than those with an annual household income of £16,100 or less. There was no difference, however, between respondents in the two lowest income groups, suggesting that, in York, respondents under the household income threshold of £21,250 were all similarly affected by food insecurity.

In York, other structural factors, beyond low income, were implicated in experiences of food insecurity. The survey identified a clear association between housing tenure and food insecurity: respondents who were private renters were six times more likely to be food insecure than homeowners, while those in social housing were 11 times more likely. After accounting for income, the risk of food insecurity for those in private and social housing/council tenancies was similar, with each being around three times more likely to experience food insecurity than homeowners, suggesting an independent relationship between living in rented housing and greater risk of food insecurity in York.

Unlike in Bradford, the research in York collected data on food bank use alongside food insecurity. The findings aligned with Macleod and colleagues' work in Glasgow (MacLeod et al, 2019) and Loopstra and Tarasuk's survey in Canada (Loopstra and Tarasuk, 2015) to show that only a minority of those experiencing food insecurity accessed food banks. In the sample, of those who reported experiences of food insecurity, only one fifth had used a food bank.[4] Nevertheless, food insecurity was highly associated with food bank use, and the characteristics of those who used a food bank and those who reported food insecurity were similar. Like food insecurity, food bank use was strongly related to low income and housing tenure. People with a household income over £21,250 per annum were 10 times less likely than those with an income of £16,100 or less to have ever used a food bank. Respondents renting from the council or a housing association were more likely to have used a food bank than those who owned their own home, and this relationship persisted when accounting for both income and food insecurity status, suggesting that housing tenure is itself a determinant of food bank use.

Lived experiences of low income, social security and food

'Making do' on a low income

There is a long history in the UK of research on women's experiences of poverty, detailing the strategies women employ to get by on a low income and drawing attention to the high proportion of the limited budget of low-income families used for 'fixed costs' (costs where neither the amount nor the timing could be controlled by the family, most often the mother) (see Charles and Kerr, 1988; Popay, 1989; Glendenning and Millar, 1992; Graham, 1993, among many). The findings from qualitative research with parents, particularly mothers, in Bradford and York, aligned with this literature, as well as with more recent qualitative research on lived experiences of food and poverty (Cooper et al, 2014; Lambie-Mumford and Snell, 2015; O'Connell and Brannen, 2021). Parents detailed the severe financial constraints of life on a low income and described the complex budget management strategies employed to make ends meet, including attending multiple varied outlets ("shopping around") to search for low prices and "offers"; visiting budget supermarkets; and buying items at the back of the shelf with the longest date mark. Among a significant minority of participants, buying secondary produce – "wonky" fruit and vegetables; out-of-date, reduced-cost items; and end of-the-day unsold vegetables and fruit in markets – was an important strategy in purchasing sufficient food on a low income.

Structural economic factors other than income, such as housing and food availability, were also important in affording and accessing adequate food. Food was characterised as part of a series of competing financial demands on monthly budgets (see also Millar and Glendinning, 1992; Graham, 1993), and rising food prices amid stagnant incomes in recent years severely constrained parents' ability to afford adequate food – described here by Martha, a parent of two children: "It is harder to afford everything like we used to, and we are often overdrawn or at the edge of our budget for the same lifestyle as a couple of years ago when we seemed better off – the cost of everything has gone up dramatically."

In keeping with the quantitative findings, the high cost of housing was noted by multiple participants to be problematic, since it consumed a large proportion of monthly income and further constricted household budgets. Jayne, a parent of three children, told me:

'My partner and I both work full time, but due to rent and council tax there is very little left over. We are constantly overdrawn, despite not spending money on anything other than bills and food. Despite us both working we have a combined income of less than £25,000 a year, with almost half our wages going on rent.'

As a result, for some parents, like Mary, a lone parent of one child, food became a flexible element in the household budget and time-consuming strategies, such as visiting multiple supermarkets, were required to reduce costs: "The cost of living in York is so high, mainly rent, accommodation and council tax, that you have to make savings in other areas such as food. You have to spend time shopping around to get the best deals." Household debt and monthly expenditure were mentioned frequently in discussions of accessing and affording food. Higher rents could explain the independent relationship between housing and food insecurity in York, while the increased outgoings attached to higher costs of living in York (although not in Bradford) could explain why the relationship between food insecurity and food bank use persists even after accounting for both housing and household income.

Parents living on low incomes felt that an appropriate range of healthy foods was only available to those of higher social and economic status and described experiences of shame and low self-esteem attached to food insecurity. In York, increased costs of living in a highly unequal city, oriented towards tourism, pushed families towards debt and made more affordable food difficult to access. Indeed, many parents spoke of relying on credit cards to purchase food. The greater the proportion of household income required for housing costs and food, the more likely that those on lower incomes will struggle to make ends meet.

Social security and (in)adequate nutrition

Conversations with parents underscored the extreme difficulty of accessing and affording a nutritious diet for themselves and their family while living on social security. In Bradford, where the quantitative data showed a clear link between receiving means-tested welfare benefits and experiencing food shortages and hunger, mothers described the inadequacy of the income received on social security for affording food amid competing household costs. In York, the detrimental impact of Universal Credit on food security was sharply exposed by the testimonies of participants. The statutory delay of five weeks on payment of a first Universal Credit claim left families with no income whatsoever and, in the absence of any means to purchase food, people were forced to seek help from food banks. The income provided by Universal Credit, when it did come through, was often too low to enable families to purchase a nutritious diet – as described by Joanna, a lone parent of two children: "The reality is that on Universal Credit I cannot provide the recommended amount of fresh fruit and vegetables per day for my children, and I go without more times than not so they can have my share."

It was clear that in the two English cities of Bradford and York experiences of food shortages and hunger were closely associated with inadequate incomes from wages and benefits amid high and sometimes rising living costs. This was particularly stark in York (possibly due to the later time frame) where housing tenure was associated with both food insecurity and food bank use, independent of income. Food was the most malleable component of household outgoings and, when money was tight and other bills needed to be paid, the amount of money spent on food was reduced. Parents went to great lengths to maintain adequate diets for their children and, where possible, themselves, but while food – or lack of it – was the symptom, insufficient household income – poverty – was the cause. This analysis underscores that, contrary to behavioural narratives responsibilising food bank use, and stigmatising those who use them, food insecurity is intimately associated with systemic factors of low income, social security and housing tenure. In the following sections I unpick the systems and discourses that maintain food insecurity despite clear policy options for addressing it.

Language on food and poverty

Parents who experienced food shortages struggled to reconcile structural barriers to accessing food in the context of poverty with an ethic of individual independence. Parents highlighted their "willpower", optimism and complex household resource management strategies enabling them to live through and, in the case of one participant, move away from food insecurity. The ability to "live within your means" and prudently "manage money" was presented by Suzy, a parent of two children, as a form of virtuous active unemployment:

'My mum is on benefits 'cos she has got quite severe mental health problems. I've got three brothers and she manages money really well. She gets little money and she still drives a nice car; she still cooks fresh meals every day, she always has done so. I think it is just about managing the money, because she does manage her money brilliantly, she has never had a problem with it, and she has been on benefits for maybe four years now.'

Accordingly, household resource management was heavily moralised. The superior resource management of some participants was juxtaposed with the financial incompetence of those struggling to afford food, exemplified by both Hana and Suzy:

'I am fortunate that I have never been on benefits and that we have an income. My husband works in a bank and he has had people calling him saying they need money; he has advised them that they should be careful about money.' (Hana [translated from Urdu])

'Chris [her partner] does all the money for us. But Chris is really good at budgeting, 'cos we don't actually earn a lot of money between us, but he budgets the money pretty well. … Yeah 'cos I am not sure she [a friend who went to a food bank] were really, she would have her money straight away and then spend it, she wouldn't think about the rest of the week or the rest of the month. She wouldn't go out and do a proper shop, she would think I've got my money, I haven't had a decent meal for a while and buy a takeaway, blow it like that.' (Suzy)

There was, however, also an alternative narrative surrounding food insecurity which, rather than denigrating those in poverty, claimed to promote their best interests. This paternalistic narrative, exemplified by Amy, a parent of two children, pivoted on the idea that poor people are either unable or unwilling to exercise 'good choices' or fulfil civic duties (Whitworth, 2016) and must be guided by those with a superior understanding of their interests: "I'd like to be able to invite a family who is struggling to feed their household to dinner sometimes. It would be nice to set up a community to do that." Paternalistic narratives, while often well-meaning, deny the agency of people living on a low income and may obfuscate the systemic causes of food insecurity through individualistic portrayals of poverty, accompanied by charity-based responses. Amy's preferred response to food insecurity in her community was to feed "a family who is struggling". Consideration of the underlying causes of why a person might struggle to provide food for their household was absent from the discussion, neglecting the systemic change required to address household food insecurity. In this way, the donation and redistribution of food at a community level operated, like in food banks, as a 'moral safety valve'. It reduced the 'discomfort evoked by visible destitution in our midst by creating the illusion of effective action …

and legitimating personal generosity as a response to injustice rather than encouraging systemic change' (Poppendieck, 1999: 26–7).

What can Foucault tell us about food, poverty and power?

Chapter 2 discussed at length Foucault's concept of neoliberal governmentality, a specific construction of neoliberalism which foregrounds the exercise of power and control over populations. What came across most clearly from the narratives of people living on a low income in Bradford and York was the surveillance, discipline and coercion they experienced as a consequence of their poverty. Lives and choices were restricted not only by an inadequate social security system, low wage and insecure employment, and high living costs but also in more insidious and arguably more deep-seated ways. This chapter continues the discussion in Chapter 2, drawing on the testimonies of people, largely women, living in poverty.

Disciplinary state

The most explicit and comprehensive form of power exercised on participants was that of the state. Lived experience was modified and behaviour manipulated by state policies and institutions. This coercive strand in state policy was directed with greatest fervour towards those in the most severe poverty, configuring in the place of a welfare state a disciplinary state (see Jones and Novak, 1999). Conditionality,[5] inherent to accessing support from the social security system, intimately shaped the lives of those on low/ no income. Daily activities oriented around the obligation to apply for a sufficient number of jobs per week while simultaneously managing a very small household budget and caring for children:

Danielle: Well, if you're signing on, if you forget your book, or if you forget to put down your work ...
Jade: You're meant to search.
Danielle: Searching for a job, three, four a week at a time.
Jade: And you'll have no money, it will stop and you're just stuck with it.

The bureaucratic and apparently inflexible system was also, at the same time, unpredictable and unreliable. Benefit sanctions[6] were portrayed as unwarranted, arbitrary and punitive, forcing claimants into destitution and eroding agency:

Gail: If they sanction you, they take away your money.
Danielle: Yeah, they do stop it.

Moderator: So is that why people are going to food banks?

Danielle: It is getting a lot worse from what it were, it is a lot worse.

Universal Credit was described as "not working": errors within the opaque system of processing payments penalised claimants, reducing or curtailing income. Participants described how the Universal Credit administration process was poor at responding to queries in a timely or personal way and how system errors were exacerbated by 'moral distancing' (May et al, 2019) inherent to the system. For instance, online Universal Credit journals that claimants were required to complete appeared to be responded to inconsistently by different members of staff, despite the pretence of a personal service. Sophie, a lone parent of two children, described the long-term financial impact of the apparently inflexible system:

'When my partner moved out they expected me to live on about £400 a month taking into account that his wage was supposed to be in that month. But it didn't work out like that and they basically turned round and said "tough, that's how it works", that's pretty much their words. I was in minus, still in minus now, trying to play catch up with the companies, and paying off things, paying off my rent – I think I've got until March to pay it, two months' worth of rent, as well as bills that build up.'

The ability of individuals to manage the income received was monitored continuously through a system of surveillance, which stretched beyond government to the economy, linking Jobcentre Plus to utility companies. For instance, failure to pay utility bills could result in a deduction of income from social security: "I didn't pay mine [water bills] for a year but now it is coming out of my benefits. You get reductions off your benefits, which means you are lower" (Jade).

Chronicity of state surveillance

The absence of a direct financial relationship between other state institutions, such as schools and hospitals, and participants mitigated the immediate disciplinary power of the state. The power of the state continued, however, in a subtle manner, embedded within everyday practices. Schools and hospitals were important sites of surveillance and potential channels through which the state could monitor and shape the private sphere. State institutions worked in partnership to intervene in cases of child food insecurity, not necessarily in line with the wishes of parents. Fiona, a provider of services, as a part-time nurse, and living on a low income, described the process by which this could occur:

'You do tend to have social services and stuff involved. A lot of the families where we think there are issues, social services are there. A lot of the time, it is better if there is a younger child who is under a health visitor because then we can get help through to them. Because sometimes the school pick it up as well, the children are not getting the meals that they need.'

Financial relationships could exist with schools through obligated payments for school trips, meals, school uniforms, and classroom supplies. Some participants were keenly aware of what they saw as their failure as parents – especially as mothers – in reneging on these financial obligations and the condemnation from the wider community of parents that may ensue. Speaking to Ruth, a parent of one child, I was told:

'The problem is that all these contributions get labelled as "voluntary contributions", so you go on to the payment panel to deal with it and then you find out that the voluntary contribution is like seven to eight quid, when you get messages like this sent out saying stuff like, "If we don't get enough contributions then the trip will be cancelled." It just puts so much pressure on.'

The all-pervasive dynamics of capitalism

The fluidity between institutions of the state and capitalism, exemplified by Jade's experience, mentioned previously, of having money deducted from her benefit payments because she was in arrears on her water bills, illustrated the increasing blurring of bureaucratic practices through which welfare is now delivered. The 'welfare state' is no longer a straightforward entity; welfare today is administered by the public, private and third sector (see May et al, 2019), with specific aspects of service provision contracted out to voluntary sector providers and private companies for profit (see Hall, 2011: 720), (Atos, Capita and Maximus being some of the most high profile examples). This prompts consideration of whether it is the state or, in fact, capitalism that is the pre-eminent form of disciplinary power in the lives of participants. In its delivery of welfare (and outsourcing of welfare delivery to the private sector), the state emulates many of the characteristics of the market, surveilling and auditing claimants, and defining success by arbitrary markers of efficiency and cost-cutting. However, the state's subordination to capitalism arguably goes further than this: the state is 'ensnared in the reproduction of capitalism relations' (Livingstone, 2017: 9), 'limited and sharpened by the fact that it exists as just one node in a web of social relations' (Holloway, 2002: 13), which it is constantly, and unsuccessfully, trying to control. Holloway describes the all-pervasive dynamics of capitalism: 'the existence of capitalism implies a dynamic of development which attacks us constantly, subjecting our lives more directly to money, creating more and more poverty, more and more inequality, more and more violence' (Holloway, 2002: 50). Post-war developments in the economy and welfare, including high employment levels, access to easy credit and improved state welfare support mitigated the worst excesses of capitalism (see Livingstone 2017: 9). However, these stabilising forces are being decisively eroded by neoliberalism – the post-war welfare settlement (see Glennerster, 2020) is being dismantled and reformed, and the labour market is becoming increasingly precarious through zero-hours contracts and low wages – revealing the 'insecurities and alienation in our social form' (Livingstone, 2017: 9) and underscoring the inadequacies of the state in mediating the antagonisms of capital. The volatility and insecurity of neoliberal capitalism indeed shaped the day-to-day existence of participants, creating a perennial sense of fragility and giving rise to antagonism between communities or individuals, to be discussed later.

Nevertheless, the state is not innocent in this process of increasing inequality and insecurity purportedly borne of the market. Actual markets do not work independently of the state but require the external power of the state and law to regulate them (Hall, 2011: 716). Moreover, the roles of capital and the state in using and legitimating classifications based on class, gender and race – categorisations which maintain inequality and preserve a low-paid labour force necessary for capitalist (re)production and 'growth' – have always been closely entwined (detailed by Shilliam [2018] in his explication of the racialisation of the deserving and undeserving poor). As argued by Beverley Skeggs (2019: 30), 'nothing much has changed [since the 15th century] in terms of the legitimating legacy for capital, only the methods'.

Pastoral power in food banks

Power was exercised within and in relation to the food bank both in direct and via insidious, indirect, ways. As explained in Chapter 3, receipt of a food parcel and associated support from the food bank was, in the majority of cases, dependent on referral from a third-party agent. The criteria according to which an individual was entitled to referral to a food bank appeared to be tied to ideological constructs of the deserving – entrepreneurial, active, hardworking – and undeserving poor (see also May et al, 2019), constructs which could, on occasion, be racialised – as discussed in Chapter 5. A series of bureaucratic, supposedly inflexible rules further governed access to the food bank once a voucher had been secured. Service users were limited to a certain number of food parcels in a set time period, purportedly to preclude dependency on the food bank. On presentation of the food bank voucher (itself disclosing extensive personal information, including the name of the service user, household composition, gender, ethnic group, age and reason for food bank use), the service user was required to explain to a member of staff why the food parcel was required before receiving food. In this way, the food bank emulated a key characteristic of both state welfare bureaucracy and pastoral power (described in Chapter 2): 'it exercised the need to know people's minds, souls, and details of their actions' (Nettleton, 1997: 211).

Within the food bank, the service user was processed through a system which disassociated acts of care and welcome from the receipt of the food parcel, allowing those distributing the parcel to remain emotionally disconnected from service users. Describing her trip to a food bank, Danielle told me:

'Now you go upstairs and talk to them, so they get all your details, then you've got to take your voucher, go outside, around the back … so you go upstairs and they stamp your voucher and then you take it outside and around the back. This is the plan, you've got the thing there, you get your food and that's it, you're left on your own.'

The inability of service users to reciprocate the gift of food (a food parcel) could precipitate a form of 'claims stigma' (Walker, 2005). Individuals who failed to reciprocate gifts, either through personal gratitude or in-kind donations – such as volunteer labour – might incur sanctions in the form of condescension or rejection.

Nevertheless, the 'more than food' identity of food banks, involving not only care but also sign-posting, budgeting courses and holiday hunger programmes, purportedly endorsed a more holistic conception of the person. Food banks provided intellectual and emotional as well as material support. They intended to support – to save – not only the physical self, through the provision of food, but also the intellectual or spiritual self (as touched on in discussions of faith-based food charity in Chapter 4). Self-improvement was an integral part of – condition of – receiving a food parcel. The system of sign-posting and onward referral, accompanied by increasingly robust relationships between third-party referral agents, including Jobcentre Plus schools and GPs, and local food banks, fostered the chronicity of the support and supervision made mandatory for service users.

Sousveillance, self-regulation and the Other

Notwithstanding the powerful systems and processes of control – the repressive and constructive power of the state, the volatility and insecurity of neoliberal capitalism, and the interplay of disciplinary and pastoral power in food banks – applied to the parents I spoke to, the arenas in which power was most effectively instrumentalised were those of the community and the self. The community was the site of a highly gendered form of surveillance, concerning the ability of mothers to care for their children according to certain (public health) standards. Participants, like Suzy, described adopting surveillance roles surrounding potential child food insecurity: "I knew that she were embarrassed to say that she were a bit skint. Whatever we made, sometimes I would dish some up for her little boy and take it down. 'Cos sometimes I used to wonder if he was getting enough." In this way, some participants entered into an inverted form of 'sousveillance' (Mann et al, 2003), surveying not state institutions but each other, and intervening to avert or correct deviant behaviour through social sanctions. Of particular interest to those conducting such surveillance were the financial affairs of neighbours and friends. While this could precipitate benign – albeit unsolicited – interventions to supposedly protect the welfare of children, it could also take a more malign form. Resentment against members of the community who were perceived to be receiving more favourable treatment could spill over into vindictiveness when mistrust was directed towards individuals (Manji, 2017). Social vindictiveness towards identifiable members of the community could be highly racialised – aimed at migrant neighbours and "Asians", as exemplified by both Gemma and the conversation between Jade and Becky in Bradford:

'It is like my next-door neighbour, they're from – I can't remember where it is. They both work but they both claim [social security] as well which is quite annoying when there is me and my husband and he works every hour God sends to get money to bring home just to live off and next door they have got all this money, they have just got a brand new 60-inch telly, a U-shaped sofa.' (Gemma)

Jade:	Yeah, you can't go down to Asda and buy fresh burgers. They've now got up to three aisles, halal food. Don't get fresh burgers, you can get mince, but they only put 16 packets of mince out in the morning and then 16 in the afternoon, if they have all gone there is no more mince.
Becky:	Does that explain it because when I nipped down to Asda there was only one packet of mince left?
Jade:	Yeah, 'cos they are not putting them all out.
Moderator:	So why are they doing it? Why are they changing it?
Jade:	Because the Asians are complaining that our meat is next to their halal meat.

The most potent channel through which control of the individual operated was the beliefs, behaviour and discourses of participants themselves. Feelings of shame in respect of poverty was a common theme, most explicit in discussions around accessing food banks. In this context, shame was co-constructed through the convergence of an individual's internal sense of inadequacy and externally imposed disapproval for failing to satisfy societal expectations of economic self-reliance: "I have degrees and I have qualifications; I have all this stuff and I can't get into jobs that I need to get into. I feel like I'm letting my husband down because I'm not really earning anything at work" (Ruth). The most widely adopted method to avert shame involved individuals' attempts to align themselves with dominant discourses, in particular the 'culture of poverty' (Lewis, 1966), and define themselves in opposition to the demonised Other. Individuals who were apparently unashamed of accessing food aid were subject to disparagement. Openness about food insecurity was itself assumed to reflect an absence of need – of deservingness – and these people were considered to be "playing the system". Suzy told me: "There is one kid that we know at school and the mum brags that she goes there to get things, 'I don't go food shopping because I just go to food bank'." This discourse was common among those who were not currently living through food insecurity as well as among those who were. Sabira described episodes of severe food insecurity; however, when discussing food banks (which she avoided) she aligned herself with societal discourses individualising poverty:

| Moderator: | Do you think it is a universal thing, people feeling shame and pride and not wanting to go to a food bank? |
| Sabira: | No, some people go because they want free stuff, people always want free stuff. |

Parents who expressed anxieties around food insufficiency, but had not personally experienced hunger, constructed a food insecure Other in opposition to themselves. The food insecure Other was culpable for their food insecurity, which was itself attributable to personal failings, notably their incompetent or selfish use of household income and poor cooking skills. Participants contrasted their own superior resource management abilities with those of their image of the food insecure person, carefully explaining the complicated budgeting strategies they employed to avoid food insecurity. With this ascendency of individualistically determinist explanations thereby disappeared compassion. The plight of those living in poverty and struggling to afford food was reconstituted as being due to wilful attitudes or personal incompetence. Accordingly, such citizens could only be responded to with social ostracism and denunciation.

A racialised Other?

Notwithstanding examples of racism surrounding food and poverty evident in Bradford – the blame ascribed to "Asians" for changes in food supply at supermarkets and the racialised social vindictiveness toward neighbours – stigmatisation of a racialised Other was a minority view. Only one of the many people I spoke with, Gemma, explicitly described a racialised, in this case Muslim, Other. This Other was accused of committing benefit fraud, which was portrayed as a reason for the Other's relative affluence compared to the poverty in which Gemma lived. This construction of a racialised Other was, however, fervently contested by another (White) participant:

Kate: Are you sure what you are saying is true?
Gemma: Yeah.
Kate: Cos this does not sound like refugees to me.
Gemma: No, not refugees.
Kate: What then?
Gemma: They are from, oh I don't know where they are from, not refugees.
Kate: So immigrants.
Gemma: Muslims, yeah.
Kate: They don't get benefits, they are usually very poor. I know it is easy for us to judge.

The predominant interpretation of an 'Other' by Pakistani British participants was not of another person but of another place. Pakistan was an important reference point for many of the Pakistani British people I spoke with. Perception that Pakistan, not England, was a place of extreme poverty limited the extent to which participants accepted or acknowledged their own food insecurity and, or the food insecurity of others, like Sabira: "But we always had something, in England you always have something to eat, no one goes hungry forever." The more affluent Pakistani British participants described directing charity, especially donations from zakat (see Chapter 2), to poverty in Pakistan, rather than the UK: "There isn't poverty in the UK as there is in the third world. Most [Muslim] charity is donated and most of the money from zakat goes there [Pakistan]. The UK is comparatively well off: people have health and a roof over their head"(Ghada).

The testimonies of parents in and at risk of food insecurity illuminated the variable modes and processes of power which shaped their lived experiences, including those of food. This was not limited to the disciplinary power of the state and the market, but also included coercion in food banks, as well as the infiltration of people's – often gendered and sometimes racialised – subjectivities and self-conceptions by governing discourses. The most influential form of coercion appeared to operate not via the state or civil society but the self, in the form of self-regulation and self-surveillance. The pauperisation and obedience of the poor may, hence, be created and cemented by state policy and by an economic structure whose inequalities in the ownership of wealth and the distribution of income are self-perpetuating, but it is, in fact, maintained by a set of social relations that keep this system in place (Jones and Novak, 1999). It is when the (dominant) economic and political system is most under threat, when its claim to fairness is most visibly denied by the distress and unfairness it manifestly creates – most starkly brought to light by troops of people walking through the doors of food banks – that poor people are subject to the most criticism and attack, from both the establishment and their peers (Jones and Novak, 1999).

Conclusion

> There must be a degree of pressure [for people to participate in wage labour] and that which is attended with the least violence will be the best. When hunger is either felt or feared, the desire of obtaining bread will quietly dispose the mind to undergo the greatest hardships, and will sweeten the severest labours. ... The wisest legislature will never be able to devise a more equitable, a more effectual, or in any respect a more suitable punishment than hunger is for the disobedient servant.
>
> Reverend Joseph Townsend, 'A Dissertation
> on the Poor Laws', cited in Poynter, 1969

Reverend Joseph Townsend's commentary from 1789, the year of the French Revolution, is as relevant today as it was in the 18th century. The contemporary British social security system impoverishes and punishes people who are unable to find well-paid work (see Wright et al (2020) on the 'social abuse' wrought by the British social security system); it creates hunger among all types of households – people who are too unwell too work, people with young children, people who are unable to find employment, and many more. Food insecurity, which pervades Britain today, is in fact a reflection of deep and desperate poverty created by punitive social security and exploitative employment: food, as the most malleable element in the household budget, is reduced when income is low and other bills need to be paid.

Yet a key difference between Townsend's analysis and the contemporary situation is that, today, it is not only hunger itself that propels people into insecure and exploitative wage labour, but both actual hunger and the appearance of hunger. Thus, central to the preservation of the political and economic status quo, in which aristocrats populate the Cabinet while people die of starvation and despair because of benefit sanctions[7] (Butler, 2020), is the shame and stigma intimately associated with hunger. People living on a low income, like Gemma, denigrate and differentiate themselves from their peers in an attempt to escape the poverty and food bank use that is so highly stigmatised. Simultaneously, obedience to the status quo is maintained through multiple interconnected systems of surveillance and coercion. State surveillance within and between institutions – Jobcentre Plus, schools and hospitals – requires citizens to emulate 'homo economicus', by engaging in 'active unemployment' (Garthwaite, 2017), submitting job applications and existing within the monthly structure defined by the Department for Work and Pensions.

Discipline and coercion is also embedded within some food banks and soup kitchens. In food banks, neoliberal processes and practices – the referral system, classification and surveillance of service users, and moral distancing between staff and users – cultivate a highly bureaucratic and stigmatising form of welfare, one which demarcates the deserving from the undeserving poor (see also May et al, 2019). There is, however, another form of power in food banks: pastorship or 'pastoral power', a particular type of affective and individualising power outlined by Foucault in his lecture notes from the Collège de France (Foucault, 2008). Food banks exhibit some of the characteristics of pastorship as it materialised in the 16th- and 17th-century Christian Church: they care for each and every user of the food bank singly and, in order to do so, require detailed knowledge of the circumstances and intentions of food bank users; they assure – or at least attempt to assure – individual salvation; and they do not just command obedience and sacrifice but are purportedly prepared to make sacrifices for their subjects. Pastoral power in food banks is thus a fundamentally individualising power. Personalised support and care is offered to food bank users on an individual basis, according to their disclosed needs. Poverty thereby becomes an individual rather than a systemic condition which can be 'solved' through self-improvement (see also Möller, 2021). Theorisations of pastoral power, in which individual subjects are 'cared for' by food bank volunteers, are perfectly compatible with moral distancing and bureaucratic forms of exclusion, discussed in Chapter 3. The arena and remit of pastorship in food banks is clearly demarcated and is itself a consequence of wider bureaucratic practices, including the referral system in which detailed information is collected on food bank users, as well as processes of 'moral distancing' (May et al, 2019). In many food banks, there was clear separation between volunteers checking vouchers and distributing food parcels, and volunteers providing care in some form; the affective relationship essential to pastoral power could thereby operate simultaneously with the moral distancing enabled by the food bank voucher. While volunteers did make sacrifices for their subjects, giving up their time to work in the food bank, this sacrifice was clearly couched within the bureaucracy of the food bank. Volunteers 'sacrificed' their time for a limited period only and, unlike service users who were required to disclose detailed personal information, there was no equivalent expectation from volunteers who were often distinguished from service users by branded aprons and name badges, and who saw their role as asking questions rather than sharing intimate information about themselves. In this way, pastorship individualised the poverty of food bank users and aligned with a stigmatising culture of arbitration and exclusion manifesting in the referral system.

In Bradford and York, people living in poverty opposed their own attitudes and behaviours to those of the food poor Other, who was profoundly stigmatised and whose food insecurity was attributed to personal failings. This Other was highly gendered, as discussed further in Chapter 7, but they could also, on occasion, be racialised. Jock Young (2003) highlights the rise in widespread resentment and tension resulting from economic and cultural globalisation. He argues that globalisation exacerbates both relative deprivation and crises of identity: such a combination is experienced as unfair, humiliating and threatening, and results in behaviour which is vindictive rather than instrumental. Such social vindictiveness was evident – albeit to a limited extent – in Bradford, as an increasingly degraded working class surveilled and scapegoated migrants for declining conditions and their own precarity (see also Standing, 2011). In this way, resentment within communities was situated within a neoliberal structural context, in which wider developments contributed to divisiveness and anomie.

Chapter 7 further examines the influence of religion and ethnicity on the lived experience of food in contexts of poverty. It argues that the experiences of Pakistani British and White British people must be considered against a backdrop of historical and contemporary racism, but also proposes that possibilities for solidarity and resistance to neoliberal norms may emerge through eating and sharing food among and between ethno-religious groups outside of food aid.

Notes

[1] Hall (2011) in fact argues that at the heart of classical liberalism was a 'splitting' along the lines of race and wealth: progress was accompanied by the need to contain any 'threat from below'; tolerance, reform, moderation and representative government for the English race operated in parallel with colonial governmentality, discipline, violence and authority for recalcitrant 'other' native peoples abroad; and emancipation and subjugation were promoted simultaneously. Hall argues that 'in these different ways, liberalism became a "world mission" harbouring an un-transcended gulf between us and 'the others', the civilized and the barbarians' (Hall, 2011: 170). We find this repeated today in the 'soft' face of compassionate conservatism and Cameron's 'Big Society' coupled with the hard edge of cuts, workfare and the gospel of self-reliance.

[2] The association was strongly statistically significant.

[3] Means-tested benefits are any welfare benefits where your eligibility is determined by the amount of income and capital you have. Means-tested benefits are available to people who can demonstrate that their income and capital are below a certain level. The means-tested benefits are: Income-based Jobseeker's Allowance; Income-related Employment and Support Allowance; Income Support; Pension Credit; Tax Credits (Child Tax Credit

and Working Tax Credit); Housing Benefit; Council Tax Support; Social Fund (Sure Start Maternity Grant, Funeral Payment, Cold Weather Payment); Universal Credit.

4   Looking at this a different way, 23 per cent of respondents reported experiences of food insecurity but only 8 per cent said that they or a member of their household had used a food bank.

5   Conditionality, or conditional welfare arrangements, requires people to behave in a certain way to access welfare goods, such as cash benefits, housing or support services. These behavioural conditions tend to be enforced through penalties or 'sanctions' that reduce, suspend or end access to these goods. See: Dwyer (2019).

6   A benefit sanction is a financial penalty imposed on a claimant meaning a loss of income when someone does not meet conditions like attending Jobcentre appointments. Claimants who miss one Jobcentre appointment have their payments reduced or removed for 28 days. If they make the same mistake three times, the penalty is 91 days. Nearly a quarter of all Jobseeker's Allowance (JSA) claimants were sanctioned between 2010 and 2015, sometimes for trivial reasons (NAO, 2016). The British sanction system is the second harshest in the world (Immervoll and Knotz, 2018) with penalties of up to 100 per cent removal of benefit income for up to 3 years.

7   In 2019, Phillipa Day, who had been diagnosed with a personality disorder, took a fatal overdose after her social security payments were cut. In 2018, Errol Graham starved to death while seriously mentally ill. His benefits were stopped when he failed to attend a work capability assessment and did not respond to calls, letters or home visits from the DWP. When his body was found, Errol weighed four-and-a-half stone (30kg) and his family said he had used pliers to pull out his teeth. In 2014, Jodey Whiting, who suffered multiple physical and mental health issues, took her own life after her benefits were stopped. Cases where people claiming benefits died or came to serious harm have led to more than 150 government reviews since 2012. See: Homer (2021).

7

Racial inequality or mutual aid? Food and poverty among Pakistani British and White British women

'We had times when the bailiffs were knocking on the door. Money was always pretty tight towards the end of the month and it was during this time that food was very short. But even when life was very hard and money short, I wouldn't go to a food bank – because of shame, pride and embarrassment. You don't want people to see you like that. There may be people you know there who will talk.'

Sabira

Introduction: Sabira's story

I met Sabira in 2017. She was separated from her husband and had three young children. She was in her late twenties and had lived in the same area of Bradford all her life. Her parents, to whom she was close, lived nearby. She described her ethnicity as Pakistani and her religion as Islam but, when asked about the influence of her faith on her experience of poverty, she stressed that was, "not to do with Islam. I'm just a bubbly person; I'm optimistic and I know I'll get through hard times".

Sabira described several episodes of what may be classed as food insecurity. Her ex-husband controlled their household income and would spend the vast majority it – "I don't know where the money went" – leaving very little for food and other household bills. When there was no money for food, Sabira would make a meal from whatever there was in the cupboards – fairy cakes using margarine, eggs and flour, or scrambled eggs – or she would seek support from her parents, whose assistance was given willingly – "I would always be able to go to my mum's". Her mother would provide food and emotional support – although never money – and, occasionally, Sabira would ask her father for financial assistance. While parental support was given freely, Sabira stressed that she would endeavour to "repay the debt": "I would work really hard; I would clean and cook, it would be nothing to make an extra chapatti – four rather than three. They really appreciated it, they all said afterwards how helpful I was."

Despite numerous episodes of severe hardship, Sabira had never used a food bank, or any formalised food aid provision, and was adamant that she never would. She didn't know anyone who had been to a food bank. Her friends who, like her, had been at "rock bottom", without money to buy food for themselves and their children, had never been and would never go to a food bank: "They were all too embarrassed." In response to food shortages, these women would either seek support from family and friends or they would "keep it quiet out of shame and embarrassment". Chapter 5 described how Whiteness intimately shapes the character and performance of food charity in the UK; White, and sometimes Christian, norms permeate food aid, especially food banks, and may be implicated in the apparent under-representation of Black and minority ethnic groups. This chapter considers whether and how ethnic and ethno-religious identities may influence the likelihood of reporting food insecurity, as well as the broader lived experience of food, poverty and food aid use.

Exploring ethnic differences in food insecurity

In the US, communities of colour are disproportionately affected by hunger. Food insecurity is almost three times higher among African American households (26 per cent) and Hispanic households (24 per cent) compared with White households (11 per cent), and regional and local-level data estimates food insecurity among Native American populations to be anywhere between 30 and 50 per cent (Blue Bird Jernigan et al, 2013). In *Feeding the Other*, Rebecca de Souza (2019) exposes the racial inequality in food insecurity in the US that becomes manifest in food pantries, spaces in which service users are largely Black and Hispanic, and volunteers and paid staff are predominantly White.

In the UK, the racial demography and lived experience of food insecurity is less clear cut. This is, in part, attributable to the historical absence of routinely collected national-level data on food insecurity, prior to the publication of the 2019–20 Family Resource Survey (FRS) (in 2021); it is arguably also, however, a consequence of the relative neglect of race and ethnicity in research on UK food insecurity.[1] Chapter 5 detailed racial inequality in UK food insecurity, as set out in the FRS, which identified very high food insecurity among Black/African/Caribbean/Black British households (19 per cent) and relatively low food insecurity among Indian households (5 per cent) and White households (7 per cent) (DWP, 2021). Analysis of the nationally representative 2016 Food and You survey by Loopstra and colleagues (Loopstra et al, 2019b) similarly illustrated differences in food insecurity by ethnicity. The relatively small size of the survey forces the researchers to use crude categories of ethnic group: 'White' and 'Other ethnic group'/'non-White'. Using these categories their analysis suggests that adults who describe themselves as belonging to a 'non–White' ethnic group are more likely to report food insecurity than adults identifying as 'White'. The researchers also find that the association between food insecurity and ethnicity is associated with moderate food insecurity but not with severe food insecurity, suggesting that ethnicity may be a less important factor in food insecurity than other characteristics, such as income, health status and gender.

My own analysis of survey data in Bradford suggests that the picture may be both more complex and more localised. The BiB1000 dataset, which includes a measure of food insecurity, is smaller than the Food and You Survey analysed by Loopstra and colleagues; however, reflecting the demography of Bradford, the dataset encompasses a highly multi-ethnic population, allowing for a more nuanced analysis of the interaction of ethnicity and food insecurity, particularly among the two largest groups in the dataset: Pakistani and White British women. In the sample of 1,280 women living in Bradford, 49 per cent describe themselves as Pakistani and 37 per cent as White British; 4 per cent identify as Indian and 2 per cent as Black (Power et al, 2017d).[2] As a consequence of the varying sample size of the different ethnic groups within the survey, in-depth statistical analysis of food insecurity is only viable for Pakistani and White British women. Nevertheless, some simple assessment of food insecurity among Black, Bangladeshi, Indian, Mixed ethnic, as well as Pakistani and White British, women is possible. I found a significant difference in food insecurity between the six ethnic groups. A very high proportion of Black women (32 per cent) reported food insecurity, while a very low proportion of Indian women (5 per cent) were food insecure. There was a considerable difference in reported food insecurity between the ethnic groups traditionally collectively categorised as South Asian: Pakistani (10 per cent), Indian (5 per cent) and Bangladeshi (13 per cent), raising concern about the validity of lumping these groups together into one category.

In the BiB1000 survey, Pakistani women were less likely to report food insecurity than White British women. While Pakistani women were the majority group in this survey (comprising 48.9 per cent of the sample), they are a large but still minority group in Bradford and a minority group in the UK: at the time of the 2011 Census, 20 per cent of the population in Bradford classified themselves as of Pakistani ethnic origin (ONS, 2011) and 2 per cent of residents in England and Wales belonged to the 'Asian/Asian British: Pakistani' group. Thus, contrary to the racial demography of food insecurity in the US and the findings of Loopstra and colleagues (Loopstra et al, 2019b), in Bradford, a minority ethnic group appears to be at lower risk of food insecurity than the majority ethnic group.[3]

The demography of – or risk factors for – food insecurity also differed between Pakistani and White British women in Bradford. Among Pakistani women, the mother being older increased the risk of her reporting food insecurity, while among White British women, the younger the mother the greater her risk of being food insecure. Being a lone parent ('cohabitation status'), as opposed to living with the child's father or another partner, increased the risk of being food insecure among White British women but had no effect on food insecurity among Pakistani women. The most marked difference between Pakistani and White British women was variation in the strength of the relationship between socioeconomic measures and food insecurity. The association between multiple socioeconomic measures (unemployment, receipt of social security, and perception of financial insecurity) and food insecurity was considerably stronger for White British than Pakistani women. For instance, accounting for other demographic factors, such as age and cohabitation status, food insecurity was associated with receiving social security among White British women but not among Pakistani women. The probability of food insecurity was 26 per cent for White British women in receipt of means-tested social security compared with 13 per cent for those not in receipt of social security. By contrast, for Pakistani women, the probability of food insecurity was 11 per cent for those in receipt of means-tested social security and 9 per cent for those not in receipt. Unemployment was only associated with food insecurity among White British women and not among Pakistani women. As discussed in Chapter 6, a woman's perception of her financial insecurity had the strongest association with food insecurity of all the different socioeconomic measures, and this was the case among both Pakistani and White British women. The association was, nevertheless, stronger for White British than Pakistani women.

Chapter 6 argued that food insecurity is primarily a function of poverty. It showed the ways in which daily existence, including the ability to purchase adequate food, may be constrained by income. It set out the various systems and processes of power which operate in the lives of women in and at risk of food insecurity to demonstrate how food insecurity is implicated in a wider framework of neoliberal governance which, via an inadequate and punitive welfare system and low wage economy, causes a large segment of the population to experience hunger. The finding that food insecurity and its causes vary by ethnic group, in this case between Pakistani and White British women, does not necessarily imply that the arguments of Chapter 6 do not hold true. It does suggest, however, that a conceptual framework which neglects ethnicity and race provides only a partial portrayal of food and poverty today.

What is 'race'? Social and historical constructs of race and ethnicity

So far in this chapter I have discussed race and ethnicity as though they referred to fixed or natural categories. In the quantitative surveys, I have drawn on ethnic categories which are inflexible and discrete: a woman is White British or Pakistani. But ethnicity is not a natural or fixed category; it does not have a biological essence but is a result of discursive, social and historical processes, formed in articulation with other constructions (often gender and class) (see Grossberg, 2007; Alexander, 2009) and highly dependent on the context in which the definition is made (Senior and Bhopal, 1994). As argued by de Souza, 'racial groups are social creations and reflect a process and external ascription that are constituted in structures and everyday practices' (de Souza, 2019: 57–8). Stuart Hall, the late and highly influential cultural and social theorist, characteristically points to the emergence of the possibility of a 'Black' identity within a specific historical moment: 'The fact is "black" has never just been there either. It has always been an unstable identity, psychically, culturally, and politically. It, too, is a narrative, a story, a history. Something constructed, told, spoken, not simply found ... black is an identity which had to be learned and could only be learned in a certain moment' (Hall, 1996: 116). De Souza describes the contemporary racial stigma in the US in which 'Blackness' is tacitly associated with 'unworthiness' (see Shilliam (2018) on equivalent constructions in the UK), an association which is deeply historically embedded in the institution of chattel slavery and the associated rituals and customs that supported the master–slave hierarchy (Feagin, 2013). Racism and capitalism are arguably intimately entwined; American sociologist, Joe Feagin observes that racism and capitalism evolved collectively as part of the same 'political economic system that took root in European countries and their colonies in North America'; he argues that, 'in this early period, thus, modern capitalism was systemic racism and systemic racism was modern capitalism' (Feagin, 2013: 25).

The concept of 'race' was first applied to humans in the 18th century as an arbitrary classification to aid understanding of evolution and examination of variation. The aim was to extend to humans a taxonomic classification below the level of species (Senior and Bhopal, 1994). In the 19th and 20th centuries, spurious and highly racist scientific and medical arguments were employed as an explanation for the alleged mental and physical inferiority of Black and minority ethnic people in Europe and the US (Washington, 2006). Today, while scientific explanations of racial inferiority have been discredited, differences in health and income across ethnic and racial groups continue to be rationalised via cultural or genetic explanations (Goldberg, 2009), including poor work ethic or lack of personal responsibility; key components of social disadvantage, such as material disadvantage and particularly racism, are relatively neglected (Nazroo, 1998; 2003). Race is, today, marked by an 'active suppression of "race" as a legitimate topic in public discourse ... racial stigma flourishes because of the "collective forgetting" that has occurred via the sanitizing of collective memories and national narratives' (de Souza,

2019: 58), as well as the imposition of supposedly objective, fixed categories which shape much (quantitative) analysis of racial inequalities (including the quantitative analysis in this book). A history of slavery, theft and colonisation in Europe and the US is rewritten as one of industrialisation, urbanisation and wealth.

This rewrite of history, as well as the interplay of systemic racism and capitalism, is manifest in the economic history of Bradford. In the mid-19th century, Bradford's economy was built on the wool trade, with the city being described as 'the wool capital of the world'. Related industries such as engineering and services (for example, finance) developed alongside the wool industry. One of the key social consequences of the rapid industrialisation of the area throughout the 19th century was a huge increase in population, achieved primarily through immigration, initially from Ireland and subsequently from Germany, Central and Eastern Europe and, from the 1950s onwards, from Asia and the West Indies, as described in Chapter 1. Changes to the local textile industry in the mid-1950s precipitated a sharp increase in South Asian migration into Bradford. This migration consisted of a first wave of male workers, actively recruited by the owners of mills to counteract staff shortages at a time of expansion in demand, followed by the migration of workers' families (Bradford Heritage Recording Unit, 1987). The wool textile industry declined considerably in the latter part of the 20th century, with important implications for the employment prospects of large sections of the city's population. Groups who had previously relied on low-skilled manufacturing work requiring few qualifications were particularly hard hit by the relative decline of the manufacturing sector and less well placed than others to take advantage of growth in areas such as financial and personal services. The occupations of Bradford's workforce continue to reflect its manufacturing past, with a relatively high proportion concentrated in elementary and operative occupations.

The 2001 'riots' in Bradford and Oldham exposed the extent of racial stigma in parts of Northern England. The spread of unrest in 2001 was linked to increasing racial violence, longstanding mistrust and disillusionment with the police, the overt and taunting presence of the British National Party and other far-right groups, and entrenched poverty and unemployment in Bradford and Oldham (Ray and Smith, 2002: 4). At the time of the riots, more than half of Pakistani British and Bangladeshi British households lived in the most deprived 10 per cent of wards in England, compared with only 14 per cent of White households; Pakistani British and Bangladeshi British men were two and a half times more likely to be unemployed than White men and those in work received only two thirds of the average earnings of White men (Modood and Berthoud, 1997).

Despite this wider context, the official reports published in the aftermath of the 2001 riots focused largely on broader issues surrounding the management of public services (Cantle, 2001; Burnley Task Force, 2001; Ritchie, 2001). These reports promulgated an ideology of 'community cohesion' organised around crude functionalist ideas of social integration in which all should come to share a common social identity. These ideas were underpinned by new modes of 'racialisation' (Miles, 1989) in which South Asian communities of Northern England were pathologised. Discourses of gang culture, forced marriages, drug abuse, intergenerational conflict, resistance to integrating and speaking English, and being Muslim were mobilised, especially post 9/11 (11 September 2001), to explain away racism and to justify dubious, stigmatising policies. Simultaneously, second and third generation South Asians were increasingly constructing new identities,[4] differentiating themselves from their parents, yet continuing to be Muslim/Pakistani/ Kashmiri and British (Bagguley and Hussain, 2003). It was against this wider context of racism and deprivation that I spoke with women in Bradford about their lived experiences of food amid poverty. The following section reports on these conversations.

Lived experiences of food, poverty and food aid

Apparent variations among Pakistani British and White British women

The quantitative data in the BiB1000 survey indicated variation in food insecurity between Pakistani British and White British women. My conversations with White British and first and second generation Pakistani British women in Bradford suggested considerable differences in experiences of food among *all* women living on a low income in the city. Experiences of food insecurity ranged from anxiety that money and food would not last throughout the month until payday, to immediate, severe and chronic hunger – starvation – among one or more members of the household, usually the mother.

Gail had lived on the same estate in Bradford since she was a child. She had struggled at school and left with few qualifications. After giving birth to her first child in her early twenties, she had found it increasingly difficult to find employment. When I spoke to Gail, she was receiving social security and had eight children, ranging from 12 years to 11 weeks, which placed extreme pressure on the very small household budget. Life was a constant struggle to ensure that the children, especially the youngest, had food and nappies: "If I've not got food in to feed the seven kids and she [the baby] needs nappies or milk, the money will go on her." It was common for Gail to go whole days without eating, existing on cups of sweetened tea, to ensure there was enough food for the rest of the household.

Unlike Gail, Gemma had never missed a meal because of food shortages but towards the end of the month – before payday when money was short – it was a familiar occurrence to struggle to afford food and, in response, to seek familial support or eat cheap frozen food:

'It is like with us, I won't say that I'm great with food and stuff, sometimes we really do have bad weeks where we do struggle but literally, we've never been to a food bank, but we have always looked in the freezer to see what we got and, if we didn't have enough to make a big meal, he'd ring his mum and say, "Have you got a bit of this that I can borrow". Just to put in to add it up. Like the other week, the kids had fish fingers, chicken nuggets, sausages. We got it all in on a Thursday, because he gets paid on a Friday. On Thursday we were like, "we've got no food", so we just threw everything together.'

A desire to conceal food insecurity from others outside of the household was overwhelming among the women I spoke with in Bradford (as was also the case in York); there was keen awareness of the stigma attached to food bank use and the shame associated with not being able to afford food. Food shortages resulting from poverty were concealed from family members, the local community and local welfare services. Lucy hid her experiences from her close family, "I wouldn't even be able to tell my own sister that I had to go [to a food bank]", while Sanjeeta described how people living in deprivation in Bradford "hide it [food insecurity], they are ashamed".

There did, however, appear to be a difference between women describing themselves as 'White' or 'White British' and those who identified as 'Pakistani' or 'Pakistani British' in their likelihood of reporting food shortages or issues in accessing sufficient food for themselves and their household. It was notable that, apart from Sabira, no woman describing herself as 'Pakistani British' disclosed current or past episodes of food insecurity and none of the Pakistani British women I spoke with, including Sabira, said they had used formal food aid, such as a food bank. This was in contrast to those women describing themselves as 'White' who did disclose food shortages and using food aid. The possibility of food insecurity was assertively rejected by many of the Pakistani British women I spoke with: the price of food was described as "not a problem for us" and I was told "we can afford whatever we need" or "we have no problem affording food".

Why does there appear to be lower food insecurity among Pakistani British than among White British women?

The survey data and the conversations with women in Bradford would suggest lower reporting of food insecurity, if not lower food insecurity itself, among Pakistani British compared with White British women in the city. It is possible that this could be attributable to lower poverty among all or some of the Pakistani British women interviewed, placing them at reduced risk of food insecurity, or that racial stigma affected their likelihood of disclosing insufficient access to food, particularly to a White British researcher. It is also possible that other factors underpin this difference – if a difference really does exist – such as family support, religious frameworks, or varied strategies employed to make ends meet within the household. Below, I briefly discuss these possible theories and consider whether ethnicity, race or religion may shape the likelihood and lived experience of food insecurity.

Lower poverty

There was no notable difference between the Pakistani British and White British women interviewed in terms of socioeconomic status. Across all the women there was variation in levels of poverty but no ethnic pattern to this, implying that the apparently lower food insecurity reported by Pakistani British women was not attributable to higher wealth – this aligned with the quantitative findings in the BiB1000 survey, in which the relationship between food insecurity and ethnicity persisted after accounting for socioeconomic status (when controlling for age and cohabitation status). Reflecting this, the women I spoke with intimated that financial difficulties were experienced by members of Bradford's Pakistani British community as well as the White community. The commonality of Sabira's experience – "even when life was very hard and money very short, I would not go to a food bank" – was apparent in Maisa's remark: "I have not heard of anyone going to a food bank – but anyway it would be hush hush in the South Asian community. There is so much honour and pride and providing food for the family is just so important." This aligns with data at a national level, which shows clearly and uncontrovertibly that Pakistani British households have lower incomes and higher unemployment than White British households (Gov.uk, 2021). On both a national and local level, therefore, apparently lower food insecurity among Pakistani British women than White British women is not necessarily attributable to differences in poverty.

Strategies employed to 'make ends meet' within the household

In Chapter 6, I outlined the elaborate and time-consuming strategies women in Bradford and York employed to 'make ends meet' within their household – such strategies cut across ethnicity, race and religion. Approaches included tight control of material resources and keen attention to budgeting and financial planning, alongside cooking food from scratch, cooking in bulk and creating a meal from food available in the household. Basma, who had recently migrated to Bradford from Pakistan for marriage, described the communal preparation and consumption of food in her household, while

Suzy and Kate discussed the importance of "cooking from scratch": "There are 13 people in my house and we all cook and eat together. I am the main cook but everyone else helps and cleans up. We prepare [food] together, everyone supports. There are different chefs for different foods" Basma (translated from Urdu).

Kate: It seems that just cooking from scratch is the key.
Suzy: And it is much cheaper as well.
Moderator: Yeah?
Suzy: You can make things in bulk and sort of freeze them.

There appeared to be a greater tendency among Pakistani British than White British women to cook a single meal for the entire family and eat communally, often attributable to living with extended family members. However, contrary to the assumptions made by service providers in Bradford that food insecurity was lower in Pakistani British households not only because of a greater tendency to cook in bulk but also because of a higher frequency of cooking "cheaper" types of food, such as "lentils", South Asian participants described eating a wide variety of foods, including pizza, and fish and chips. Lentils tended to be cooked only a couple of times a week and most meals incorporated meat.

Where variation did exist in approaches to 'making ends meet' within the household these were shaped by poverty not ethnicity. For households living in severe poverty, like Jade's, cooking using fresh ingredients or in bulk was subordinated to cooking "not healthy stuff but just what I get really": "I've got ten people in my house and trying to cook on a budget is – I get a packet of pasta, a tub of sauce, and that's your tea." Like Sabira, then, who when confronted with no food or money made cupcakes for her children, Jade's main priority was to feed her household with whatever food she could access.

Familial and social support

Family, predominantly parents and occasionally grandparents, were critically important to survival in hard times. Family members provided emotional, childcare and material support, most often food, and alleviated isolation. For Sabira and Gemma, family was a source of food and entwined emotional support:

'To cope [with food shortages], I went to my mum's for emotional support and for food – I would always be able to go to my mum's.' (Sabira)

'His [her partner's] mum has just got a big fridge so she has brought a load of food over and said, "We got this and we don't want to throw it away". So it is sat in the freezer and it is like, "We are alright now".' (Gemma)

Well-established family networks were central to the day-to-day life of most of the Pakistani British women I spoke with to a greater extent than the White British women. This was in part a consequence of housing and migration circumstances. The Pakistani British women I talked to lived largely with or very close to extended family members (predominantly members of their husband's family due to patterns of migration from Pakistan to the UK for marriage); family members shared caring and food responsibilities within the household and provided accessible support networks. Among Pakistani British women who did not experience financial difficulties in accessing food, there was no reticence or shame in sharing food and caring responsibilities or requesting assistance from extended family members – most notably in the case of women who were unable to purchase food from local shops due to language or knowledge barriers and who drew on family members to do so on their behalf. However, family members were not necessarily an unproblematic source of help. Seeking help transgressed the ethic of independence which permeated some – especially, but not limited to, White British – families. Requesting help from the family could, thereby, undermine a participant's sense of agency and self-esteem, as explained by Jade: "I don't see my mum; I don't really talk to her. I don't really want to ask her for help, because I don't want her to see me like this." Some women who drew on parental support in times of food shortages either described previously assisting their parents with material resources or substituting their unpaid labour for the resources received, thereby retaining a sense of independence and self-worth through reciprocation.

Alternatively, the ability to seek assistance from family members could be precluded by intergenerational poverty: parents and grandparents also experiencing (food) poverty were unable to support their children with food or money. While it was notable that only White British women discussed this obstacle to support, it was unclear whether this difference was attributable to their lower likelihood of living in multi-generational households, in which the effects of poverty may be more evenly distributed, or deeper poverty among successive generations of the families of White British women I talked to in Bradford.

Mutual support systems were almost completely mediated through women, reflecting and reinforcing the gendered organisation of care within families. Most of the day-to-day help received by participants came from other women. Their mother and their partner's mother played an especially important role in this informal economy of care, providing childcare and material support, in kind rather than cash. Beyond the family, members of the community – whether based on geography, gender, class or ethnicity – provided essential food and emotional support. Friends and key community figures, such as Julie and Wendy, provided food parcels or money, sometimes at a cost to their own living standards: "If it weren't for Julie last Christmas – she gave us a food bank parcel – if it weren't for Julie, we would have had no meal, we wouldn't have eaten all week" (Katie).

Moderator:	What makes it [food insecurity] better? What is a better situation?
Danielle:	Wendy.
Jade:	She tries to help out, you try to help out the community, don't you?
Wendy:	Yeah.
Jade:	Even if she makes herself poorly, she still helps.
Wendy:	No, 'cos I've seen their …
Jade:	It is like Jesus!

Key members of the community, like Wendy, who provided food and emotional support to others, were also those who themselves experienced hardship, underlining the extent to which low-income individuals in Bradford were integrated within local communities and the wellbeing of each individual member was intimately associated with the wellbeing of the whole community. Yet, the nature of community support appeared to vary by ethnic group. Exchange of food and money among White British women in Bradford was apparently based on visible need; by contrast, Pakistani British women described exchanging food with neighbours and friends, who were largely also Pakistani British women, regardless of (apparent) food need. Cooked food was routinely passed directly over the garden fence or shared with visitors. Many women, including Maisa and Uzma, described cooking more food than was required for household members to share with others. Maisa said, "If you live in the heart of an Asian community food is always circulating. Neighbours give to neighbours; you cook a little extra as standard and give to others", while Uzma told me "We regularly give food to neighbours. If you are cooking a special meal you will always give some to your neighbours. There is no expectation that they will reciprocate but it is nice if they do".

Food was routinely exchanged and constantly circulating among Bradford's Pakistani British population. The ethnic identity of friends and neighbours had no influence on whether or not food was shared; however, the congregation of Pakistani British households in certain areas of Bradford, largely consequent upon migration patterns and house prices, meant that in practice food was largely shared among this one ethnic group rather than between ethnicities.

Religious frameworks

Chapter 4 discussed the interplay of food aid and religion in the UK. It described how Christian beliefs of hospitality, participation and salvation motivated food charity in food banks and soup kitchens in York and Bradford, services predominantly staffed by White volunteers in these two cities, and showed how religion provided a moral prism which shaped how food was distributed and, on occasion, influenced who received food. Among women in Bradford, religion appeared to inform the lived experience and exchange of food only among those who described their ethnicity as Pakistani or Pakistani British and their religion as Muslim. Unprompted, Pakistani British women explained the influence of Islam on the circulation of food among members of Bradford's Pakistani community. Participants reported that food was most commonly shared during religious festivals, especially Ramadan and Eid, when food was exchanged by friends and neighbours and donated to and received from mosques. Describing this, Maisa said, "In Ramadan, I cook for four or five families to be generous. In Ramadan, there is a particular blessing for providing food for the fasting person. It is called Iftar". Hana added: "We don't celebrate birthdays but during Eid we have a big party and we invite all our neighbours".

Islam also informed the redistribution and exchange of food outside of religious festivals. As described by Abida and Maisa, sharing food with neighbours and visitors was considered fundamental to living an Islamic life. Etiquette and courtesy were interchangeable with religious etiquette and religious courtesy, which was applied to Muslims and non-Muslims alike. While this could be informed by the potential inequality of another's hunger alongside wealth and plenty – for instance, in the case of Abida – the discourtesy of asking about food insecurity meant that, in reality, food was exchanged regardless of need.

> 'It is part of Islam to give to your neighbours, even if your neighbours are non-Muslims. It is written in the Qur'ān that you must give to them if you have a full stomach and they have gone hungry. But you give anyway, even if you don't know if they are hungry – you can't ask!' (Abida)

> 'Food is a big part of religion: providing food for your guests. It is religious courtesy, religious etiquette. My mum would always say, "You should make sure you have loaf of bread and eight eggs at home at all times so that you can provide if people come over". Islam is a way of life: you are conditioned to follow practices; it is etiquette and courtesy. There is a concept of sharing food, you cook enough so that you can pass some to your neighbours.' (Maisa)

In *Hospitality and Islam: Welcoming in God's Name*, Mona Siddiqui (2015) argues that hospitality is fundamental to Islam (as, she points out, it is to all the Abrahamic religions). She looks at the Qur'ān and other areas of Islamic thought to trace signs and words of hospitality which are both actions and exhortations to establishing more generous and giving relationships (Siddiqui, 2015: 12). Hospitality in Islam, Siddiqui explains, is:

> first and foremost a duty towards others, and a way of living in which we are constantly reminded of human diversity. There are overlapping discourses on food as a blessing to be shared with others and food as a means of enjoying the company of others. There are multiple commandments to give charity and shelter, to feed others, to look after widows, neighbours, travellers and orphans. We must give and be generous because this is how God is and God's giving knows no limits. (Siddiqui, 2015: 12–13)

Critically, hospitality is not a domestic, sentimental affair but 'about knowing that reaching out to others is an act of worship, thus challenging, humbling and spiritually transformative' (Siddiqui, 2015: 17).[5] Hospitality among Muslim women in Bradford was, as in Siddiqui's analysis, honoured and exercised as divine imperative. As an act and an attitude to life it could be radical, a practice of selflessness and openness not only to friends, families and guests but also to strangers; an 'attitude of simply being with others irrespective of whether they are strangers or friends' (Siddiqui, 2015: 15). There were no equivalent discussions of hospitality among White British women in Bradford whose lived experience of food insecurity and food exchange appeared to be informed by a secular ethics of independence, alongside antithetical ideas of mutual aid, discussed later.

Racial or gendered stigma?

Potentially more important than religion in determining apparent variations in experiences of food insecurity and poverty among White British and Pakistani British women was the stigma surrounding food insecurity and the ways in which the character of this stigma varied by race and ethnicity. Pakistani British women spoke of the shame associated with failing to provide adequate food for household members and guests, stressing the importance of this within South Asian families specifically. For Abida, having "food on the table" was not only "very important" but "the culture in Asian families", while Uzma explained: "I would rather have good food on the table than go on holiday or have flashy gadgets. Living within your means is key. ... Providing adequate food is just so fundamental to South Asian families." While not explicitly described as such by participants, it is possible that this was a racialised form of stigma. The Pakistani British women I spoke with lived in low-income households in areas which were among the most deprived in Bradford and nationally. They lived among communities and households that had been at the centre of the Bradford 'riots' in 2001 and which had suffered decades of racism at an institutional and a local level. Their poverty had been pathologised and individualised by local and national media, by government, and by racist groups in Bradford and elsewhere. The inability to afford food for household members and guests may be one of the most visible forms of poverty (made even more conspicuous by food banks). In a context in which poverty among Pakistani British people was not only stigmatised but also racialised – framed as a consequence of migration, having a (too) large number of children, resistance to integrating and speaking English, inherent intergenerational conflict, and poor educational performance (see Hussain and Bagguley, 2013) – it is unsurprising that poverty and food insecurity was concealed by Pakistani British women. The stigma and shame associated with food insecurity among Pakistani British women in Bradford was presented as a major reason for the avoidance of food aid. Intense shame associated with financial insecurity and food insufficiency prevented even women experiencing severe food insecurity from accessing support outside of the immediate family; none of the Pakistani British women I spoke with had used a food bank or knew anyone who had – as told by Sabira: "Three of my friends who had kids were at rock bottom and really struggling to get food but would not go to a food bank. They were all too embarrassed and would seek support from elsewhere."

The shame of using a food bank was not limited to the individual but also impacted on the family, who would intervene before food charity was sought. Maisa told me: "There would definitely be some form of intervention before it got to the stage where someone was going to a food bank. The family would intervene and help out financially." As discussed in Chapter 6, the stigma of using food aid was, however, an almost ubiquitous experience among women in Bradford and York. Only a small minority of White British women I spoke to had used a food bank; food aid was widely described as a "last resort", "avoided nine times out of ten" (Jade), and the experience of going to a food bank was humiliating and stigmatising. For Gemma, for instance, food aid would only be used on condition of anonymity: "If I really needed to go to the food bank I would go but I probably would not tell anyone that I know. I would feel embarrassed."

The people I spoke to about food and poverty in York and Bradford were largely 'poor' women whose lived experiences, including stigmatised experiences, were closely shaped by their identity as women and mothers. The shame which ensued from failing to provide food for household members and visitors was keenly felt by these women, who were largely responsible for care and food within the household. Among all the low-income women I spoke with in Bradford and York, the food poor Other, when discussed at all, was constructed as female. This stigmatised, food poor female Other was presented as responsible for her food insecurity by virtue of her personal failing to manage food and money responsibly and, on occasion, also her selfishness.

Researching the lived experience of benefit receipt among women in Canada in the late 1990s, sociologist Elaine Power (Power, 2005) similarly highlighted the gendered stigma of poverty. She identified two ways in which (lone) mothers may be constructed and disciplined as Other: as 'welfare bums' who are not in the labour market; and as 'flawed consumers' without the financial resources to participate in a consumer society. The construction of the female Other by women in Bradford and York was reminiscent of Power's 'welfare bums' and 'flawed consumers': the female Other used food banks because of both her irresponsible use of money and her lack of shame. There was, however, a further way in which low-income women were constructed and disciplined as Other: as the negligent mother, failing to adequately feed her children because of her own incompetence or selfishness. All examples provided were of women, whose dependence on the state and selfishness were seen to deprive their children of care and food. This gendered stigma surrounding food insecurity, bound up with ideals of motherhood, induced guilt and shame in some mothers, unable to meet the standards of parenting in a consumer society:

> 'We've just got through Christmas and obviously had to use credit cards 'cos we couldn't afford Christmas, which is not what I wanted to do but when you've got a little boy, you want to get him something and if you can't get him something then it's just awful.' (Ruth)

Many women contrasted their own work ethic and resource management with those of the constructed food poor Other woman. Central to this was the view that 'poor' women respond to personal and societal changes in ways that other women do not. This narrative conflicted with the structural obstacles to purchasing an adequate diet on a low income experienced by women in Bradford and York, and may have influenced all low-income women, regardless of their ethnicity, to conceal food insecurity. Appreciating this intersection between class and gender inequality was critical to understanding the lived realities of the women I spoke with, and to developing accurate representations of power relations in modern society (see also Skeggs, 2019). Women strove to achieve an identity of respectability as a vehicle for acceptance within the moral order (see Skeggs, 1997 for an in-depth discussion of female 'respectability' as a technology for the maintenance of the moral order). In their quest for respectability, many women utilised stigma as a classificatory form of power (see Tyler and Slater, 2018) based on class and gender, to reproduce social inequality – a social inequality in which they themselves lacked power and were subject to control and exploitation by capitalism and the neoliberal state. It is possible that Pakistani British women experienced both a racialised and gendered stigma in regard to food insecurity, reflecting their intersectional identities as minority ethnic, 'poor' women. The tendency among the women I spoke with to describe the dishonour of failing to provide food for the household as a uniquely South Asian characteristic may suggest that intersecting identities created a heightened class, gendered *and* racial stigma surrounding food insecurity.

Divergent ethical frameworks? An ethic of independence, Islamic hospitality, or mutual aid

Underpinning the lived experience of food in contexts of poverty among women of different ethno-religious and ethnic groups were multiple, overlapping ethical frameworks, informed by both secular and religious principles. An ethic of independence, shaped by neoliberal governmentality, underpinned the individualisation of food insecurity. This encouraged women to conceal their own poverty and construct a food poor (female) Other in opposition to themselves, who was highly stigmatised. Alternatively – and as identified by Mellin-Olsen and Wandel (2005) in their study of Pakistani Muslim women in Oslo – among Pakistani British Muslim women in Bradford, hospitality, informed by Islam, was of importance and enjoyment. Food and eating were arguably the most important vehicles for the expression of (Islamic) hospitality – life was more than food and eating but there was no life without food and eating, and, thus, on a daily basis, the theological and philosophical significance of what was eaten and with whom food was shared connected 'the ordinary life with the higher life' (Siddiqui, 2015: 13). Commitment to hospitality underpinned exchange of food between households; this may have had the benign impact of mitigating food insecurity; however, perversely, for Pakistani British women, its effect was also to heighten the stigma of failing to provide food for family and guests.

The redistribution of food within communities in Bradford was not only underpinned by Islamic hospitality but also by systems of mutual aid (which were arguably related conceptually to hospitality), largely mediated through women. Embodied by social and familial solidarities, these systems of mutual aid were fundamental to the maintenance of food security in hard times. Family members provided emotional, childcare and material support, and helped to avoid isolation. Familial and social solidarity was sustained through food technologies, most notably among (although not limited to) Pakistani British women in Bradford, whose routine sharing of food appeared to mitigate food shortages while simultaneously augmenting the interdependency of the community. While there was no explicit suggestion that this form of self-organising was also an act of a resistance, it would fit into a long tradition of social and community organising and self-reliance among Black and minority ethnic communities, motivated by institutional racism and the absence of adequate government support (see Bryant et al, 2018: 124–81). Conversations with women in Bradford, thus, suggest that new ethical possibilities which counteract and resist neoliberal individualism may be inculcated via social and familial solidarities – mutual aid – centred around food in marginalised communities.

Alternative ethics of food charity: social solidarity and mutual aid

Chapter 2 cited scholarship proposing the possibilities for 'care' and mutuality in food aid (Williams et al, 2016; Cloke et al, 2017; Lambie-Mumford, 2017), while Chapter 3 outlined a diversity of organisational approaches and ethical frameworks (both individual and organisational) in food charities. These discussions in both chapters encourage the question: can a radical mutualistic approach, apparent within working-class and minority ethnic communities, also be found in food aid? Service user reports of shame and embarrassment within food banks (see van der Horst et al, 2014), as well as the low use of food banks by people experiencing hunger (MacLeod et al, 2019; Pybus et al, 2021), call into question the propositions of Williams et al (2016), Cloke et al (2017) and Lambie-Mumford (2017) that food banks may be benign, productive spaces for those in poverty (rather than just for those distributing food and instruction). Notwithstanding the chapter's acknowledgement of heterogeneity in the design and delivery of food aid, Chapter 3 revealed institutionalised classism in some food charities (especially emergency food projects), while Chapters 4 and 5 detailed racism in food aid. In many of these providers, and particularly in food banks, the development of new political beliefs and identities that challenge neoliberal austerity may not be possible in such a context where shared understandings, and the coordination of action based on this, are precluded by institutionalised inequalities.

Conversations with people in York, and to a significantly lesser extent in Bradford, about experiences of food charity suggested that the development of new political beliefs and identities forged through solidarity in a shared encounter is, however, possible in some food aid – and even, on occasion, in food banks. The difference in the nature of some food charity in the two cities may have been partly attributable to the time difference (three years) between the primary research in Bradford and York, a period which witnessed not only the steep growth of Trussell Trust and independent food banks, but also the development of other food aid providers, especially community cafes and community food hubs. As a consequence, the food aid support network drawn on by those in York was broader and more diverse. While many of the York participants used or had used Trussell Trust and independent food banks – albeit with some reporting using these as a last resort – it was more common to visit community food hubs and community cafes which provided free or low-cost communal meals and which often operated a food bank-type service in which free food was available in an area of the building for anyone to take. The food and community available at some of these food aid providers was highly valued and considered essential to food security. Describing a community cafe which provided free and fresh food to take away on a daily basis, Sophie, a lone parent of two children, explained:

> 'This place is really important to me and to meet other people just too. I'd call them friends there, you can go and then chat. It's not like a normal coffee shop either where you can't come and go, some of them don't say "hi" to you and aren't as pleasant. This place has more customer service. They want you there. They like you to be there, you can sit there with a coffee and nurse it, which I tend to do, for a good couple of hours!'

These food providers, whether in the form of a community cafe, a community garden or a holiday hunger club, were non-judgemental and inclusive (it is worth noting that these types of provision tended to be open access, rejecting referral systems). They recognised and responded to human frailties and vulnerabilities, and facilitated socialisation among people in similar situations, as explained by Beverly:

> 'In a nearby church they put on like a "Let's Lunch" thing. Well, you know, really, for anyone to come to. But it meant, for a little in the holidays, you didn't need to struggle. You know, and you got to go and see other people and not be stuck in the house if you didn't have any money.'

Unlike in Bradford, where the idea of sacrifice was a notion voiced largely by service providers describing the sacrifice of their time and energy in volunteering at food banks,[6] in York, sacrifice was applicable to service providers *and* service users. Service users contributed via food or money to support food projects, where possible, as told by Annie:

> 'Without them we'd seriously struggle. Like for lots of other people, they've been a huge rescue to us. Especially with that month where I couldn't have fed my children, if it wasn't for these food places. I always put money in, even if it's just a tiny amount, just to give that back. And even now I still need to use it.'

This sense of solidarity and common experience, cultivated via food sharing (and occasionally financial donations) with and within community food aid, contributed to the politicisation of people experiencing food insecurity and fostered resistance to neoliberal norms and policies. Amid the egalitarian, sociable and non-judgemental environment of a community cafe or community garden, people experiencing food insecurity talked to each other and spoke out against the economic injustices and government policies that produced their (food) poverty, calling on others living in poverty to join campaigns for food justice. Speaking to Sandy, a lone parent of one child, at a community cafe, I was told: "The politicians need to listen to us: everyone deserves a living wage. These things – the sharing food – is just a stop gap. We need to go to the source and everyone deserves to live, properly." Grassroots food poverty networks (alliances between local organisations addressing poverty and food insecurity, and people with lived experience of poverty) could be powerful breeding grounds for political awareness and campaigning on food inequalities. Sophie regularly picked up free food from local community cafes for herself and her two young children; she had been in receipt of social security since her first child was born and, from personal experience, was keenly aware of the destitution created by social security, especially by Universal Credit. She was involved with the local food poverty alliance (later taking over leadership), which provided a platform for publicly confronting the neoliberal policies which created food insecurity. Speaking at an alliance event, Sophie called on others with direct experience of poverty to get involved:

'But if we don't stand up, who will? If we don't speak up, who's going to speak up for us? Things only change if we speak up and we put forward, and we all help each other, even little things that each individual does make a big impact all put together. Please come and help us, please get involved. There's lots of meetings, there's a national organisation to try and fight this cause, to try and make it fair, everybody on Universal Credit, who's on full benefits, will feel the pinch, will feel this increase coming up. To most people £20 here and there isn't a lot of money but for people like you and me, it makes a big difference between whether we can do that or can't do that, so to speak. Please get involved, please contact us, even just to find out more to help get some awareness, just share some [Facebook] posts maybe, please get involved, we need you to help.'

While an ethic of care and mutuality, and the politicisation and resistance it may incubate, was predominantly characteristic of community hubs and cafes (open access provision in which food distribution was embedded alongside cooking, eating and chatting), progressive possibilities were not necessarily limited to certain types of organisation. For instance, some soup kitchens and community cafes could be highly condescending towards and coercive of service users (see Chapters 3 and 6), despite offering a form of 'open access' provision. Equally, the fieldwork in Bradford and York intimated possibilities for mutualistic ethics to be co-constituted in some independent and Trussell Trust food banks, illustrating the role of individual ethics, rather than organisational ethos and managerial control, in shaping welfare practices (see Williams et al, 2012). Trussell Trust food banks could, on occasion, embody cooperation within and among local communities, as described by Julie, living on a low income in Bradford:

'I am actually friends with the person who started the [Trussell Trust] food bank, he delivers to me so I don't [have to go], because I don't have any transport. So if I go over there, he will bring me home. He will ring me up and say, like the other day, he's got a big bag of rice because they can't divide it.'

Food banks could offer support and care, motivated by solidarity and empathy with those using the service. Melissa, a lone parent of three young children, described the welcome and care received in the food bank: 'That's real nice, they [the Trussell Trust food bank] get the kids involved and stuff like that. Because it's open Monday, Wednesday, Friday, half 11 to half 1 and if you need something to eat they will give you a meal.'

Like many community cafes and community hubs, food could be donated to Trussell Trust and independent food banks by the community that the organisation intended to serve, underpinning a mutualistic ethos within working-class communities, which was in fact facilitated by the food bank. Speaking to Stephanie, the manager of a food bank, I was told:

'We have somebody from this estate, he is not coming in this week 'cos he is on holiday but he comes in every week with two bags at least of food. He is just an ordinary bloke, newly retired and he says, you know, we always say "that's great, thank you", but he says, "I know what it is like, I've been there, I've been hungry and there was nothing like that to help me. I've done alright for myself now, I'm retired, I've got a reasonably comfortable life, I want to give something back", and the way he does it is by bringing in some food each week.'

In stark contrast to 'morally distanced' (May et al, 2019), hierarchical interactions inside certain food charities, outlined in Chapters 3, 4, 5 and 6, there was, thus, evidence of mutual aid within some food providers. Food was shared by those providing and those using the services; indeed, there was often little distinction between the two: the community serving and seeking food was interdependent. These projects could arguably (or cynically) be seen as an example of 'moral neoliberalism' in a communitarian guise (Muehlebach, 2012). In the wake of the withdrawal of social service programmes, these organisations were providing much needed food and support to people in poverty; volunteers, motivated by socialistic principles, were interpreting their unwaged labour as an expression of social solidarity. In this way, the neoliberal state nurtured selflessness in order to cement some of its most controversial reforms. And yet, many of these projects explicitly rejected neoliberalism through their egalitarian ethos – marked by an absence of surveillance and barriers to entry; by the tendency for projects to be self-organised among local, often working-class, communities; and by both the donation and receipt of food by people living in poverty. Further, these organisations could be incubators for growing awareness of and resistance to the neoliberal policies that created food insecurity. As both sites of social solidarity and places of politicisation, such community food aid appeared to be motivated by ideas of human nature as social, cooperative and moral, and of society as interdependent – ideas propagated by strains of revolutionary theory, historically most evident in anarcho-communist Peter Kropotkin's 1902 *Mutual Aid* (Kropotkin, 1987a), described in Chapter 2.

Political resistance to neoliberalism through dialogue and campaigning was essential in undermining the stigma so associated with food insecurity and food charity. Conversations within food projects among service users and between users and providers (often both members of the same working-class community) drew attention to the structural causes of food insecurity and the need for structural solutions, subverting individualistic narratives of poverty and highlighting commonality of experiences among marginalised communities. The potentially stigmatising process of receiving food charity was further undermined by the ethos of the projects themselves: open access, self-organised and non-hierarchical. Notwithstanding the food bank exceptions outlined above, these community projects differed markedly from many Trussell Trust and independent food banks, resisting capture of the ethics and praxis of neoliberal governmentality, the latter marked by hierarchy, auditing and systems of classification.

Nevertheless, these projects did not completely resist the dynamics of neoliberal capitalism. Many self-organised, community food providers were partially or wholly reliant on surplus food from organisations such as FareShare or local branches of national supermarkets. As noted in Chapter 3, the critical analysis applied to government was not transferred to corporations, who were often looked on favourably. Partnerships with retailers were often perceived by food charities to be apolitical, despite the profound power inequalities at play; these projects thus became ensnared in the reproduction of capitalism through their acceptance and distribution of surplus food (see Livingstone, 2015; 2017). There were also questions surrounding the efficacy of acts of resistance against the state, which were largely discursive; these small-scale, localised food projects posed little real challenge to a state whose ability to give and withdraw support to people living in poverty was supreme. And yet, these small, self-organised projects did represent an alternative way of being, in parallel with the neoliberal state, and could be places where resistance to the status quo was nurtured.

Conclusion

National and local survey data as well as discussions with people of varying ethnic groups in the two cities of Bradford and York suggest there are ethnic differences in food insecurity in the UK. It is also clear, however, that stigma – and especially racial stigma – along with pride in one's cultural heritage and identity may affect the likelihood of reporting financial difficulties in accessing food. The lived experience of food among women in Bradford and York is shaped by their poverty, their ethnicity, their religion and their gender. It was notable that the stigmatised, food poor Other was often presented by participants as female: her construction was reminiscent of Power's (2005) 'welfare bums', economically inactive and reliant on the state, and 'flawed consumers', without the financial resources to participate on behalf of themselves and their children in a consumer society. There was also a further way in which low-income women were constructed and disciplined as Other: as the negligent mother, failing to adequately feed her children because of her own incompetence or selfishness.

Mutual aid, embodied in social and familial solidarities in marginalised and stigmatised communities – particularly pronounced among Pakistani British women in Bradford, where it can be informed by religious frameworks, including Islamic conceptions of hospitality – may mitigate food insecurity and explain its lower prevalence. Yet mutual aid can also be found in some food aid providers – providers which evolve from the community they serve, and which are largely open access and non-hierarchal. These alternative, co-operative ethics embodied by some forms of food aid and some marginalised communities – along the lines of gender, ethnicity, religion and class – are not necessarily a rejection of the state (anarchy) or a pure example of communal ownership (communism). Within community food aid and social and familial networks, however, cooperation, redistribution and reciprocity according to need operated in parallel with and in spite of the state, and altruism, not individualism, was the predominant human characteristic. Mutual aid in both community food aid and marginalised communities was, thus, premised upon ideas of human nature as cooperative and altruistic, and of society as interdependent – ideas that can be found in the work of anarcho-communists, notably Kropotkin.

These examples of mutual aid provide an exemplar of how relationships and forms of exchange may operate differently. It is possible that the performance of mutual aid within the Pakistani British community in Bradford was bound up with experiences of racism and discrimination.[7] It is also viable that, despite the intentions of some community food aid to be sites of politicisation and solidarity, the very existence of these organisations enabled further retrenchment of the welfare state, so heightening inequality. Nevertheless, the profound impact of these ethical frameworks – founded upon mutual aid, encouraging and valuing cooperation and interdependency – on the lived experience of food and food redistribution, in spite of dominant narratives individualising and stigmatising poverty, offers hope for a more progressive future.

These ideas have been relatively neglected in the 20th century due to the dominance of a left-of-centre social democracy. However, they have found expression within social movements particularly from the 1960s onwards – the peace, women's, LGBTQ+, environmental and anti-capitalist movements being the most notable – and are characterised by a rejection of hierarchy, organisation from the bottom up, commitment to individual and collective self-realisation, and more radical forms of democratic organisation (Goodway, 2012). Fundamentally, such ideas emphasise that means determine ends: living out relationships with other people, marked by fellowship, respect and cooperation, fosters the spirit of the progressive society sought. Thus, through everyday living, sharing and socialising people can form the structure of a new society within the shell of the old. The persistence of this mutual aid in spite of neoliberal governmentality fuelling aggressive individualism and hierarchy provides hope that an alternative approach to food and poverty is not only possible but is happening now.

Notes

[1] The relative neglect of some marginalised groups, including minority ethnic groups, in UK food insecurity research may be consequent on the nature of the research field itself: empirical and analytical responses to food insecurity have been shaped by disciplinary speciality and focused on specific aspects of the 'problem' – for instance, the relationship between food bank use and welfare reform. This has resulted in a fragmented evidence-base, one which neglects relationships between food insecurity and wider inequalities, and fails to interrogate the broader context to – what appears to be the new phenomenon of – food insecurity. It is also arguable that tacit acceptance of the post-racial within the academy (see Bhopal, 2018) has led to a neglect of race and ethnicity as factors of importance in analyses of food insecurity.

[2] I use the terms that the survey employs to describe different ethnic groups, i.e. White British, Pakistani, Indian, Asian other, White other, Black, Mixed, Other. In this section, I therefore do not use the prefix 'British' as seen elsewhere throughout the book.

[3] In the FRS, Indian households reported the lowest food insecurity of all ethnic groups, indicating that, as in Bradford, a minority ethnic group is at lowest risk of food insecurity on a national level. However, unlike in Bradford, in the FRS, Pakistani households reported higher food insecurity (10 per cent) than White households (7 per cent); the latter reported the second lowest food insecurity after Indian households.

[4] See Stuart Hall on identities as situated, imagined and multiple: 'Identity is formed at the unstable point where the "unspeakable" stories of subjectivity meet the narratives of history, of a culture' (Hall [1987] 1996: 115).

5   While focusing predominantly on Islam, Siddiqui (2015) points to the similarities between Christianity and Islam in their conceptualisation and approach towards hospitality. She writes, 'The writings of the [Christian] Church Fathers on poverty have parallels with Muslim mysticism as to how prayer and poverty are so closely aligned in the way we think about God and our reliance on God' (Siddiqui, 2015: 17) and notes that 'for many Christians, hospitality is about seeing the face of Christ in every stranger and living God's triune grace-filled kingdom on this earth' (Siddiqui, 2015: 16).

6   See also: Power et al (2017b).

7   See Bryant et al (2018)'s discussion of self-organising in Black and minority ethnic communities in response to discrimination and institutional racism (Bryant et al, 2018: 124–81).

8

Seeds beneath the snow

When I first started the research for this book in 2014, we were in the bitter – and it turned out to be prolonged – winter of austerity. Instead of blaming reckless financial entities for the runaway speculation and short-term selling that had triggered the 2007–08 financial crisis, the Conservative-led government penalised disabled people, lone parents, public sector workers and the low paid through drastic cuts to the welfare state. These people, who had nothing whatsoever to do with the crash, would be compelled to pay for it (Jones, 2020).

The government's 'Hostile Environment', introduced in 2012, was already taking hold. This highly racist policy, an unashamed attempt to reduce immigration, tasked the NHS, landlords, banks, employers and many others with enforcing immigration controls. It aimed to make the UK unliveable for undocumented migrants, withdrawing any access to the safety net, and ultimately to push them to leave. The Windrush Scandal, revealed by *Guardian* journalist Amelia Gentleman in 2017, illustrated the true horror of this stigmatising policy (Gentleman, 2019). British citizens, the children of Commonwealth citizens who migrated to Britain between 1948 and 1971, people who had lived, parented and paid tax in the UK for decades, began to receive menacing text messages and threatening letters from the government. The communications told them, contrary to their own understanding, that they were illegal immigrants:

> They went into work one day to be told that their new illegal status meant they no longer had a job. People with ongoing health troubles turned up to scheduled treatments to be presented with a bill of tens of thousands of pounds before they could be seen. A visit to the jobcentre revealed that the benefits they were entitled to had been denied or revoked. They were even refused food bank vouchers. (Eddo-Lodge, 2019)

In 2016, the British people voted by a margin to leave the EU. The 'Yes' vote, propelled by xenophobic slogans, a particular construction of 'British' identity, and the purported threat of an invasion of immigrants on British shores, served as a licence for explicit racism. The leave result was followed by a significant rise in the number of racist and hate crimes reported to the police and other anti-racism organisations. Brexit became an 'us versus them battle' in which 'white privilege was used to separate those who belonged from those who did not, and racism was used as the vehicle to promote this' (Bhopal, 2018: 156). Boris Johnson's electoral victory in 2019, won on a platform of 'getting Brexit done', legitimated the separation of 'us and them' and further institutionalised racist language and policies at the heart of the establishment. In the US, the election of Donald J. Trump as the 45th president gave a very public platform to deep-seated and longstanding systemic racial inequities and racially motivated violence, most horrifyingly exemplified by the murder of George Floyd on 25 May 2020.

Meanwhile, the cuts introduced by the Conservative-led administration in 2010 chipped away at the livelihoods, lives and hopes of millions of people. Austerity made poverty more acute, but it also – and most likely unintentionally – made it more visible as thousands and then millions of people sought food charity. Writing now in 2021, amid the second wave of the COVID-19 pandemic and in the wake of the Black Lives Matter movement, it is clear that the world is a changed place from 2014. The pandemic prompted an outpouring of solidarity as people, confined to their homes, became more aware of the daily existence and needs of those on their doorstep. Small-scale, grassroots 'mutual aid' groups sprang up across the country, often geographically defined by a single street or block of flats. Research by More in Common, a charity founded in memory of the late Labour Party MP Jo Cox, who was murdered by a member of the far-right during the Brexit campaign, identified a marked shift among the general public during the pandemic towards solidarity and communitarian views and away from individualistic ideas of self-reliance. More than half (57 per cent) of respondents reported an increased awareness of the living conditions of others, while 77 per cent felt that the pandemic has reminded us of our common humanity (Juan-Torres et al, 2020). The resurgence of the Black Lives Matter movement in 2020 led to increased awareness of systemic and institutional racism and heightened scrutiny of racist structures and discourse at all levels of society, alongside renewed interrogation of Britain's colonial and imperialist history.

However, while the world may today be a different place in some ways from the distant days of 2014, deep-rooted and longstanding inequalities and prejudices remain. COVID-19 has not only exposed but also amplified inequalities of race, gender and class in the UK, entrenching poverty and poor health among already disadvantaged groups, while advantaging those with decent, secure incomes (Marmot et al, 2020; Women's Budget Group, 2020; Brewer and Patrick, 2021). Despite the steep rise in the number of people claiming Universal Credit, the stigma surrounding social security remains as pronounced as ever (Power et al, 2020a). Simultaneously, the Black Lives Matter movement is far from universally supported. While roughly half of Britons (51 per cent) support the aims of the movement, one in five oppose it; support for the movement is highly stratified according to age – for instance, 18–24-year-olds are much more likely to support the movement than people aged 55–75 (Ipsos MORI, 2020). Most damagingly, opposition to the movement is also embedded at the heart of government. In October 2020, Kemi Badenoch, the Black British Conservative Party Minister for Equalities, told MPs:

> Some schools have decided to openly support the anti-capitalist Black Lives Matter group, often aware that they have a statutory duty to be politically impartial. … We do not want teachers to teach their white pupils about white privilege and inherited racial guilt. Let me be clear that any school that teaches those elements of critical race theory as fact, or that promotes partisan political views such as defunding the police without offering a balanced treatment of opposing views, is breaking the law. (Kemi Badenoch, quoted in Wood, 2020)

The remark made by Liz Truss, the White British Minister for Women and Equalities, that, "Too often, the equality debate has been dominated by a small number of unrepresentative voices, and by those who believe people are defined by their protected characteristics and not by their individual character" (Truss, 2020), coupled with Kemi Badenoch's opposition to the Black Lives Matter movement, makes clear that we are a long way from meaningful legislative action – or even meaningful political debate – to address racial inequalities and White privilege.

The COVID-19 pandemic precipitated sharp rises in unemployment and poverty across the UK, leading to an outpouring of community care in which hundreds of individuals and groups established ad hoc food distribution services to assist those who could not afford or access food. Amid this context of flux and expansion, the traditional food aid/food bank/food insecurity narrative continued unchanged. According to this narrative, food banks are compassionate spaces run by benevolent volunteers, responding to growing and desperate need; food banks should not be needed but they are; and food insecurity is a consequence of government austerity since 2010. This final part of the narrative, drawing attention to the structural causes of food insecurity, is an advancement on previous accounts of compassion and care detached from the root causes of food insecurity, reflecting a decisive shift in recent years in the strategy and advocacy of the Trussell Trust, away from the notion of 'compassionate communities' and towards policy change.[1]

What is missing from this conversation is a more nuanced and thoughtful consideration of why food aid might exist in the UK, including the role of religious motivation, as well as acknowledgment of the deeper, more entrenched root causes of food insecurity: low wages, unaffordable housing, racism, sexism and longer histories of colonialism, imperialism, exploited labour and gendered oppression. Absent from the discussion is much reflection on the ways in which food aid maintains the neoliberal policies and ideologies – individualism, surveillance and White privilege – it claims to counter and meaningful acknowledgment of the multi-faceted identity of food charity in the UK, encompassing beacons of radicalism and mutual aid. This book has attempted to shine a light on these relatively neglected dimensions of the debate. I will conclude by briefly setting out some key reflections based on these ideas, before closing the chapter with three examples, informed by recent fieldwork in the US, of how food aid may promote a radical, egalitarian agenda. As a White British woman with no experience of poverty, I do not believe it is appropriate for me to present 'solutions' to the issues identified in this book – these must necessarily come from the people most affected by poverty, classism, racism and poor access to nutritious food[2] – but I hope that these North American examples can illuminate how things can be done differently, and thereby potentially inform progress in the UK.

The murky alliance between neoliberalism and food charity

By the 1990s a new consensus had been forged, one defined by the late cultural theorist Mark Fisher as 'capitalist realism', the 'widespread sense that not only is capitalism the only viable political and economic system, but also that it is now impossible to imagine a coherent alternative' (Fisher, 2009: 2). The subversion of social democracy and rise of neoliberalism, rooted in the monetarist agenda of the 1970s (of Prime Minister Jim Callaghan and his chancellor, Denis Healey) but all-consuming during Margaret Thatcher's premiership from 1979 to 1991, dramatically reshaped the role and responsibilities of the voluntary sector, laying the groundwork for the growth of food charity in the 21st century. Although Blair's government attempted to humanise Thatcherism – introducing a minimum wage and hiking public investment – it simultaneously accelerated the intrusion of the private sector into public services and slashed taxes on big business. The electoral victory of a Conservative-led government in 2010 cemented Thatcher's legacy, augmenting a fresh, ideologically charged onslaught to drive back the frontiers of the British state and remould society in favour of the wealthy and powerful. Essential to this programme of spectacular and spectacularly unequal change was promotion of a 'scroungers and strivers' narrative, problematising 'the poor' rather than the policies which created poverty.

The predominant voluntary sector approach to hunger and destitution created by government policy – food parcels or meals distributed in person to those in need – largely failed to address the root causes of food insecurity and hence, as in North America, the sector perpetuated its own continuation and growth. Historical resistance to the institutionalisation of food aid at both the local level, as evident in Bradford, and on a national scale was arguably fatally undermined by the COVID-19 pandemic, as local and national government collaborated with and financed food charity to manage growing need. The Trussell Trust may have rejected government funding, but it actively colluded with big business, accepting multi-million-pound corporate donations from Tesco, Asda and British Gas.[3] The Trussell Trust chose to strengthen its alliance with corporate Britain rather than engage in more radical political reform; in a context of rapidly rising unemployment, the business community provided money and food donations in exchange for positive publicity. Hunger was upheld as a *cause célèbre* for numerous corporations, while the Trussell Trust (and FareShare, who were also beneficiaries of multi-million-pound corporate donations) secured, like North American emergency food aid, 'bigger buildings, more trucks, strategic growth goals, and intricate ties to those firms that aggravate the hunger problem in the first place through their labour practices' (Fisher, 2017: 262).

Between 2014 and 2019, I spoke with representatives from many different types of food aid. Despite considerable diversity in operations, staffing structures, funding and religious affiliation, a distinctive characteristic of a significant minority of these conversations was the stigma and condescension that some service providers expressed towards those using their services. These narratives, which often sat uneasily alongside forms of 'care' in the food aid encounter, drew legitimacy from and further legitimated a neoliberal paradigm which presupposed a certain conception of the citizen or the 'self' (Rose, 1992): this citizen was independent, entrepreneurial and economically successful, unlike the dependent, lazy and foolish people using food aid. In so doing, some service providers pathologised and individualised food insecurity, obscuring the systemic issues which gave rise to food aid use. In food banks these stigmatising narratives were made real – they were tangible and visible – via a particular system of food distribution. Food banks embraced neoliberal market principles in the distribution of food, closely surveilling, categorising and controlling hungry people through bureaucratised processes of food distribution. The referral system gave physical form – the food bank voucher – to the notion of the deserving and the undeserving poor. And yet, it was the very existence of these complex bureaucratic food bank processes that allowed these stigmatising and divisive narratives to persist unchallenged. Staff discourses concealed their own ideological values within the bureaucratic and unchallenged systems of the food bank. Food distribution processes and practices were embedded at the level of 'common sense' (May et al, 2020) and rationalised as a progressive response to mitigating chronic poverty and associated 'dependency' on the food bank.

This separation of those deserving of support, by virtue of their compliance with the expectations of the ruling power – hard work, obedience and abstinence – from those undeserving – highly conspicuous in some food aid – has been used unashamedly by government since the late 1970s, and particularly since 2010, to justify cuts to working-age social security. However, this instrumental binary has long historical roots, stretching back as far as the 16th-century Elizabethan Poor Laws, embedded in the theological tradition of Calvinism, and a defining feature of 19th-century liberalism (Dean and Taylor-Gooby, 1992). These narratives – realised through discourse and systems – complicated the development of solidarity among people seeking food, and between those providing and using services. How could fellowship be formed in a context in which people were divided, not only by bureaucratic processes, but also by the idea that some people were undeserving of food – they were not allowed to eat – because of their own character and behaviour?

Food charity in the UK is dominated by Christian organisations. Food banks, soup kitchens and community cafes are situated in churches and run by Christian groups, while the largest provider of food banks in the UK, the Trussell Trust, is motivated by Christian ethics. By adopting responsibility for poverty, destitution and population welfare, religious charities, like their secular counterparts, are colluding with neoliberal state transformation. Although they may not necessarily consider themselves superior to state welfare services, religious food charities do believe they bring unique – and positive – attributes to charitable food distribution. They build relationships with and care for those in need, living out Christianity's ethos of egalitarianism and hospitality through food aid and, on occasion, they may seek to offer physical and spiritual salvation to hungry people through food and opportunities for reform in accordance with the (Calvinist) ethics of modern, global post-industrial capitalism. It is clear that in contemporary faith-based food charity (particularly in food banks and soup kitchens) there is a productive merging of Christianity and capitalist subjectivity, alongside participatory and communistic Christian ethics. These Christian codes coexist, influencing what is said, as well as what is practised, although with the two not necessarily in alignment.

It is less clear whether there is a comparable alliance between Islam and capitalism in contemporary food charity. Islamic organisations operate food banks, soup kitchens and community cafes; they donate food and money to community organisations; and participate in local networks of mutual aid. This may be motivated by Islamic ideals of *khayr*, the performance of 'good deeds' through charitable acts in order to improve the self and one's relationship with God (Atia, 2013). In my fieldwork, however, there was no explicit evidence that this was the case – that, for Muslims, the purpose of food charity was to improve their own character and their relationship with the divine – and, unlike some Christian providers, there was no suggestion that Muslims looked on food charity as an opportunity to reform others in line with Islamic principles. This is not to suggest that, because Islamic food projects do not appear to seek to reform the character of 'the poor', Islam is resistant to capitalist subjectivity – as the work of Atia (2013) attests; however, in this case study, Muslim food aid did not seek to instil neoliberal ethics of entrepreneurialism and self-help in those using their services.

Food aid can be racist

Food charities in the UK exist within a highly racist and racially unequal social and economic context. Against this background, they were never likely to be race-neutral organisations; however, they have evolved into entities which often – and arguably unintentionally – uphold White privilege. Whiteness is the default identity, informing the nature of the food distributed, and represented in staff, users and senior management, as well as the standard against which the Other – inferior, deviant, exotic, or simply noteworthy – is measured. The marked absence of culturally appropriate food in many food charities subliminally contributes to a narrative that a White ethnocentric 'healthy' diet is the only healthy diet that exists. The omission of culturally appropriate foods motivates the question: who is – and who is not – in the decision-making position to determine what foods are available for people seeking food aid (see Suzanne Babb in Power et al, 2021b)? White ethnicity nonetheless remains invisible and unexamined in debates on UK food charity and food insecurity. It is seen as neither problematic (as a potential source of racism) nor as a mode of marginalising and stigmatising those 'poor' Whites – 'chavs', 'underclass', 'white trash' – who represent an undesirable form of Whiteness. Racism and classism towards marginalised 'poor' White ethnicities in some food aid stigmatises and demonises these people, in ways not too dissimilar from the stigmatisation and criminalisation of working-class minority ethnic groups within some food charities and in society at large.

Racial divisions between working-class communities have been mobilised by successive governments to realise certain policy goals – for instance, legitimating cuts to social security and public services, and fuelling White nationalism and calls for British self-determination (see Shilliam [2018] for a historical analysis). The centrality of White working-class identities to the realisation of particular policy goals is nowhere more apparent than in the case of Brexit. The 2019 Conservative Government's idea of an independent nation brought about by Brexit is founded in White privilege and a certain notion of the White working class. This is expressed in divergent attitudes to White and Black activism. The Black Lives Matter protests are described by senior government ministers as 'dreadful' (Parveen, 2021), while class in northern regions – a code for White working class – is upheld as a greater inequality than racism (Syal, 2021). This particular construction of the White working class remains, however, distinct from persistent and unchanging undesirable forms of Whiteness, personified by Traveller communities, recent Eastern European migrants, and White people in receipt of social security. To understand how food charity maintains racial precarity and racial divisions sown by successive governments in the UK, it is necessary to not only problematise Whiteness, but to interrogate its power through the lens of class.

The lived experience of food is shaped by class, gendered and racial stigma

The extensive fieldwork in the two English cities of Bradford and York underscored the reality that food poverty or food insecurity is one aspect of multi-dimensional poverty. Food is the most malleable element in the household budget and, therefore, when income is insufficient to cover outgoings, food is reduced. Despite this obvious reality, food poverty and insecurity is highly stigmatised. Contemporary discursive constructions of the 'food poor' in media and politics are often informed by ideas rooted in Calvinism, ideas which underpin and are embedded within, not just neoliberalism of the 20th and 21st centuries, but liberal industrial capitalism of the 19th century. These ideologies, personified in 'homo economicus', promote hard work, independence and competition as forms of virtue; those who fail to attain these ideals are condemned and stigmatised.

The stigmatisation of people living in poverty, so prevalent today, is thus not a new phenomenon in Western Europe and North America, geographical entities highly shaped by Calvinist theology. Like in 19th-century Britain, in which fear of the workhouse was instrumentalised to 'motivate' people to work long hours in the harsh and dangerous conditions of the mills and factories, in the 21st century, fear of the food bank coupled with a punitive and demonising social security system drives people to accept insecure and poorly paid employment. However, today, the power of the state to punish and shame its citizens is not only evident in government policies and systems but embedded throughout the whole of society – it finds its way into communities, families, friendships and even our own self-perception. A distinctive feature of poverty in the 21st century is not only the condemnation of 'poor people' by their peers but the condemnation of people living in poverty by themselves.

Food poverty stigma is, nevertheless, also influenced by inequalities of gender and race, inequalities themselves grounded in histories of colonialism, imperialism and gendered oppression. In Bradford, recent histories of racially motivated violence against South Asian people, coupled with a policy environment in which the practices of minority ethnic groups can be pathologised, may have contributed to a racial stigma which induced Pakistani British women to conceal both their poverty and their food shortages. Surprisingly, given the considerable literature on gendered aspects of the welfare state and the informal caring work performed by women (see Lewis, 1983; Pascall, 1986; Glendinning and Millar, 1987; Millar and Glendinning, 1992; Graham, 1993; Skeggs, 1997, among many), gender has been relatively absent from research on contemporary food insecurity in the UK. It was clear, however, from conversations with people on a low income in Bradford and York that the lived experience of (food) poverty is intimately shaped by gender, as well as by race and class. It was the woman's, not the man's, responsibility to ensure there was adequate food for household members and guests and, when money was tight, it was the woman who went to great lengths – often sacrificing her own consumption – in order to maintain a pretence of sufficiency. Condemnation of the 'food poor' Other was largely directed towards mothers, who were portrayed as failing to care for their children according to certain public health standards. There was a strong belief that the state or other members of the local community had the right to intervene in these women's private lives to purportedly protect the wellbeing of their children.

It is interesting to note that, despite the clear relationship between food insecurity and income poverty in the UK, the predominant voluntary sector response to rising food insecurity has been food rather than cash based. Why is this? Why give someone a prescribed parcel of food or a pre-prepared meal when their reason for needing that food is a lack of money to buy food rather than the absence of food itself? I acknowledge that, in some circumstances, food may be an appropriate response to food insecurity – for instance, in a day centre or homeless shelter intended for people living on the streets without cooking facilities, a hot meal may be necessary (although in these circumstances surely what is most needed is secure housing?). For people who do have a home and a kitchen, however limited, but do not have money to buy food or pay for electricity, the most logical response is to give these people money, with which they can go to the shops or to a cafe, and buy the food they would choose to eat, like everyone else. In the dominant representational fields of media, politics, academia and the voluntary sector, however, this cash-based response is not considered the most logical approach; rather, poverty is medicalised, reconstructed as a question of nutrition – as food insecurity – which must necessarily be responded to with food.

IFAN has made considerable progress in recent years, shifting the debate away from wholly food-based third sector solutions to food insecurity to responses which incorporate 'cash-first' approaches. These approaches aim to assist people using food banks in accessing any available government financial entitlements through advice and support (such as local authority hardship funds intended to provide immediate cash grants to people in urgent need) via distributing cash-first referral leaflets in food banks. These resources, co-developed with local communities, indicate where and how someone can access financial support and are intended as an alternative to emergency food assistance. While IFAN's pioneering cash-first approach has been adopted by many food banks across the UK, there remains resistance among some food banks and their donors to distributing money rather than food parcels direct to service users. Old stigmatising tropes surrounding the use of money on the 'wrong' items – alcohol, cigarettes, sugary and fatty food – persist. These paternalistic and offensive notions are ultimately founded in middle-class beliefs that 'the poor' do not know what is best for them.

Food distribution can be a mode of resistance

What was noticeable from my fieldwork, conducted between 2014 and 2019, and is even more apparent as I write in 2021, is the immense diversity that characterises community food aid in the UK. Food aid may be dominated by very large, hugely wealthy, corporatised and hierarchical charities – notably FareShare and the Trussell Trust – but it is increasingly composed of a ragtag bunch of very small-scale community groups and organisations. Examples of these include a local councillor running a cheap cafe once a week, a community centre holding a meal for all those in the local area twice weekly, and a lone parent setting up a shop to sell fruit and vegetables at wholesale prices in an area that otherwise lacks fresh food.

These grassroots, small-scale initiatives are largely open access, they tend to resist (sometimes assertively) collecting data on who visits for food, they can include the collective production of food such as via communal gardening, and they are often set up by people with direct experience of poverty – or at least people who are embedded within the community they seek to serve. These organisations and groups can be political spaces, in which people come together as equals over a cooked meal, a piece of cake, a cup of tea, or spades and soil to share their ideas on housing, social security, health services, public transport, international affairs, religion, government, parenting and loneliness. Like all forms of food aid, these spaces will not solve food insecurity, but they may undermine the stigma associated with it and be a site where ideas, activism and protest among and between people of all incomes may germinate.

And yet, the progressive possibilities inherent to some food charity may not necessarily be limited to small-scale, grassroots providers. The fieldwork in the two English cities of Bradford and York underscored the equivocal ethics of established and bureaucratic food charities, such as Trussell Trust and some independent food banks. These organisations could employ complicated and sometimes controlling bureaucracies in their distribution of food, heightening the stigma of poverty. However, they were simultaneously ambivalent spaces of 'care', providing support and respite to food bank users. While emotional sensitivity (in the form of pastoral power) could be a method to shape acquiescence to dominant codes and practices in the food bank, care was also motivated by a sense of solidarity and concern for those using the service. This was particularly apparent in some Christian food banks and soup kitchens, in which volunteers used food to emphasise our 'communism of being' (Allen, 2016), living out Christian principles of egalitarianism and hospitality to strangers and rejecting an individualistic understanding of human beings (see Siddiqui [2015] on Christian hospitality) – in many ways emulating the mutualistic ethics of some small-scale secular providers. Food banks, like other grassroots community food projects, could also be radical, political spaces. They could challenge the policy decisions which create food insecurity, administer support and advocacy to tackle the reason for someone's visit to the food bank, and foster mutuality and solidarity in communities through the provision of localised care and the circulation of food. Such comparability between what may on the surface seem to be highly dissimilar types of food charity underscores the ethical complexity of the food aid sector.

Resistance is not, however, dependent on the development of specific food initiatives; it can be found in everyday living – in sharing and eating food among families, friends and communities, and in hospitality to neighbours and strangers, sometimes informed by religious ethics, such as Islamic hospitality. Food maintains bonds: to ancestral homes and traditions; across ethnicity, class, gender, disability, religion, language and culture; and to our sense of self. It can be a vehicle through which to reject dominant narratives of self-reliance, and to recognise our interdependency with each other and the natural world.

Another way is possible

It is overwhelmingly obvious that to reduce food insecurity it is necessary to address its root causes: poorly paid and insecure employment, unaffordable housing, 'No Recourse to Public Funds' status, and a social security system which creates and maintains destitution. These socio-political arrangements and neoliberal policies which give rise to multiple and intersectional inequalities, are embedded within longstanding power inequalities which promote and capitalise on deep-rooted sexism, racism and classism to divide communities and exploit people, in the form of labour, for profit. Solving food insecurity requires not only targeted campaigns on specific and particularly destructive policies, such as the five-week wait for Universal Credit, but opposition to these broader inequalities and inequities. Community food aid, despite its limitations, can be part of oppositional movements.

Janet Poppendieck, the North American sociologist best known for her seminal critique of food pantries, *Sweet Charity*, wrote in the final part of that book:

> In my most optimistic scenarios, I envision turning our kitchen and pantries into free spaces, places where people can meet and interact across the gulf of race and ethnicity, not as givers and receivers in ways that widen the gulf, but as neighbours and fellow citizens in ways that strengthen social bonds. (Poppendieck, 1999: 317)

Despite most evidence pointing to the contrary (see Fisher, 2017; Riches, 2018; de Souza, 2019, among many), in March and April 2018, I travelled the East Coast of the US to explore whether community food aid could be 'free spaces' of communality and solidarity across race, class, gender and geography, and to find out what we in the UK could learn – even if it was only what *not* to do – from North American food charity. I spoke with agricultural and migrant justice organisations in Vermont; charities campaigning for improved school food in Massachusetts; food pantries providing health services and workshops on narrative change and influencing strategies in New Jersey; and a multitude of organisations in New York City working to bring about social and health justice through food distribution and advocacy. Among the many organisations I spoke with, three stood out for their radical – and immensely varied – approaches to tackling hunger and promoting racial and economic food justice. I will close this book by briefly describing each of these organisations and what I learnt from them, with the hope of helping British food charities to chart a different path.

Neighbors Together: addressing hunger through housing reform

On a crisp, bright April morning I took the subway from central Manhattan to Rockaway Avenue station in Brooklyn. I emerged from the underground to find a world so different from the tall flashy buildings and confident wealthy commuters I had just left in Manhattan that I could scarcely believe I was only a 20-minute train ride away. People, predominantly African American people, without homes and visibly without health care, populated the streets; there was a sense of abandonment of not only these people but of the area in which they continued to reside. A short walk from the subway I found Neighbors Together, its busy and noisy canteen in full lunch flow, serving hot food to a queue of people snaking around the building. I was shown around the canteen by two members of staff, Nathalie and Amy, before being ushered into a small office to learn about their activities and campaign work. After describing their twice-daily community cafe for anyone in the local area, and the varied services they offered to members – advice and legal assistance around taxes, benefits, food stamps and health insurance; a mobile unit for medical testing and other medical services; psychological support; and legal advice on immigration – they turned to their Community Action Program.

The organisation aims to address hunger at a systemic level, Nathalie explained, by operating a member-driven programme of campaigning. Around 10 years ago, informal conversations with members over a shared meal in the Community Cafe began to increasingly touch on one recurring theme: housing. There was a major lack of affordable housing in New York City, and many of the shelters in which Neighbors Together's members slept were unwelcoming, dirty, undignified and often a pathway to drug and alcohol addictions. The collective analysis of members and staff at Neighbors Together was that housing was a stabilising force in people's lives; maintaining a job, going to school or college, or protecting your physical and mental health was near impossible when living on the streets, moving between different shelters on a daily or weekly basis.

Neighbors Together resolved to focus its Community Action Program on housing, at both a city and state level, and they have had great success in doing so. In 2009, the organisation led a major campaign to raise awareness and institute regulation of the hidden and highly exploitative network of three-quarter houses in New York City, buildings that rent beds in apartments and houses for profit, falsely claiming to provide supportive and other services (Mobilization for Justice, 2021). Amy described the exploitative and duplicitous system, in which tenants were encouraged to live in three-quarter housing by landlords on false pretences – sobriety, paid employment, further housing – but often evicted with no warning and for spurious reasons. The three-quarter housing system was historically entirely unregulated, she explained, with tenants utterly devoid of rights, but the system was simultaneously fuelled by housing subsidies (the $215 state rental allowance would pay for a monthly bed in a three-quarter house).

Neighbors Together worked in partnership with legal services and the New York Police Department to secure the rights of their members living in three-quarter housing while high-profile media coverage (the front page of the *New York Times*: Barker, 2015) opened the door to a legislative bill introducing stringent regulation. Neighbors Together introduced further legislative action to tackle multiple other housing inequities in New York, including improving the availability of affordable housing in New York City and reforming rent laws to enhance the rights of renters state-wide. They have collaborated with members to understand and address challenges and discrimination surrounding housing vouchers (a federal housing/rent assistance programme) and, confronted with opposition to their legislative bills from the executive branch (notably from the Mayor of New York City), they have initiated direct action with their members against the mayor.

Amy and Nathalie are not naïve about the obstacles they face in introducing housing reform in a city (and country) which holds individual property rights as sacred. Nathalie talks frankly about their powerlessness in campaigning on housing amid a hostile executive branch and strong private sector lobby: "It is very difficult for a non-profit to make change, particularly when those with legislative influence and power are resistant to change." Amy continues: "Housing is thought of as a private sector issue. In theory, it could be a public entitlement or democratically controlled and not something that is commodified but seen as a human right." They are, nevertheless, adamant that they will "focus on housing for as long as they need to". Where they cannot effect city and state-wide change through legislative action, they assist members on a one-to-one basis to access supported public sector housing.

As I leave through the Community Cafe, now busy cleaning up from lunch and preparing for the evening session, Nathalie thanks me for coming – we are all energised by the conversation even if it did identify as many challenges in their work as successes – and says something that sticks with me as I return on the subway to Manhattan: "Neighbors Together are member driven, by the people who need to have a voice. The message is so much more powerful when it comes from someone who really understands."

WhyHunger: "This is about root causes and systemic change, not changing behaviour"

At first glance, WhyHunger (see WhyHunger.org), the high-profile American NGO, supported by glamorous celebrities, and boasting a central Manhattan address, seems a world away from Neighbors Together and Rockaway Avenue. On closer inspection, however, the two organisations are remarkably similar: both focus on the systemic causes of hunger, both promote alliance-building as a pathway to change, and both emphasise the fundamental importance of including people with direct experience of poverty, hunger and discrimination in conversations and campaigns on food insecurity.

I'm introduced by Alison, Senior Director of Programmes and the (immensely generous) architect of my visit to both WhyHunger and Neighbors Together, to Suzanne and Lorrie, Directors of WhyHunger's US programmes. In a windowless room illuminated by sketches, flow charts, and idea bubbles covering the walls and depicting various theories of change, Alison, Suzanne and Lorrie describe the radical work of WhyHunger. Like food aid and food justice organisations in the UK, WhyHunger sees a key part of its role as naming and openly discussing the root causes of hunger. However, in stark contrast to the Trussell Trust, FareShare, and the multiple food poverty governing and coordinating bodies that have proliferated in the UK over the past decade, which can restrict their conversations on the causes of food insecurity to recent welfare reforms, WhyHunger critically assess the deeper, longer and arguably more contentious roots of hunger in the Global North – slavery, racism and land dispossession; industrial capitalism and the exploitation of labour; gendered and racial stigma; unequal property rights and unaffordable housing. As I have noted many times in this book, ethnic and racial inequality has, to date, been relatively neglected in UK debates on food insecurity and food aid. Early on in our conversation, Suzanne articulates the roots of contemporary racial inequality in the US so lucidly and powerfully that I will quote it in full here:

'A key element of our movement is racial inequality. The country is fractured along race lines, with Black people and native American people systemically disadvantaged. The country was founded on the backs of Black and native American people, and their exploitation remains a key part of society, inequality and economic growth today. Ethnic minority groups are more likely to be in poverty and to have poor health outcomes. They are more likely to work in the food industry and workers in the food industry are highly likely to themselves experience hunger.

Black people in the US today, who are the descendants of slaves, have the highest rates of disease and poverty. Their disadvantage is historically embedded: servitude continued after freedom was granted – the convict leasing law allows Black people to be arrested for no reason and forced to work on a farm. The person who made this arrest – not necessarily a police officer – can demand their labour. Today, exploitation and servitude can be worse than slavery. In slavery Black people were seen as property and therefore their life is valuable; today, Black people are worthless and so worked to death on farms.'

This critical analysis, shared and scrutinised with grassroots community food providers across the US is, for WhyHunger, fundamental to "moving forward". Only through a frank and often self-critical assessment of the root causes of hunger is it possible to develop responses which go beyond the band-aid solutions of many US food banks and food pantries. WhyHunger seeks to assist community food providers transition from a charity-only model to engagement with social justice, via participation with their wider progressive network of community food organisations. They encourage organisations to engage in leadership of the network, supporting leadership development among grassroots groups, and provide opportunities for community food providers to participate in narrative change, examining and overturning dominant stories around hunger. They help organisations partner with others from whom they can learn, collaborating around food justice, food sovereignty and racial inequity.

Like Amy and Nathalie at Neighbors Together, Alison, Suzanne and Lorrie recognise that their task is not a simple one. Not only are they challenging the tendency among American NGOs for individualism rather than collectivism (encouraged by corporate funding policies), but they are confronting centuries of divide-and-rule tactics, Lorrie explains:

> 'When we started organising around economics rather than race people found this much more threatening. There is a history to this: there was indentured servitude for White and Black people before we identified as White and Black. Both were enslaved. Awareness of race and White supremacy was used strategically as a dividing tactic, to undermine economic revolt. The idea of White supremacy was created. Class consciousness is not something that people talk about in the US. If we could build solidarity across class this could be powerful.'

As the conversation draws to a close, Alison explains that they are currently focusing on building partnerships and alliances with organisations outside the food aid sector, including labour movements and organisations advocating for economic justice, to raise class consciousness and draw attention to poverty as a driver of hunger. In a country in which democratic socialism can be portrayed as radically left-wing (Smith, 2020), illuminating the role of class in shaping experiences and driving hunger is no easy task but WhyHunger have spent their 46-year career tackling unfashionable systemic issues, fostering alliances around these causes based on trust and mutual accountability, and they are not to be deterred now.

Diggers' Mirth Collective: anarchist farming and food markets in Vermont

> 'Food access[4] is not our mission. It is just a very natural part of what we want to be doing. We expect that we will all benefit from this work. We are not a movement but more a success rate from a project that comes from necessity, or from cooperation.' (Jude)

I'm sitting with Jude, one of multiple owners of Diggers' Mirth Collective Farm, in a light and peaceful room at the InterVale Centre, an environmental NGO, in Burlington, Vermont. It's early March 2018 and I've spent the past week in the unexpectedly freezing city of Burlington to learn about the work of InterVale and its partner organisations. I have interviewed local food pantries alongside Vermont's largest food bank; talked to advocates for migrant rights on dairy farms; and attempted to assist with seed planting in InterVale's humid polytunnel.

Jude is the final person I am speaking to before I leave for Massachusetts. She tells me that Diggers' Mirth Collective was founded in 1992 as a cooperative farm on land leased from InterVale. The farm is owned and run collectively; risk and equity are shared. What is most notable about the farm is its ideology: the farmers identify themselves as anarchist and see themselves as part of an alternative economy – Jude explains: "we charge what we feel is a fair price, not what we can get. For instance, our stuff at the Coop supermarket [their main buyer] is cheaper than it needs to be."

Diggers' Mirth are keen promoters of sustainable agriculture: each year the farmers cultivate approximately two thirds of the field and grow cover crops in the other portion to ensure soil regeneration. A majority (85 per cent) of their sales are wholesale, largely to the bourgeois cooperative supermarket in downtown Burlington; however, they also sell their produce in two farmers' markets, one in downtown Burlington and the other in "the much poorer area of" Old North End. Diggers' Mirth worked in partnership with local community groups to set up a farmers' market in the northern part of the city that rejected the stereotypes of expensive food sold by White people for White, wealthy people. Jude tells me that it is:

'Different to the other Burlington farmers' market where the produce is more expensive – in the Old North End the plots are cheaper so the food prices are lower. People can use their EBT [Electronic Benefit Transfer[5]] cards in the farmers' market. We were one of the first to pilot it in the US. People can double the amount of fresh fruit and veg' purchased if they use the EBT card.'

Jude is firm in her belief that the farmers' market is no 'solution' to food insecurity and hunger, rather it is a place in which, "people come to hang out. The attendance is very seasonal, it waxes and wanes. People pop by if they are in the neighbourhood or on their way to other things".

The farmers' market in Old North End is accompanied, in the summer months, by a "mobile market, a veggie truck":

'It [the truck] takes two different routes and plays disco music', Jude is animated when describing the mobile market, 'it is like an ice cream truck. We sell stuff at the same price as in the Old North End market, effectively it is really low priced. We show up at people's door and people want it, kids like the agency of having something in front of them they can buy. Everybody that we encounter is into it. It is happenstance that people would know we were there but it's an opportunity for neighbours to meet each other for the first time. People are stoked by it.'

Diggers' Mirth Collective make no profit from the veggie truck, although they do break even; it is viable because of their other sources of income, particularly regular contracts with the downtown cooperative supermarket.

The mobile food truck operates only in the summer months and, in charging for food, will inevitably exclude those who are destitute, but the food truck and the farmers' market do achieve something immensely valuable and often absent from food charities or food access schemes, they "bring people together in a cool way" (Jude) across the gulf of race and ethnicity, class and geography, offering accessible, nutritious food and nourishing solidarity and community. In the closing chapter of *Feeding the Other*, de Souza (2019) recounts the activities of Appetite for Change (AFC), a social enterprise that blends business and justice to address food access and equity. She argues that:

> AFC's work resonates with J.K. Gibson-Graham's (1996) claim that community economies are expressions of 'diverse economies,' which cannot be pegged as capitalism because they contest and resist particular features of neoliberalism. These economies can be spaces of ethical action, not just places where we submit to the bottom line. (239)

The work of Diggers' Mirth similarly captures J.K. Gibson-Graham's (1996) idea of alternative economies. The collective explicitly resisted the individualistic and profit-motivated ethics of neoliberalism; it was the most radical expression within the "diverse economy" of Burlington that I came across on my travels. Its anarchist philosophy underpinned both its agricultural and food distribution work; the goals of cooperation, egalitarianism and sustainability were integral to the organisation's identity and its mission, as powerfully articulated by Jude:

> 'We don't think of this work as an external mission, it is integral to who we are. I would give away everything if I could but I need to earn an income. When social movements become successful it is not because they are prescribed, but because they have a mission and work collectively.'

Diggers' Mirth was, thus, above all, a space of ethical action – of growing, sharing and eating food in a sustainable and inclusive manner. It was not communistic – food was sold, not shared according to need – and, unlike WhyHunger and Neighbors Together, it did not explicitly confront racial injustice or address White privilege. Diggers' Mirth Collective was not by any means a 'solution' to food insecurity nor could it overturn longstanding economic and racial inequities underpinning contemporary forms of poverty. However, in selling food at cost-price to diverse communities and by replacing dominant neoliberal codes and practices with ones of cooperation and inclusivity, the collective allowed providers and recipients to engage in new ways of being, to relate to each other not as 'givers and receivers in ways that widen the gulf, but as neighbours and fellow citizens in ways that strengthen social bonds' (Poppendieck, 1999: 317).

Seizing uncertainty

Among a significant minority of service providers I spoke with in Bradford and York, food insecurity was portrayed as self-inflicted, the product of defective behaviour, which permitted scrutiny of the authenticity of need presented in food aid. Nevertheless, while this was distinctly the dominant narrative, it was *not* the majority view; among the remaining majority, views were variegated, narratives diffuse and ambivalence about the causes and consequences of food insecurity was apparent. It is in these ambivalent spaces that the potential exists for dialogue on systemic inequities – and, most importantly, the opportunity to *listen* to each other – within communities and across classes, ethnicities, genders and religions. It is in these discursive cracks that the seeds of resistance to neoliberal narratives of competition and self-help may germinate.

Notes

[1] In recent years, the Trussell Trust has been a vocal critic of welfare reform, regularly drawing attention to the fact that the single most common reason for needing food reported by those using its food banks is a problem with benefits and collaborating with anti-poverty charities to call for social policy changes (for example, JRF, 2020).

[2] In the UK, see the collaborative social policy work of Covid Realities and the APLE Collective.

[3] These corporate partnerships extended existing collaboration between the Trussell Trust and business, notably a partnership between the Trussell Trust and the US technology conglomerate CISCO to manage their data systems (Trussell Trust, 2021b) and £20 million of sponsorship (jointly with FareShare) from the grocery giant Asda.

[4] 'Food access' is the common term for 'food aid' work in the US.

[5] Electronic Benefits Transfer (EBT) is an electronic system that allows a Supplemental Nutrition Assistance Program (SNAP) participant to pay for food using SNAP benefits.

Appendix: methodology

Bradford

The study in Bradford had three key components: analysis of the Born in Bradford 1000 (BiB1000) survey data; interviews and focus groups with food aid providers and public health professionals; and focus groups with women in or at risk of food insecurity. I discuss each in turn.

Survey sample

Born in Bradford study

Born in Bradford (BiB), a prospective birth cohort study, was established in 2007 in response to concerns about the high infant mortality rate in Bradford compared with other UK cities, and high levels of childhood morbidity, including congenital anomalies and childhood disability (Small, 2012; Wright et al, 2012). The study recruited pregnant women (and their partners) at the Bradford Royal Infirmary. Women were recruited from the maternity unit between March 2007 and December 2010 as they attended the clinic for an oral glucose tolerance test, routinely offered to all pregnant women in Bradford between 26 and 28 weeks' gestation. All babies born to these mothers and all fathers were eligible to participate; mothers were only excluded if they planned to move away from Bradford before the end of their pregnancy. Over 80 per cent of the women invited for the study accepted the offer to participate. Ethical approval for the data collection was granted by Bradford Leeds NHS Research Ethics Committee (Ref 07/H1302/112). Table A1 provides baseline characteristics for the mothers in the sample. As demonstrated with t-tests and Pearson chi-square tests in Table A1, differences between Pakistani and White British mothers (as collectives) are statistically significant.

The BiB1000 study

BiB1000 is a nested cohort of the BiB birth cohort. It was established in 2008 in response to evidence gaps in knowledge regarding the impact of exposures during pregnancy and early life, especially among South Asian children (Bryant et al, 2013). All mothers recruited to the full BiB study between August 2008 and March 2009, who had completed the baseline questionnaire, were approached to take part in the BiB1000 study during their routine 26–28-week glucose tolerance test. A sample size of 1,080 was calculated based upon the statistical ability to detect a difference in infant

Table A1: Baseline characteristics BiB1000 sample

Demographic variables	BiB mothers	Pakistani mothers	White British mothers
N	11 396	5127	4488
Ethnic group			
White British	39.4%		
Pakistani	44.9%		
Indian	3.8%		
Asian Other	2.9%		
White Other	2.6%		
Black	2.2%		
Mixed	1.9%		
Other	1.7%		
Could not categorise/missing*	0.6%		
Mean age (years)	27.8	28.2	27.2
		$t(9580)=-9.01, p<0.001$	
Marital status			
First marriage	64.7%	91.8%	30.9%
Single	29.6%	1.2%	64.2%
Other	5.7%	7.0%	4.9%
		$\chi^2(2)= 4500, p<0.001$	
Educational level mother			
< 5 GCSE	21.5%	25.8%	20.0%
5 GCSE equivalent	30.6%	31.1%	34.1%
A level equivalent	14.4%	12.5%	17.0%
> A level	25.6%	25.9%	19.2%
Could not categorise/missing*	7.9%	4.7%	9.7%
		$\chi^2(3)= 116.41, p<0.001$	
Managing financially			
Living comfortably	26.5%	26.6%	26.4%
Doing alright	41.3%	41.5%	40.2%
Just getting by	23.9%	23.6%	26.2%
Finding it difficult or very difficult to manage	7.6%	7.7%	6.8%
Could not categorise/missing*	0.7%	0.6%	0.4%
		$\chi^2(3)= 10.28, p=0.016$	
Receiving means tested benefits			
Yes	40.7%	46.9%	37.9%
No	59.0%	52.8%	61.8%
Could not categorise/missing*	0.3%	0.3%	0.3%
		$\chi^2(1)= 78.88, p<0.001$	

*There are only a small number of missings (N=25) in the BiB dataset and, therefore, this category relates mostly to women who could not be categorised (N=625 'other'), with a very small number of 'don't know' and 'foreign unknown' (see Fairley et al, 2014).

growth of 0.67 z-scores in weight at age over one year, and allowing for a 5 per cent annual attrition (Bryant et al, 2013). However, once recruitment had begun (and was highly successful), the team decided to oversample the population by up to 70 per cent to optimise the amount of data available across all assessments (Bryant et al, 2013). Trained bilingual study administrators collected information from mothers in participants' homes, hospital-based clinics and in local Children's Centres. Anthropometric measurements were taken and structured questionnaires were self-completed. Routinely collected data were extracted from the maternity IT system (eClipse) and the Child Health system in Bradford and Airedale Primary Care Trust. Ethical approval was obtained from the Bradford Leeds NHS Research Ethics Committee and all participants provided written informed consent prior to inclusion in the research.

Of 1,916 eligible women, 1,735 agreed to take part in the study. Of these, 28 mothers gave birth to twins. Seventy-seven per cent, 75 per cent 74 per cent, 70 per cent and 70 per cent of participants were followed-up at 6-, 12-, 18-, 24- and 36-month assessments respectively. Forty-seven per cent of participants completed all assessments, with 17 per cent having formally withdrawn from the research. Table A2 provides baseline characteristics for the mothers in the BiB1000 sample. The sample characteristics closely reflect those of the full BiB cohort. The two largest ethnic groups in the sample are Pakistani (49 per cent) and White British (37 per cent), followed by Indian (4 per cent), Other Asian (2 per cent) and Other White (2 per cent). Overall, 86 per cent of the mothers live with the baby's father or another partner, higher than the 65 per cent of married mothers in the full BiB cohort. Cohabitation is highly dependent on ethnicity: 74 per cent of White British women cohabit compared with 95 per cent of Pakistani women. Slightly raised compared to the full BiB cohort, around 35 per cent of the mothers have an educational level equivalent to five GCSEs, and 24 per cent have a lower level of education. Pakistani mothers were more likely to be in the lowest or the highest education group than White British mothers and more Pakistani than White British mothers reported receiving means-tested benefits (45 per cent versus 37 per cent). As in the full BiB cohort, the majority of participants reported to be financially managing well/alright (68 per cent). As demonstrated with t-tests and Pearson chi-square tests in Table A2, all these differences between Pakistani and White British mothers (as a group) are statistically significant.

Creating a food insecurity dataset

Data on household food insecurity was matched with demographic data from the BiB baseline questionnaire. Household food insecurity was assessed when babies were approximately 12 to 18 months old by trained bilingual

Table A2: Baseline characteristics BiB1000 sample

Individual characteristics	BiB1000 mothers at 12-month wave	Pakistani	White British
N	*1280*	*624*	*480*
Ethnic group (baseline)			
White British	37.34%		
Pakistani	48.87%		
Indian	4.07%		
Asian Other	2.26%		
White Other	2.19%		
Black	2.01%		
Mixed	1.25%		
Other	2.01%		
Mean maternal age at delivery (baseline)	27.49 (sd 5.61)	27.70 (sd 5.13)	26.91 (6.10)
		t(30) = 71.5505 p<0.000	
Mother's education (baseline)			
<5 GCSE equivalent	23.93%	27.13%	21.90%
5 GCSE equivalent	34.78%	33.60%	39.60%
A-level equivalent	14.71%	12.01%	17.34%
Higher than A-level	26.58%	27.26%	21.17%
		$\chi^2(5) = 33.6716 \, p<0.000$	
Subjective poverty (baseline)			
Living comfortably	26.49%	27.71%	23.78%
Doing alright	41.91%	40.59%	43.34%
Just about getting by	23.03%	24.61%	24.11%
Finding it difficult or very difficult to manage	8.56%	7.09%	8.77%
		$\chi^2(3)=3.8519 \, p<0.278$	
Receiving means-tested benefits (baseline)			
Yes	40.55%	45.19%	37.27%
No	59.45%	54.81%	62.73%
		$\chi^2(1)=8.6791 \, p<0.003$	
Cohabitation status (baseline)			
Living with the baby's father or another partner	86.29%	95.11%	74.49%
Not living with a partner	13.71%	4.89%	25.51%
		$\chi^2(1)=124.8164 \, p<0.000$	

Table A3: BiB1000 sample characteristics for food insecurity at 12 months

Food insecurity	BiB1000 12-month wave	Pakistani	White British
N	1280	624	480
Food secure	1101 (86.02%)	560 (89.74%)	393 (81.88%)
Moderate food insecurity	133 (10.39%)	50 (8.01%)	62 (12.92%)
Food insecure with hunger	39 (3.04%)	12 (1.92%)	22 (4.56%)
Food insecure with severe hunger	7 (0.55%)	2 (0.32%)	3 (0.62%)

community researchers using the 18-item US National Household Food Security Survey Measure (HFSSM) (Hamilton et al, 1997a). Women were categorised into four categories of food insecurity. Table A3 sets out how the sample divides into the four categories.

A total of 313 women were excluded from the analysis due to missing data or responding 'don't know' or 'refuse to answer'. The high number of missings is mainly explained by attrition rates. As touched on above, only 75 per cent of the 1,735 mothers in the BiB1000 study were followed up at 12 months when the food insecurity questionnaire was conducted (Bryant et al, 2013). Within the BiB1000 12-month survey wave, 14 women were excluded from the food insecurity analysis due to missing data or responding 'don't know' or 'refuse to answer'. There were no systematic differences between missings and sample participants. This is in line with existing food insecurity analyses: results from Pearson chi-square tests show that adults with and without reliable and complete 24-hour dietary recall, or with and without family income data do not differ by food insecurity status (Dixon et al, 2001).

Small sample sizes in the two 'severe' food insecurity categories ('food insecure with hunger' and 'food insecure with severe hunger') precluded the use of the four-category food insecurity variable in regression analyses. As a consequence, the three food insecurity categories were amalgamated into a single variable ('food insecure') and the regression analysis utilised a binary food insecurity variable: food secure and food insecure.

Variables used in the analysis

The outcome was 'food insecurity', explained previously. The exposure was multiple sociodemographic factors: self-assigned ethnicity (White British and Pakistani, due to predominance of these ethnic groups in the sample); cohabitation status; number of people living in the household (measured at the 12-month survey wave of the nested BiB1000 study); maternal age; occupation of the father;[1] receipt of means-tested benefits; perception of financial security; and maternal education.

Statistical analysis

The regression analyses were preceded by description of (a) the full food insecurity survey, (b) maternal characteristics in relation to food insecurity status, (c) food insecurity in relation to social security status, and (d) food insecurity in relation to household size. Logistic regression analysis was used in the full sample and within the two largest ethnic groups, White British and Pakistani, to calculate unadjusted Odds Ratios (ORs) of food insecurity in relation to all covariates separately. In addition, adjusted ORs for (i) food insecurity in relation to all covariates combined in a multivariate model [Model 1] and (ii) food insecurity in relation to all covariates with p<0.1 in Model 1 [Model 2]. P<0.1 was adopted as a threshold rather than p<0.05 in response to the small sample size. Average Marginal Effects were calculated to facilitate interpretation of results. All analyses were conducted using Stata 14.0.

Interviews and focus groups

Food aid providers: 2014–15

Three focus groups with individuals (N=9) who had experience with food security programmes/policy at a governance level were conducted in June 2015. Ethical consent was obtained from the University of York Department of Health Sciences Research Governance Committee (HSRGC) (Ref HSRGC/2015/98A). A sampling frame was drawn up by the author in conjunction with senior members of Bradford District Metropolitan Council Public Health team to include individuals who had experience with food security programmes/policy. These included councillors in Bradford; members of the Public Health team; members of NHS services in Bradford addressing food/health; nutritionists, dieticians and members of local Clinical Commissioning Groups; and third sector organisations with experience of food-related coordination/policy.

Forty people were identified as meeting the inclusion criteria. There was an element of subjectivity in the final (purposive) sample. A number of people did not reply to the invitation to join the study, and others declined to be involved. Those who did not reply or declined to contribute were more likely to work in the NHS or third sector organisations. No incentives were offered for participation. The participants in the focus groups and interviews were key stakeholders in community food aid and food insecurity in Bradford. The focus groups and interviews were semi-structured and conducted by a 'White British' female interviewer (myself) and a 'White Other' male member of the Bradford Council Public Health team; the data were recorded on a Dictaphone and transcribed verbatim.

The interview method was chosen to develop a detailed understanding of the varying community-based responses to food insecurity within the context of the theoretical framework and the specific demographic and geographic setting. The interviews were carried out by myself alone, between September and November 2015. Interviews were conducted in Bradford involving individuals from third sector organisations with experience of food security programmes at a community level (N= 18). Ethical consent was obtained from HSRGC (Ref HSRGC/ 2015/160A). Sample organisations were chosen purposively from the 67 food aid organisations identified in a scoping exercise to form a representative sample, which included various types of organisations and multiple religions. In line with the religious demography of Bradford, the faith-based organisations in the sample were Christian and Muslim only. Interviewees within the sample organisations were also chosen purposefully to capture perspectives that would best represent each organisation's viewpoint. Publicly available information was used to compile a contact list. Invitations to join the study were sent by myself to the appropriate person within an organisation. Organisations that failed to respond were removed from the sample. Others declined to be involved or suggested another organisation in their place. If this occurred, the organisation was contacted only if it was considered an appropriate replacement. Reasons given for declining to participate included a perception of limited relevant experience and failure to see the study's value. No incentives were offered for participation.

Interviews were semi-structured. The topic guide was informed by the available literature, discussion within the project team and themes that arose from the focus groups. The interviews were recorded on a Dictaphone and transcribed verbatim. In order to avoid leading the respondent towards a particular construction or viewpoint there were a limited number of questions (five). However, prompts were used where necessary to further a line of conversation or investigate views on specific topics considered to be related to community-based food aid and food insecurity.

Data analysis

Identical methods were used to analyse the focus group and the interview transcripts, which allowed for triangulation and comparison of the results. To ensure rigour, reduce subjectivity and present a fair representation of all views, the data analysis involved three stages. Each stage fed into the next and so informed the final analysis. This multi-stage analysis was informed by Dwyer's approach in his qualitative study of 'welfare service users' (Dwyer, 2002: 273). The transcripts were uploaded to Nvivo 10 to facilitate the analysis and ensure it was systematic and comprehensive. The analysis process involved:

1. Summaries of individual transcripts: each transcript was summarised in order to understand the narrative of the focus group or interview as a whole. This also offered an opportunity to begin a basic thematic analysis of the text.
2. Overview grid of all transcripts: the grid facilitated an analysis of the range of opinions across the transcripts in relation to specific questions and provided an indication of similarity/differences of opinion. The grid enabled a fair and equal representation of all opinions and reduced the potentially disproportionate influence of forceful or articulate voices.
3. Thematic code: the code, written with reference to Boyatzis (1998), was identified by:

    a. the code label;
    b. a definition of what the theme concerns. A theme:
        i. included multiple codes in a coherent schema;
        ii. constituted a topic that re-occurred frequently throughout the text;
        iii. could be related to questions and issues of theoretical importance, as identified in the literature;
    c. a description of how to know when the theme occurs.

Sample

To preserve anonymity of participants and, as required by HSRGC approval, details about the organisations and individuals in the sample are anonymised. The focus group sample consisted of nine participants in total. It was biased towards stakeholders involved in food insecurity and community food at a governance level, including four employees of Bradford District Metropolitan Council and a local councillor. The interview sample of 18 organisations was biased towards emergency food aid providers.

Focus groups with low-income families 2016–17
Setting: Little Horton, Bowling and Barkerend, and Bradford Moor

The study was conducted in Little Horton, Bowling and Barkerend, and Bradford Moor: three inner city areas in Bradford. The wards have a higher birth rate than Bradford District or England, and are very ethnically diverse, with residents of Pakistani heritage forming the largest ethnic group (48.6 per cent) and a minority White British population (24.8 per cent) (Dickerson et al, 2016). An increasing number of families arriving from Central and Eastern European countries, especially Poland, Slovakia and the Czech Republic, augment the diversity of the areas. Mortality and morbidity rates are higher than those in both Bradford District and England, and include a relatively high infant mortality rate (Dickerson et al, 2016). Employment in all three areas is low: 26.3 per cent, 22.9 per cent and 18.4 per cent of residents are in full-time employment in Bowling and Barkerend, Little Horton and Bradford Moor respectively, compared with 38.6 per cent in the UK as a whole (ONS, 2011).

Together, the three wards comprise the Better Start Bradford (BSB) areas. BSB is a community project, based in Bradford, allocated £49 million by the Big Lottery Fund to implement 22 interventions to improve outcomes for children aged 0–3 in three key areas: social and emotional development; communication and language development; and nutrition and obesity (BSB, 2017).

The researcher worked with BSB to recruit participants and conduct the focus groups. The research setting was, therefore, in part a pragmatic choice: BSB's pre-existing relationships and activities/interventions in the area facilitated relatively rapid recruitment for and execution of the focus groups. Nevertheless, the choice of research setting was not simply pragmatic. The demography and high deprivation of the wards allowed for recruitment of an appropriate population, one which was both ethnically diverse and more likely to be at risk of food insecurity than the general population of Bradford.

Study design

The study aimed to investigate perceptions and experiences, and fulfilling the research aims required an in-depth exploration of a sensitive topic (experiences around food in the context of poverty), a topic which may not be commonly discussed by participants and which may need to be 'teased out' through careful, open-ended questioning (Morgan, 1997). Focus groups were conducted within pre-existing groups, in a setting familiar to the participants. With the assistance of BSB, existing group activities in Bradford in which it would be appropriate to hold focus groups were identified. Members of these groups were invited to participate in the study; no incentives were offered for participation. The researcher worked with BSB to ensure a diversity of groups and participants and, specifically, to include:

• White British and Pakistani British women with dependent children;
• women who spoke only Urdu, women who were bilingual and women who spoke only English;
• women living in low-income households, including those in severe poverty.

The focus groups were held between July 2016 and January 2017. Three focus groups were conducted and, as a consequence of recruitment difficulties, one interview. The focus groups were recorded on a Dictaphone and transcribed verbatim. The focus groups were semi-structured. The opening stage was conducted as an interview within a group (Morgan, 1997). Rather than presenting a question for whole group response, the moderator began by concentrating on a single participant, and subsequently requesting group members to respond. This approach aimed to involve all participants fully in the group and encourage each participant to give a meaningful response, with the goal of hearing from everyone (Morgan, 1997). As the focus group progressed the researcher acted as a 'moderator' for the group (Wilkinson, 2004), rather than as an interviewer, posing the questions, maintaining the flow of the discussion and enabling members to participate fully.

Focus group 1 included participants with varying levels of English language ability. All participants were of Pakistani origin; however, while some (N=4) were bilingual (Urdu and English), others spoke only Urdu (N=3). Because of this, the focus group was conducted as two smaller conversation groups within the larger group, with the Urdu speakers spoken to separately via a translator. Although there are significant limitations to dividing the group in this manner, it was preferred to excluding some members of the group on the basis of language or breaking up the flow of the conversation entirely with a translator translating all dialogue – English and Urdu – to all group participants.

Sample and ethical considerations

A total of 16 people participated in the focus groups. The sample included eight Pakistani British women and eight White British women living in Little Horton, Bradford Moor, and Bowling and Barkerend. Seven Pakistani British women were married to men in employment. Only one Pakistani British woman was in employment. Six White British women were married or cohabiting with a partner; one was employed; four had partners who were employed and three were solely reliant on social security.

Ethical consent was obtained from HSRGC (Ref HSRGC/2015/121A). Given the vulnerability of some of the participants and the sensitive nature of the topic, ethical considerations were prominent in the design and conduct of the focus groups (and interview). The moderator aimed to ask participants about their personal experiences; however, the line of questioning was discontinued in situations where the participant appeared distressed. The moderator was also conscious of her position of power in her relationship with participants, in terms of both academic knowledge and her role in setting the agenda of the group, deciding the boundaries of time and indicating acceptable discussion points. The researcher attempted to address this power imbalance by foregrounding the right of the participant to withdraw at any time and providing the participant with considerable scope to determine the direction of the discussion. Participants were provided with full information about the study before agreeing to take part and informed consent was attained before the start of each focus group. Finally, the focus groups and interview were recorded and transcribed anonymously. Descriptions of the sample use pseudonyms, identifying material is removed and direct quotes are published with pseudonyms.

Data analysis

The data analysis involved three stages and was informed by Dwyer (2002), as described previously. In analysing the empirical data, a theoretically informed coding framework was constructed. General themes were broken down into sub-themes and used to analyse all transcripts. Nvivo 10 was used to group quotes for each sub-theme, with some quotes categorised within multiple sub-themes.

York

Research approach and aims

The study in York was based on two years of participatory research with people living in poverty – and at risk of food insecurity – and service providers responding to food insecurity and poverty. The dominant framing of poverty, including food poverty and insecurity, forefronts elite political and politicised accounts, which accentuate behavioural drivers of food insecurity, portraying it as an individual rather than a societal-level phenomenon (Garthwaite, 2016b); the voices and insights of those directly affected by food insecurity often remain absent in these conversations. This study placed experts-by-experience, as both service providers and service users, at the centre of the research design and delivery. By doing so it sought to open up a space for the emergence of alternative narratives of food poverty and insecurity, while also constituting a direct confrontation to unequal power structures which contribute to the marginalising of the perspectives of people living in food insecurity and poverty. The study was not only intended as a route through which to counter the silencing of marginalised groups but also as a means for building community capacity in confronting poverty and food insecurity. The aims of the research were motivated by service providers and service users and were as follows:

1. to assess the sociodemographics and lived experience of food insecurity, including food bank use, in the case study area;

2. to construct and conduct research on household food insecurity that reflects community priorities, and to strengthen community capacity through the design and delivery of participatory research.

Study design and setting

The study consisted of a survey, four focus groups and a community mapping exercise undertaken by the York Food Justice Alliance (YFJA) collectively. The study was initiated and co-produced by members of the YFJA, a multi-sector organisation encompassing people with lived experience of food insecurity, community food aid providers, local authority representatives, local charities, academics and other relevant stakeholders focused on tackling food insecurity and poverty in York. Accordingly, the study took place in York and prioritised questions of greatest importance to YFJA stakeholders – notably food choices and diet quality among low-income households – and the sample (households with young children) reflected an identified area of local need.

The specific components of the study, a survey and focus groups, described later, were complemented by numerous informal conversations with food aid providers and key stakeholders in York, alongside 15 participatory workshops on strategy, research and policy development. The collective of stakeholders and experts by experience (known as the York Food Justice Alliance) mapped food aid services in the City of York, supported by a research assistant.

Survey

Sample

Adult household members of children aged 4–11 years in York were surveyed about their experiences of diet, food insecurity and food bank use. Ethical approval for the study was provided by the University of York Health Sciences Research Governance Committee on 6 July 2018. The survey was disseminated via primary schools (N=25), each of which was recruited through the YFJA network, alongside being publicised through social media channels. As well as organising a community food aid response in the city, a key aim of the alliance was to generate evidence on food insecurity and experiences of food at the local level. These findings were subsequently developed into a programme of policy recommendations (see Power, 2019). The survey formed part of the evidence-gathering process and was designed to collect information on household demographics, income, diet and experiences of food insecurity and food bank use among families with primary school aged children. It was co-produced by the YFJA and researchers at the University of York through a series of three collaborative workshops designed to generate topic areas and key local priorities. Questions were defined and selected by group consensus and, where possible, existing measures were used, for example ONS income and household type categories, to ensure robustness. The survey therefore prioritises the questions and the sample (households with young children) deemed by consensus to be of greatest importance to YFJA stakeholders.

The survey used a validated two–item measure of food insecurity (Harrison et al, 2019). The two–item tool is a derivative of the experience-based 18-item US HFSSM and is widely used in clinical settings. The two-item measure allowed for robust assessment of household food insecurity while limiting the number of survey questions overall – of considerable importance given the need to ensure an adequate sample for analysis while also allowing participants to 'opt in'. In addition, the survey included a single question to assess self-reported food bank use. A free-text response box was provided at the end of the survey, entitled 'Do you have any further comments on food in York?' to explore wider food experiences, including issues of food access.

The survey was distributed via both an electronic link, disseminated via schools and shared through social media, and hard copies of the survey distributed to parents via schools. Consequently, it is not possible to calculate an accurate overall response rate; however, the response rate from paper copies of the survey distributed via primary schools was 11 per cent, highlighting the value of pursuing dual (online and offline) methods of dissemination. Overall, the survey achieved 612 individual responses, with 136 free-text responses. Exploration of demographic characteristics in the sample (Table A4) suggests an over-representation of respondents from higher-income backgrounds: 43.57 per cent (N=261) of households have an annual income of over £38,399, and 69.24 per cent (N=412) are homeowners. In England, 63 per cent of households are in home ownership, and 60.58 per cent in York (ONS, 2016; Gov.uk, 2020b). Sample sizes do, however, allow for analysis by all income groups and household tenures. Only 5.23 per cent (N=32) of households included three adults or more, so findings relating to this category should be treated with caution.

Data collection

Schools were approached by YFJA members in the first instance with verbal and written explanations of the study. Once participation was confirmed, paper copies and an electronic link to the survey were provided and disseminated to the caregivers of pupils in each school by letter and/or email. The survey was also shared via social media channels, such as Facebook. The text of the survey was accompanied by an information sheet documenting

Table A4: Sample demographic characteristics

Demographic characteristics	N (%)
Annual household income	
Less than £16,100	71 (11.85)
£16,100 - £21,249	72 (12.02)
£21,250 - £27,999	78 (13.02)
£28,000 - £38,399	117 (19.53)
More than £38,399	261 (43.57)
Total	599 (100)
Adults in household	
Single adult	117 (19.12)
Two adults	463 (75.65)
Three adults or more	32 (5.23)
Total	612 (100)
Children in household	
One child	161 (26.83)
Two children	329 (54.83)
Three children or more	110 (18.33)
Total	600 (100)

the purpose of the study, data storage and use, and the process of consent. Informed consent was obtained from all survey participants. A locked postbox was placed in each school to enable the anonymous return of paper copies of the survey. The survey was open for participation from November 2018 to February 2019.

Focus groups

Negotiation of food quality and food quantity in contexts of poverty and food insecurity was further explored in four semi-structured focus groups held in January 2019. The author worked with community groups in York and members of the YFJA to identify and recruit parents and carers living on a low income; participants were either approached directly by a member of a partner community group or informed about the focus group via leaflets distributed in community venues, including the community venues in which the focus groups were held. Participants self-identified as a parent or carer living on a low income and chose to participate in the focus groups. The focus groups were held in a familiar location, such as a community centre or a low-cost, community cafe, and lasted between one and two hours. To ensure confidentiality, the focus groups were conducted in a private room or setting in the community venue.

The focus groups were moderated by myself and a research assistant with experience of moderating group interviews. In line with the preferences of participants, no recording equipment was used; instead, written notes were taken. The opening stage of the focus groups was conducted as an interview within a group (Morgan, 1997). As in Bradford, rather than presenting a question for whole group responses, the moderator concentrated on a single participant, subsequently requesting group members to respond. This approach aimed to involve all participants fully in the group and encourage each participant to give a meaningful response, with the goal of hearing from everyone.

The topic guide was produced collaboratively with members of YFJA, constructed to explore the lived experience of food and diet in contexts of poverty and low income. Confidentiality and informed (oral) consent were maintained throughout, and all data was anonymised during transcription and analysis.

Focus group sample and ethical considerations

The focus groups included 22 participants, across four focus groups, the majority of whom were female (N=19). All participants had children and all self-identified as living on a low income. As in the Bradford groups, ethical considerations were paramount. The moderator emphasised the voluntary nature of the group and the right of participants to withdraw at any time. The moderator initiated the conversation but adopted a secondary role, allowing the discussion to develop while ensuring the inclusion of all participants. Descriptions of the sample use pseudonyms, identifying material is removed and direct quotes are published with pseudonyms.

Data analysis

I adopted a parallel mixed-methods design, in which the qualitative and quantitative data were collected separately (Teddlie and Tashakkori, 2009). Both were informed by discussions using a participatory approach and this design reflected the iterative nature of the co-production process, in which priorities and study design were tailored according to community priorities at each stage. Convergence was used to triangulate the findings at the analysis stage (Blaikie, 2009), with qualitative findings used to explain and expand on the quantitative data. Following collection of the surveys, quantitative response data were uploaded into Stata 16.1 (Statacorp, 2019) for analysis. Responses to the food insecurity questions were merged to create a single, binary food insecurity variable, according to established methods (Hager et al, 2010; Radandt et al, 2018). Quantitative data were analysed using descriptive statistics, for example, cross-tabulation, and associations estimated by logistic regression modelling, which was selected for the binary, categorical outcome data. All associations are reported as odds ratios. Free-text responses were collated and analysed using a six-stage thematic analysis framework (Braun and Clarke, 2006). Thematic categories were formulated inductively. Focus group transcripts were coded and analysed thematically by the author and a research assistant to elicit common themes related to the research aims. Data categorisations were discussed until consensus was reached.

Reflections on the methodological approach

The use of survey and interview-based methods provided considerable advantages in understanding the dynamics and lived experience of food insecurity and food aid. In a context of limited data on food poverty/food insecurity, the surveys in Bradford and York allowed for unique insights into the prevalence and demographics of food insecurity across diverse populations, in terms of income, age and ethnicity. Interview-based methods, including both focus groups and in-depth interviews, enabled the researcher to probe points of interest and gain a rich understanding of motivations for food charity and lived experiences of food insecurity and food aid. It is arguable that the detailed understanding of religious motivations for food charity and the gendered and racialised stigma that people in poverty experience on a day-to-day basis would not have been possible without interview-based methods. It is for these reasons of simultaneous breadth and depth within the constraints of a time-limited project and severely restricted capacity (one researcher undertaking fieldwork in Bradford and two researchers undertaking fieldwork in York on a part-time basis) that survey and interview-based methods were chosen. Nevertheless, there are considerable limitations to these two methodological approaches which are relevant to this study. Population-based surveys inevitably provide a crude representation of food insecurity, a complex social, economic and cultural issue, while interview-based methods (at least those that are not longitudinal) provide only a snapshot of perceptions, opinions and experiences at one point in time. An immersive ethnographic approach would have arguably provided a richer and more nuanced insight into the dynamics of food charity, in particular the ways that ideologies and beliefs actually play out on a daily basis, possibly revealing the disconnect between what is said and what is practised – a disconnect that may have been masked by the interview form. Equally, an immersive ethnographic approach may also cut through the likely rose-tinted portrayals of interviewees, whether of their food aid provision or their experience of food insecurity, providing a more truthful portrayal of poverty, religion and racism today.

Note

[1] Paternal employment was used as a marker of a woman's socioeconomic status as a high proportion of Pakistani women had never been employed.

References

Adkins J, Occhipinti K and Hefferan T (2012) Social services, social justice, and faith-based organisations in the United States: An introduction. In: Adkins J, Occhipinti L and Hefferan T (eds) *Not by Faith Alone: Social Services, Social Justice and Faith-Based Organisations in the United States*. Lanham, MD: Lexington Books, pp 1–32.

Alam Y (2015) In-group identity and the challenges of ethnographic research. In: Husband C (ed) *Research and Policy in Ethnic Relations: Compromised Dynamics in a Neoliberal Era*. Bristol: Policy Press, pp 79–104.

Alexander C (2009) Stuart Hall and 'race'. *Cultural Studies* 23(4): 457–482.

Alkon AH and Mares TM (2012) Food sovereignty in US food movements: Radical visions and neoliberal constraints. *Agriculture and Human Values* 29: 347–359.

Allen C (2016) Food poverty and Christianity in Britain: A theological re-assessment. *Political Theology* 17(4): 361–377.

Anderson S (1990) Core indicators of nutritional state for difficult-to-sample populations. *The Journal of Nutrition* 120(suppl_11): 1555–1600.

Aponte R (1990) Definitions of the underclass: A critical analysis. In: Gans H (ed) *Sociology in America*. Westbury Park, CA: Sage, pp 117–137.

Atia M (2013) *Building a House in Heaven: Pious Neoliberalism and Islamic Charity in Egypt*. Minneapolis, MN; London: University of Minnesota Press.

Back L, Keith M, Khan A, Shukra K and Solomos J (2002) New Labour's white heart: Politics, multiculturalism and the return of assimilation. *The Political Quarterly* 73(4): 445–454.

Bagguley P and Hussain Y (2003) The Bradford 'Riot' of 2001: A preliminary analysis. In: *Ninth Alternative Futures and Popular Protest Conference*. Manchester: Manchester Metropolitan University, pp 1–17.

Baker J (2003) *Eight Degrees of Charity: Rambam, Hilchot Mat'not Ani'im 10:1, 7–14*. Available at: http://www.panix.com/~jjbaker/rmbmzdkh.html

Baldwin P (1992) Beveridge in the longue durée. *International Social Security Review* 45(1–2): 53–72.

Barker K (2015) Profiting from addiction: A choice for recovering addicts: Relapse or homelessness. *New York Times*, 30 May. Available at: https://www.nytimes.com/2015/05/31/nyregion/three-quarter-housing-a-choice-for-recovering-addicts-or-homelessness.html

Barker M and Russell J (2020) Feeding the food insecure in Britain: Learning from the 2020 COVID-19 crisis. *Food Security* 12(4): 865–870.

Beatty C and Fothergill S (2013) *Hitting the poorest places hardest: The local and regional impact of welfare reform.* Sheffield Hallam University: Centre for Regional Economic and Social Research. Available at: https://www4.shu.ac.uk/research/cresr/sites/shu.ac.uk/files/hitting-poorest-places-hardest_0.pdf

Begley A, Paynter E, Butcher LM and Dhaliwal S (2019) Examining the association between food literacy and food insecurity. *Nutrients* 11(2): 445.

Bello W (2008) How to manufacture a global food crisis. *Development* 51: 450–455.

Bhopal K (2000) Gender, 'race' and power in the research process. In: Truman C, Mertens DM and Humphries B (eds) *Research and Inequality.* London: Routledge, pp 67–79.

Bhopal K (2018) *White Privilege: The Myth of a Post-racial Society.* Bristol: Policy Press.

Bigelow G (2005) Let there be markets: The evangelical roots of economics. *Harper's Magazine* 310(1860): 33–38.

Birch K (2017) *A Research Agenda for Neoliberalism.* Cheltenham: Edward Elgar Publishing.

Bird FB (1982) A Comparative Study of the Work of Charity in Christianity and Judaism. *The Journal of Religious Ethics* 10(1): 144–169.

Blaikie NWH (2009) *Designing Social Research: The Logic of Anticipation.* Cambridge, MA: Polity.

Blue Bird Jernigan V, Garroutte E, Krantz EM and Buchwald D (2013) Food insecurity and obesity among American Indians and Alaska Natives and Whites in California. *Journal of Hunger & Environmental Nutrition* 8(4): 458–471.

Boggs C (1977) Marxism, prefigurative communism, and the problem of workers' control. *Radical America* 11(6): 99–122.

Bonilla-Silva E (2013) *Racism Without Racists: Color-Blind Racism and the Persistence of Racial Inequality in the United States.* New York, NY: Rowman & Littlefield Publishers.

Bonnett A (1996) 'White Studies': The problems and projects of a new research agenda. *Theory, Culture & Society* 13(2): 145–155.

Boyatzis RE (1998) *Transforming Qualitative Information: Thematic Analysis and Code Development.* Thousand Oaks, CA: Sage.

Bradford Heritage Recording Unit (1987) *Destination Bradford: A Century of Immigration.* Bradford: Bradford Libraries and Information Service.

Bramley G, Treanor M, Sosenko F and Littlewood M (2021) *State of Hunger: Building the Evidence on Poverty, Destitution, and Food Insecurity in the UK.* London: The Trussell Trust. Available at: https://www.trusselltrust.org/wp-content/uploads/sites/2/2021/05/State-of-Hunger-2021-Report-Final.pdf

Braun V and Clarke V (2006) Using thematic analysis in psychology. *Qualitative Research in Psychology* 3(2): 77–101.

Brewer M and Patrick R (2021) *Pandemic Pressures: Why Families on a Low Income are Spending More during COVID-19.* London: Resolution Foundation. Available at: https://www.resolutionfoundation.org/app/uploads/2021/01/Pandemic-pressures.pdf

Brown W (2006) American nightmare: Neoliberalism, neoconservatism, and dedemocratization. *Political Theory* 34(6): 690–714.

Brunon-Ernst A (2012) *Beyond Foucault: New Perspectives on Bentham's Panopticon.* London: Routledge.

Bryant B, Dadzie S and Scaff S (2018) *Heart of Race: Black Women's Lives in Britain.* London: Verso.

Bryant M, Santorelli G, Fairley L, West J, Lawlor, DA, Bhopal, R, et al (2013) Design and characteristics of a new birth cohort, to study the early origins and ethnic variation of childhood obesity: The BiB1000 study. *Longitudinal and Lifecourse Studies* 4(2): 119–135.

Bryson A and Jacobs J (1992) *Policing the Workshy: Benefit Controls, the Labour Market and the Unemployed.* Aldershot: Avebury.

Bryson A and White M (2019) Migrants and low-paid employment in British workplaces. *Work, Employment and Society* 33(5): 759–776.

BSB (2017) *About Better Start Bradford.* Available at: https://betterstartbradford.org.uk/about-us/

Buckingham H (2012) Capturing diversity: A typology of third sector organisations' responses to contracting based on empirical evidence from homelessness services. *Journal of Social Policy* 41(3): 569–589.

Burnley Task Force (2001) *Report of the Burnley Task Force.* Burnley: Burnley Borough Council.

Butler P (2018a) Universal credit: What is it and what exactly is wrong with it? *The Guardian*, 25 January. Available at: https://www.theguardian.com/society/2018/jan/25/universal-credit-benefits-scheme-iain-duncan-smith

Butler P (2018b) Welfare spending for UK's poorest shrinks by £37bn. *The Guardian*, 23 September. Available at: https://www.theguardian.com/politics/2018/sep/23/welfare-spending-uk-poorest-austerity-frank-field

Butler P (2020) Disabled man starved to death after DWP stopped his benefits. *The Guardian*, 28 January. Available at: https://www.theguardian.com/society/2020/jan/28/disabled-man-starved-to-death-after-dwp-stopped-his-benefits

Cadieux, KV and Slocum, R (2015) What does it mean to do food justice? *Journal of Political Ecology* 22(1): 1–26.

Cairns B, Harris M and Hutchinson R (2007) Sharing God's love or meeting government goals? Local churches and public policy implementation. *Policy & Politics* 35(3): 413–432.

Cameron D (2009) *The Big Society.* Available at: https://conservative-speeches.sayit.mysociety.org/speech/601246

Cantle T (2001) *Community Cohesion: A Report of the Independent Review Team*. Available at: https://www.belongnetwork.co.uk/resources/community-cohesion-a-report-of-the-independent-review-team/

Caraher M and Dowler E (2014) Food for poorer people: Conventional and 'alternative' transgressions. In: Goodman M and Sage C (eds) *Food Transgressions: Making Sense of Contemporary Food Politics*. Ashgate: Aldershot, pp 227–246.

Caruso C (2019) Emergency food system: Soup kitchens and food pantries. In: Kaplan DM (ed) *Encyclopedia of Food and Agricultural Ethics*. Dordrecht: Springer Netherlands, pp 699–706.

Charles N and Kerr M (1988) *Women, Food and Families*. Manchester: Manchester University Press.

Chase E and Walker R (2013) The co-construction of shame in the context of poverty: beyond a threat to the social bond. *Sociology* 47(4): 739–754.

Cheetham M, Moffatt S, Addison M and Wiseman A (2019) Impact of Universal Credit in North East England: A qualitative study of claimants and support staff. *BMJ Open* 9(7): e029611.

Choudhury T and Fenwick H (2011) The impact of counter-terrorism measures on Muslim communities. *International Review of Law, Computers & Technology* 25(3): 151–181.

Choudhury Y, Hussain I, Parsons S, Rahman A, Eldridge S and Underwood M (2012) Methodological challenges and approaches to improving response rates in population surveys in areas of extreme deprivation. *Primary Health Care Research & Development* 13(3): 211–218.

Church of England (2019) *Statistics for Mission*. Available at: https://www.churchofengland.org/sites/default/files/2020-10/2019StatisticsForMission.pdf

City of York Council (2011) *Census 2011 – Key Statistics Update*. Available at: https://www.nomisweb.co.uk/census/2011/key_statistics

City of York Council (2019) *Indices of multiple deprivation in York*. Available at: https://data.gov.uk/dataset/a64b08cf-3b02-4d56-bcf7-fd69f24b8bf5/indices-of-multiple-deprivation-in-york

Clifford, D (2017) Charitable organisations, the Great Recession and the Age of Austerity: Longitudinal evidence for England and Wales. *Journal of Social Policy* 46(1): 1–30. doi:10.1017/S0047279416000325

Cloke P, May J and Williams A (2017) The geographies of food banks in the meantime. *Progress in Human Geography* 41(6): 703–726.

Community Food Security Coalition (no date) *What is community food security?* Available at: http://www.foodsecurity.org/views_cfs_faq.html

Connell R, Fawcett B and Meagher G (2009) Neoliberalism, New Public Management and the human service professions: Introduction to the Special Issue. *Journal of Sociology* 45(4): 331–338.

Connolly W (2005) The evangelical-capitalist resonance machine. *Political Theory* 33(6): 869–886.

Connolly W (2008) *Capitalism and Christianity, American Style.* Durham, NC: Duke University Press.

Cooper N, Purcell S and Jackson R (2014) *Below the Breadline: The Relentless Rise of Food Poverty in Britain.* London: Oxfam. Available at: https://policy-practice.oxfam.org/resources/below-the-breadline-the-relentless-rise-of-food-poverty-in-britain-317730/

Corbett S and Walker A (2013) The big society: Rediscovery of 'the social' or rhetorical fig-leaf for neo-liberalism? *Critical Social Policy* 33(3): 451–472.

Crisis (2019) *Cover the Cost: How Gaps in Local Housing Allowance are Impacting Homelessness.* Available at: https://www.crisis.org.uk/media/240377/cover_the_cost_2019.pdf

Crotty M (1998) *The Foundations of Social Research: Meaning and Perspective in the Research Process.* London: Sage.

Crossley, S, Garthwaite, K and Patrick, R (2019) *The fragmentation of poverty in the UK: What's the problem? A working paper.* Available at: https://static1.squarespace.com/static/5d3ef1aa7c54410001ea5ef3/t/5d9a73f33fc8223140de167b/1570403322350/UK+Poverty+-+what%27s+the+problem+Working+Paper+FINAL.pdf

Cummins S and MacIntyre S (2002) 'Food deserts' – Evidence and assumption in health policy making. *British Medical Journal* 325: 436–438.

Day, AE (1969) JB Priestley: Man of Letters, *Library Review*, 22(2): 59-62. https://doi.org/10.1108/eb012517

de Souza R (2019) *Feeding the Other: Whiteness, Privilege and Neoliberal Stigma in Food Pantries.* Cambridge, MA: MIT Press.

Dean H (2008) Social policy and human rights: Re-thinking the engagement. *Social Policy and Society* 7(1): 1–12.

Dean H and Taylor-Gooby P (1992) *Dependency Culture: The Explosion of a Myth.* Hemel Hempstead: Harvester Wheatsheaf.

Dean M (2014) Rethinking neoliberalism. *Journal of Sociology* 50(2): 150–163.

Desmarais AA (2007) *La Via Campesina: Globalization and the Power of Peasants.* London: Pluto Press.

Dickerson J, Bird PK, McEachan RRC, Pickett KE, Waiblinger D, Uphoff, E et al (2016) Born in Bradford's Better Start: An experimental birth cohort study to evaluate the impact of early life interventions. *BMC Public Health* 16(1): 711.

Dixon LB, Winkleby MA and Radimer KL (2001) Dietary intakes and serum nutrients differ between adults from food-insufficient and food-sufficient families: Third National Health and Nutrition Examination Survey, 1988–1994. *The Journal of Nutrition* 131(4): 1232–1246.

Dowler E (2002) Food and poverty in Britain: Rights and responsibilities. *Social Policy & Administration* 36(6): 698–717.

Dowler E and Lambie-Mumford H (2015) How can households eat in austerity? Challenges for social policy in the UK. *Social Policy and Society* 14(3): 417–428.

Dowler E and O'Connor D (2012) Rights-based approaches to addressing food poverty and food insecurity in Ireland and UK. *Social Science and Medicine* 74(1): 44–51.

Dowler EA (2014) Food banks and food justice in 'Austerity Britain'. In: Riches G and Silvasti T (eds) *First World Hunger Revisited: Food Charity or the Right to Food?* 2nd edn. New York, NY: Palgrave MacMillan, pp 160–175.

DWP (Department for Work and Pensions) (2021) *Family Resources Survey: Financial year 2019 to 2020*. DWP. Available at: https://www.gov.uk/government/statistics/family-resources-survey-financial-year-2019-to-2020

Dwyer P (2002) Making sense of social citizenship: Some user views on welfare rights and responsibilities. *Critical Social Policy* 22(2): 273–299.

Dwyer P (2019) *Dealing with Welfare Conditionality: Implementation and Effects*. Bristol: Policy Press.

Dwyer P and Wright S (2014) Universal Credit, ubiquitous conditionality and its implications for social citizenship. *Journal of Poverty and Social Justice* 22(1): 27–35.

Eddo-Lodge R (2019) The Windrush Betrayal by Amelia Gentleman and Homecoming by Colin Grant – review. *The Guardian*, 23 November. Available at: https://www.theguardian.com/books/2019/nov/23/windrush-betrayal-amelia-gentleman-homecoming-colin-grant-review

Edmiston D (2017) 'How the other half live': Poor and rich citizenship in austere welfare regimes. *Social Policy and Society* 16(2): 315–325.

Elgot J (2014) 'Selfish' food bank users spent money on booze and drugs, says Tory Julia Lepoidevin. *Huffington Post*, 27 June. Available at: https://www.huffingtonpost.co.uk/2014/06/27/food-banks-_n_5536359.html

Fairley L, Cabieses B, Small N, Petherick E, Lawlor D and Wright J (2014) Using latent class analysis to develop a model of the relationship between socioeconomic position and ethnicity: Cross-sectional analyses from a multi-ethnic birth cohort study. *BMC Public Health* 14(1): 835.

FAO (Food and Agriculture Organization of the United Nations) (2019) *Hunger and Food Insecurity*. Available at: http://www.fao.org/hunger/en/

FAO, IFAD (International Fund for Agricultural Development), UNICEF, WFP and WHO (2017) *The State of Food Insecurity and Nutrition in the World 2017: Building Resilience for Peace and Food Security*. Food and Agriculture Organisation of the United Nations. Available at: http://www.fao.org/policy-support/tools-and-publications/resources-details/en/c/1107528/

FAO, IFAD, UNICEF, WFP and WHO (2019) *The State of Food Security and Nutrition in the World 2019: Safeguarding against Economic Slowdowns and Downturns*. Available at: http://www.fao.org/3/ca5162en/ca5162en.pdf

FAO, IFAD, UNICEF, WFP and WHO (2020) *The State of Food Security and Nutrition in the World 2020: Transforming Food Systems for Affordable Healthy Diets.* Available at: http://www.fao.org/documents/card/en/c/ca9692en/

FareShare (2020) *Annual Report 2019/2020.* Available at: https://fareshare.org.uk/wp-content/uploads/2020/10/Annual-Report-2020_LowRES.pdf

Farnsworth K and Irving Z (2015) Social policy in the age of austerity. In: Farnsworth K, Irving, Z (ed) *Social Policy in Times of Austerity: Global Economic Crisis and the Politics of Welfare.* Bristol: Policy Press, pp 1–8.

Feagin J (2006) *Systemic Racism: A Theory of Oppression.* New York, NY: Routledge.

Feagin J (2013) *The White Racial Frame: Centuries of Racial Framing and Counter-Framing.* New York, NY: Routledge, pp 109–159.

Feinstein CH (1981) Population, occupation and economic development, 1831–1981. In: Feinstein CH (ed) *York 1831–1981: 150 Years of Scientific Endeavour and Social Change.* York: The Ebor Press.

Fernández-Reino M and Rienzo C (2019) *Migrants in the UK Labour Market: An Overview.* The Migration Observatory. Available at: https://migrationobservatory.ox.ac.uk/wp-content/uploads/2019/07/COMPAS-Briefing-Migrants-in-the-UK-labour-market-an-overview.pdf

Fisher A (2017) *Big Hunger: The Unholy Alliance between Corporate America and Anti-hunger Groups.* Cambridge, MA: MIT Press.

Fisher M (2009) *Capitalist Realism: Is There No Alternative?* Winchester: Zero Books.

Fletcher DR and Wright S (2018) A hand up or a slap down? Criminalising benefit claimants in Britain via strategies of surveillance, sanctions and deterrence. *Critical Social Policy* 38(2): 323–344.

Foucault M (1977) *Discipline and Punish.* Penguin: Harmondsworth.

Foucault M (1982) The subject and power. *Critical Inquiry* 8(4): 777–795.

Foucault M (1988) The ethic of care for the self as a practice of freedom. In: Bernauer J and Rasmussen D (eds) *The Final Foucault.* Cambridge, MA: MIT Press, pp 112–131.

Foucault M (2008) *The Birth of Biopolitics: Lectures at the College de France, 1978–79.* Basingstoke: Palgrave.

Frankenberg R (1993) *White Women, Race Matters: The Social Construction of Whiteness.* Minneapolis, MN: University of Minnesota Press.

Galvin R (2002) Disturbing notions of chronic illness and individual responsibility: Towards a genealogy of morals. *Health* 6(2): 107–137.

Gane N (2012) The governmentalities of neoliberalism: Panopticism, post-panopticism and beyond. *The Sociological Review* 60(4): 611–634.

Garthwaite K (2016a) *Hunger Pains: Life Inside Foodbank Britain.* Bristol: Policy Press.

Garthwaite K (2016b) Stigma, shame and 'people like us': An ethnographic study of foodbank use in the UK. *Journal of Poverty and Social Justice* 24(3): 277–289.

Garthwaite K (2017) 'I feel I'm giving something back to society': Constructing the 'active citizen' and responsibilising foodbank use. *Social Policy and Society* 16(2): 283–292.

Garthwaite K, Collins PJ and Bambra C (2015) Food for thought: An ethnographic study of negotiating ill health and food insecurity in a UK foodbank. *Social Science & Medicine* 132: 38–44.

Gentleman A (2019) *The Windrush Betrayal: Exposing the Hostile Environment.* Manchester: Guardian Faber Publishing.

Gibson-Graham, JK (1996) *The End of Capitalism (As We Knew It): A Feminist Critique of Political Economy.* Oxford: Blackwell.

Gill B (2015) *The English Indices of Deprivation 2015: Statistical release.* London: Department for Communities and Local Government, 1–37. Available at: https://www.gov.uk/government/statistics/english-indices-of-deprivation-2015

Glendinning C and Millar J (1987) *Women and Poverty in Britain.* Sussex: Wheatsheaf.

Glendinning C and Millar J (1992) *Women and Poverty in Britain: The 1990s.* Hemel Hempstead: Harvester Wheatsheaf.

Glennerster H (2020) *The post war welfare state: Stages and disputes.* London School of Economics and Political Science. Available at: https://sticerd.lse.ac.uk/dps/case/spdo/spdorn03.pdf

Glover TD (2003) Community garden movement. In: Christensen K and Levinson D (eds) *Encyclopedia of Community.* Thousand Oaks, CA: Sage, pp 264–266.

Goldberg DT (2009) *The Threat of Race: Reflections on Racial Neoliberalism.* New York, NY: John Wiley & Sons.

Goldberg DT (2013) The postracial contemporary. In: Kapoor N, Kalra VS and Rhodes J (eds) *The State of Race.* London: Palgrave Macmillan pp 15–30.

Goldberg DT (2001) *The Racial State.* Oxford: Blackwell.

Golder B (2007) Foucault and the genealogy of pastoral power. *Radical Philosophy Review* 10(2): 157–176.

Goodman D, Dupuis M and Goodman M (2011) *Alternative Food Networks: Knowledge, Practice, and Politics.* London: Routledge.

Goodway D (2012) *Anarchist Seeds Beneath the Snow: Left-Libertarian Thought and British Writers from William Morris to Colin Ward.* Oakland, CA: PM Press.

Gottlieb R and Joshi A (2010) *Food Justice.* Cambridge, MA: MIT Press.

Gov.uk (2020a) *£16 million for food charities to provide meals for those in need.* Available at: https://www.gov.uk/government/news/16-million-for-food-charities-to-provide-meals-for-those-in-need

Gov.uk (2020b) *Home Ownership.* Available at: https://www.ethnicity-facts-figures.service.gov.uk/housing/owning-and-renting/home-ownership/latest

Gov.uk (2021) *Unemployment.* Available at: https://www.ethnicity-facts-figures.service.gov.uk/work-pay-and-benefits/unemployment-and-economic-inactivity/unemployment/latest

Graham H (1993) *Hardship and Health in Women's Lives.* Hemel Hempstead: Harvester Wheatsheaf.

Graven C, Power M, Jones S, Possingham S and Bryant M (2021) *The range and accessibility of food aid provision in Bradford, and the impact of COVID-19.* ActEarly. Available at: https://www.bradfordresearch.nhs.uk/wp-content/uploads/2021/01/The-impact-of-COVID-19-on-the-provision-of-food-aid-in-Bradford_V4-Jan-21.pdf

Grossberg L (2007) Stuart Hall on race and racism: Cultural studies and the practice of contextualism. In: Meeks B (ed) *Culture, Politics, Race and Diaspora: The Thought of Stuart Hall.* London: Lawrence & Wishart, pp 27–42.

Guthman J (2008) Bringing good food to others: Investigating the subjects of alternative food practice. *Cultural Geographies* 15(4): 431–447.

Guthman J (2011) "If they only knew": The unbearable whiteness of alternative food. In: Alkon AH and Agyeman J (eds) *Cultivating Food Justice: Race, Class and Sustainability.* Cambridge, MA: MIT Press, pp 263–281.

Hackworth J (2012) *Faith Based: Religious Neoliberalism and the Politics of Welfare in the United States.* Athens, GA: University of Georgia Press.

Hager ER, Quigg AM, Black MM, Coleman SM, Heeran, T, Rose-Jacobs, R et al (2010) Development and validity of a 2-item screen to identify families at risk for food insecurity. *Pediatrics* 126(1): e26–e32.

Hall, S (1987) Minimal selves. In Appignanesi, L (ed) *The Real Me: Post-modernism and the Question of Identity.* ICA Documents 6. London: ICA, pp 44–46.

Hall S (2011) The neo-liberal revolution. *Cultural Studies* 25(6): 705–728.

Hall S, Critcher C, Jefferson T, Clarke J and Roberts B (1978) *Policing the Crisis.* London: Macmillan.

Hamilton WL, Cook JT, Thompson WW, Buron LF, Frongillo EA, Olsen, CM et al (1997a) *Household food security in the United States in 1995: Summary report of the food security measurement project.* United States Department of Agriculture.

Hamilton WL, Cook JT, Thompson WW, Buron LF, Frongillo EA, Olsen, CM et al (1997b) *Household food security in the United States in 1995: Technical report of the food security measurement project.* United States Department of Agriculture.

Harris J (1992) Political thought and the welfare state 1870–1940: An intellectual framework for British social policy. *Past & Present* 135(1): 116–141.

Harrison C, Davis J, Smallwoord T, Begum, N, Goldstein, J and Papas M (2019) Validation of a 2-item food insecurity screen among adult general medicine outpatients. *Annals of Epidemiology* 40: 39.

Harvey D (2005) *A Brief History of Neoliberalism.* Oxford: Oxford University Press.

Havely NR (2004) *Dante and the Franciscans: Poverty and the Papacy in the Commedia.* Cambridge: Cambridge University Press.

Hayek FA (1960) *The Constitution of Liberty.* London: Routledge & Kegan Paul.

Haylett C (2001) Illegitimate subjects? Abject whites, neoliberal modernisation, and middle-class multiculturalism. *Environment and Planning D: Society and Space* 19(3): 351–370.

Henman P (2004) Targeted! Population segmentation, electronic surveillance and governing the unemployed in Australia. *International Sociology* 19(2): 173–191.

Henman P and Marston G (2008) The social division of welfare surveillance. *Journal of Social Policy* 37(2): 187–205.

Hill H and Larsson J (2017) *Saved to Save and Saved to Serve: Perspectives on Salvation Army History.* Eugene, OR: Resource Publications.

Hilton B (1986) *The Age of Atonement: The Influence of Evangelicalism on Social and Economic Thought, 1785–1865.* Oxford: Oxford University Press.

HM Revenue and Customs (2009) *Health in Pregnancy Grant – Coming to the United Kingdom.* Available at: https://revenuebenefits.org.uk/pdf/HiPG_Coming_to_the_United_Kingdom_HiPG__FS1.pdf

Holloway J (2002) *Change the World Without Taking Power.* London: Pluto Press.

Holt-Gimenez E (2011) Food security, food justice, or food sovereignty? Crises, food movements, and regime change. In: Alkon AH and Agyeman J (eds) *Cultivating Food Justice: Race, Class, and Sustainability.* Cambridge, MA: MIT, pp 309–330.

Homer A (2021) Deaths of people on benefits prompt inquiry call. *BBC News*, 10 May. Available at: https://www.bbc.co.uk/news/uk-56819727

Humphreys R (1995) *Sin, Organized Charity and the Poor Law in Victorian England.* Basingstoke: Macmillan Press.

Husband C, Alam Y, Huettermann J, and Fomina, J (2014) *Lived Diversities: Space, Place and Identities in the Multi-ethnic City.* Bristol: Policy Press.

Hussain Y and Bagguley P (2013) Funny looks: British Pakistanis' experiences after 7 July 2005. *Ethnic and Racial Studies* 36(1): 28–46.

Hyatt J and Simons H (1999) Cultural codes – Who holds the key? The concept and conduct of evaluation in Central and Eastern Europe. *Evaluation* 5(1): 23–41.

IFAN (Independent Food Aid Network) (2020) *Independent food bank emergency food parcel distribution in the UK*. Available at: https://uploads. strikinglycdn.com/files/9c7292e6-4bea-410e-9e9bf9de7e22f3d1/ IFAN%20Emergency%20Food%20Distribution%20Report%20Feb%20-%20May%201920%20Published%2009.07.20.pdf

Ignatiev N (1995) *How the Irish Became White*. New York, NY: Routledge.

Immervoll H and Knotz C (2018) How demanding are activation requirements for jobseekers? Paris: OECD Social, Employment and Migration Working Papers. Available at: https://ftp.iza.org/dp11704.pdf

Inglehart R (2021) *Religion's Sudden Decline: What's Causing it, and What Comes Next?* Oxford: Oxford University Press.

Ipsos MORI (2020) *Half of Britons support the aims of the Black Lives Matters Movement*. Available at: https://www.ipsos.com/ipsos-mori/en-uk/ half-britons-support-aims-black-lives-matter-movement

Jarvis D, Porter F, Broughton, K, Lambie H, and Farnell, R (2010) Building Better Neighbourhoods: The contribution of faith communities to Oxfordshire life. Available at: https://consultations.oxfordshire.gov.uk/ ContributionofFaithCommunities/consultationHome

Jeldtoft N (2011) Lived Islam: Religious identity with 'non-organized' Muslim minorities. *Ethnic and Racial Studies* 34(7): 1134–1151.

Jenkins RH, Aliabadi S, Vamos EP, Taylor-Robinson D, Wickham S, Millett C et al (2021) The relationship between austerity and food insecurity in the UK: A systematic review. *EClinicalMedicine* 33: 100781.

Jensen T and Tyler I (2015) 'Benefits broods': The cultural and political crafting of anti-welfare commonsense. *Critical Social Policy* 35(4): 470–491.

Jones C and Novak T (1999) *Poverty, Welfare and the Disciplinary State*. London: Routledge.

Jones M and Rodney L (2002) *From Beveridge to Blair: The First Fifty Years of Britain's Welfare State 1948–98*. Manchester: Manchester University Press.

Jones O (2011) *Chavs: The Demonization of the Working Class*. London: Verso.

Jones O (2020) *This Land: The Story of a Movement*. Milton Keynes: Allen Lane.

JRF (2020) *Joint open letter to The Chancellor – Keep the lifeline*. Available at: https://www.jrf.org.uk/press/joint-open-letter-chancellor-keep-lifeline

Juan-Torres M, Dixon T and Kimaram A (2020) *Britain's choice: Common ground and division in 2020s Britain*. More in Common. Available at: https:// www.britainschoice.uk/media/iechhfpq/0917_mic_uk_britain-s-choice-exsum_dec01.pdf

Kahl S (2005) The religious roots of modern poverty policy: Catholic, Lutheran, and Reformed Protestant traditions compared. *European Journal of Sociology* 46(1): 91–126.

Kalra VS (2000) *From Textile Mills to Taxi Ranks*. Ashgate: Aldershot.

Kapoor N and Kalra VS (2013) Introduction: The state of race. In: Kapoor N, Virinder V and Rhodes J (eds) *The State of Race*. Basingstoke: Palgrave Macmillan, pp 1–12.

Kassam Z and Robinson SE (2014) Islam and food. In: Thompson PB and Kaplan DM (eds) *Encyclopedia of Food and Agricultural Ethics*. Dordrecht: Springer Netherlands, pp 1282–1291.

Kellogg's/CEBR (2017) *Hard to swallow: The facts about food poverty*. Available at: https://www.kelloggs.co.uk/content/dam/europe/kelloggs_gb/pdf/R3_Facts%20about%20Food%20Poverty%20ReportFINAL.pdf

Khunti K, Platt L, Routen A and Abbasi K (2020) Covid-19 and ethnic minorities: An urgent agenda for overdue action. *BMJ* 369: m2503.

Kim J-Y, Natter M and Spann M (2009) Pay what you want: A new participative pricing mechanism. *Journal of Marketing* 73(1): 44–58.

Kisby B (2010) The big society: Power to the people? *The Political Quarterly* 81(4): 484–491.

Knox R (1862) *The Races of Men: A Philosophical Enquiry into the Influence of Race over the Destinies of Nations*. London: Henry Renshaw.

Kobayashi A and Peake L (2000) Racism out of place: Thoughts on whiteness and an antiracist geography in the new millennium. *Annals of the Association of American Geographers* 90(2): 392–403.

Kropotkin P (1899) *Memoirs of a Revolutionist*. London: Smith, Elder.

Kropotkin, P ([1902] 1987a) *Mutual Aid: A Factor of Evolution*. London: Freedom Press.

Kropotkin, P ([1927] 1987b) *Anarchist Communism*. London: Freedom Press.

Kundani A (2007) *The End of Tolerance: Racism in 21st Century Britain*. London: Pluto Press.

Kurtz H, Borron A, Shannon J and Weaver, A (2019) Community food assistance, informal social networks, and the labor of care. *Agric Hum Values* 36: 495–505.

La Via Campesina (2009) *Campesina Policy Documents*. Ecuador: La Via Campesina.

Lambie H (2011) The Trussell Trust Foodbank Network: Exploring the growth of foodbanks across the UK (Report to the Trussell Trust). London: The Trussell Trust.

Lambie-Mumford H (2017) *Hungry Britain: The Rise of Food Charity*. Bristol: Policy Press.

Lambie-Mumford H (2018) The growth of food banks in Britain and what they mean for social policy. *Critical Social Policy* 39(1): 3–22.

Lambie-Mumford H and Green MA (2017) Austerity, welfare reform and the rising use of food banks by children in England and Wales. *Area* 49(3): 273–279.

Lambie-Mumford H and Snell C (2015) *Heat or eat: Food and austerity in rural England: Final report.* Working Papers of the Communities & Culture Network+, 6. ISSN 2052-7268. Available at: https://eprints.whiterose.ac.uk/114808/1/Heat-or-Eat-with-Annexes.pdf

Lambie-Mumford H, Crossley D, Jensen E, Verbeke M and Dowler, E (2014) Household food security in the UK: A review of food aid: Final report. Available at: https://assets.publishing.service.gov.uk/government/uploads/system/uploads/attachment_data/file/283072/household-food-security-uk-executive-summary-140219.pdf

Lambie-Mumford H, Gordon K and Loopstra R (2020) *Monitoring responses to risk of rising food insecurity during the COVID-19 crisis across the UK.* Available at: http://speri.dept.shef.ac.uk/wp-content/uploads/2020/12/Monitoring-responses-to-risk-of-rising-food-insecurity-during-the-COVID-19-crisis-across-the-UK-FINAL-1.pdf

Larner W (2000) Neo-liberalism: Policy, ideology, governmentality. *Studies in Political Economy* 63(1): 5–25.

Lawler S (2012) White like them: Whiteness and anachronistic space in representations of the English white working class. *Ethnicities* 12(4): 409–426.

Leonardo Z (2004) The Color of Supremacy: Beyond the discourse of 'white privilege'. *Educational Philosophy and Theory* 36(2): 137–152.

Levkoe CZ (2006) Learning democracy through food justice movements. *Agriculture and Human Values* 23(1): 89–98.

Lewis J (1983) *Women's Welfare: Women's Rights.* London: Croom Helm.

Lewis O (1966) The culture of poverty. *Scientific American* 215(4): 533–552.

Lipsitz G (1998) *The Possessive Investment in Whiteness.* Philadelphia, PA: Temple University Press.

Lister R (2004) *Poverty: Key Concepts.* 1st edn. Cambridge: Polity.

Lister R (2011) The age of responsibility: Social policy and citizenship in the early 21st century. In: Holden C, Kilkey M and Ramia G (eds) *Social Policy Review 23: Analysis and Debate in Social Policy.* Bristol Policy Press, pp 63–84.

Lister R (2020) *Poverty: Key Concepts.* 2nd edn. Cambridge: Polity Press.

Livingstone N (2015) The Hunger Games: Food poverty and politics in the UK. *Capital & Class* 39(2): 188–195.

Livingstone N (2017) Franchising the disenfranchised? The paradoxical spaces of food banks. In: Ince A and Hall S (eds) *Sharing Economies in Times of Crisis: Practices, Politics and Possibilities.* Abingdon: Routledge.

Long E (1774) *The History of Jamaica or, General Survey of the Ancient and Modern State of that Island: With Reflections on its Situation, Settlements, Inhabitants, Climate, Products, Commerce, Laws, and Government.* London: T. Lowndes.

Loopstra R (2020) *Vulnerability to food insecurity since the COVID-19 lockdown.* Available at: https://foodfoundation.org.uk/wp-content/uploads/2020/04/Report_COVID19FoodInsecurity-final.pdf

Loopstra R, Reeves A, Taylor-Robinson D, Barr B, Mckee M and Stuckler D (2015) Austerity, sanctions, and the rise of food banks in the UK. *BMJ: British Medical Journal* 350: h1775.

Loopstra R and Tarasuk V (2015) Food bank usage is a poor indicator of food insecurity: Insights from Canada. *Social Policy and Society* 14(3): 443–455.

Loopstra R, Fledderjohann J, Reeves A and Stuckler, D (2016) Impact of welfare benefit sanctioning on food insecurity: A dynamic cross-area study of food bank usage in the UK. *Journal of Social Policy* 47(3): 437–457.

Loopstra R, Goodwin S, Goldberg B, Lambie-Mumford H, May J and Williams A (2019a) A survey of food banks operating independently of The Trussell Trust food bank network. Available at: https://www.foodaidnetwork.org.uk/independent-food-bank-survey

Loopstra R, Reeves A and Tarasuk V (2019b) The rise of hunger among low-income households: An analysis of the risks of food insecurity between 2004 and 2016 in a population-based study of UK adults. *Journal of Epidemiology and Community Health* 73(7): 668–673.

Loopstra R, Reeves A, Taylor-Robinson D, Barr B, Mckee M and Stuckler D (2015) Austerity, sanctions, and the rise of food banks in the UK. *BMJ: British Medical Journal* 350: h1775.

Loopstra R and Tarasuk V (2015) Food bank usage is a poor indicator of food insecurity: Insights from Canada. *Social Policy and Society* 14(3): 443–455.

MacLeod MA, Curl A and Kearns A (2019) Understanding the prevalence and drivers of food bank use: Evidence from deprived communities in Glasgow. *Social Policy and Society* 18(1): 67–86.

Manji K (2017) Social security reform and the surveillance state: Exploring the operation of 'hidden conditionality' in the reform of disability benefits since 2010. *Social Policy and Society* 16(2): 305–314.

Mann S, Nolan J and Wellman B (2003) Sousveillance: Inventing and using wearable computing devices for data collection in surveillance environments. *Surveillance & Society* 1(3): 331–355.

Manzoor S (2009) Bradford reflects on many shades of Englishness. *The Observer*, 5 July. Available at: https://www.theguardian.com/stage/2009/jul/05/bradford-englishness-jb-priestley

Marmot M, Allen J, Goldblatt P, Herd E and Morrison J (2020) *Build Back Fairer: The COVID-19 Marmot Review.* The Health Foundation. Available at: https://www.health.org.uk/publications/build-back-fairer-the-covid-19-marmot-review

Marshall P (2008) *Demanding the Impossible: A History of Anarchism.* London: Fontana.

Marshall TH (1992) *Citizenship and Social Class.* London: Pluto Press.

Marxists Internet Archive Encyclopedia (no date) *Capital*. Available at: https://www.marxists.org/glossary/terms/c/a.htm

Massey D (2015) Vocabularies of the economy. In: Hall S, Massey D and Rustin M (eds) *After Neoliberalism: The Kilburn Manifesto*. London: Lawrence & Wishart, pp 24–36.

Massey D, Hall S and Rustin M (2015) *After Neoliberalism? The Kilburn Manifesto*. London: Lawrence & Wishart.

May J, Williams A, Cloke P and Cherry L (2019) Welfare convergence, bureaucracy, and moral distancing at the food bank. *Antipode* 51(4): 1251–1275.

May J, Williams A, Cloke P and Cherry L (2020) Food banks and the production of scarcity. *Transactions of the Institute of British Geographers* 45(1): 208–222.

Mayer T and Anderson M (2020) Food insecurity in context. In: Anderson M and Mayer T (eds) *Food Insecurity: A Matter of Justice, Sovereignty, and Survival*. London: Routledge, pp 1–28.

McGlone P, Dobson B, Dowler E and Nelson M (1999) *Food projects and how they work*. Joseph Rowntree Foundation. Available at: https://www.jrf.org.uk/report/food-projects-and-how-they-work

McKinney K (2005) *Being White: Stories of Race and Racism*. New York, NY: Routledge

McLoughlin S (2005) Mosques and the public space: Conflict and cooperation in Bradford. *Journal of Ethnic and Migration Studies* 31(6): 1045–1066.

McMichael P (2005) Global development and the corporate food regime. In: Buttel FH and McMichael P (eds) *New Directions in the Sociology of Global Development*. Research in Rural Sociology and Development, Vol 11. Bingley: Emerald Group Publishing, pp 269–303.

McNay L (2009) Self as enterprise: Dilemmas of control and resistance in Foucault's 'The Birth of Biopolitics'. *Theory, Culture & Society* 26(6): 55–77.

Mellin-Olsen T and Wandel M (2005) Changes in food habits among Pakistani Immigrant Women in Oslo, Norway. *Ethnicity & Health* 10(4): 311–339.

Milbourne L and Cushman M (2015) Complying, transforming or resisting in the new austerity? Realigning social welfare and independent action among English voluntary organisations. *Journal of Social Policy* 44(3): 463–485.

Miles R (1989) *Racism*. London: Routledge.

Millar J and Glendinning C (1992) 'It all really starts in the family': Gender divisions and poverty. In: Glendinning C and Millar J (eds) *Women and Poverty in Britain the 1990s*. Hemel Hempstead: Harvester Wheatsheaf, pp 3–10.

Mitchell BR and Dean P (1962) *Abstract of British Historical Statistics*. Cambridge: Cambridge University Press.

Mobilization for Justice (2021) *Housing: Three-Quarter House Tenants*. Available at: https://mobilizationforjustice.org/projects/illegal-boarding-house-project/

Modood T and Berthoud R (1997) Ethnic minorities in Britain: Diversity and disadvantage. *The Fourth National Survey of Ethnic Minorities*. London: Policy Studies Institute.

Moisander J, Groß C and Eräranta K (2018) Mechanisms of biopower and neoliberal governmentality in precarious work: Mobilizing the dependent self-employed as independent business owners. *Human Relations* 71(3): 375–398.

Möller C (2021) Discipline and feed: Food banks, pastoral power, and the medicalisation of poverty in the UK. *Sociological Research Online* 26(4): 853–870. doi: 10.1177/1360780420982625.

Morgan DL (1997) *Focus Groups as Qualitative Research*. Thousand Oaks, CA: Sage.

Morrison T (1992) *Playing in the Dark: Whiteness and the Literary Imagination*. Cambridge, MA: Harvard University Press.

Muehlebach A (2012) *The Moral Neoliberal: Welfare and Citizenship in Italy*. Chicago, IL: University of Chicago Press.

Murray C (1994) *Underclass: The crisis deepens*. London: IEA Health and Welfare Unit in association with The Sunday Times.

Murray C (1996) The emerging British underclass. In: Lister R (ed) *Charles Murray and the Underclass: The Developing Debate*. London: IEA Health and Welfare Unit, pp 25–53.

Nagel J (1994) Constructing ethnicity: Creating and recreating ethnic identity and culture. *Social Problems* 41(1): 152–176.

NAO (National Audit Office) (2016) *Benefit sanctions*. London: National Audit Office. Available at: https://www.nao.org.uk/report/benefit-sanctions/

National Union of Students (2015) *Preventing PREVENT*. Available at: https://www.nusconnect.org.uk/campaigns/preventing-prevent-we-are-students-not-suspects

Nazroo JY (1998) Genetic, cultural or socio-economic vulnerability? Explaining ethnic inequalities in health. *Sociology of Health & Illness* 20(5): 710–730.

Nazroo JY (2003) The structuring of ethnic inequalities in health: Economic position, racial discrimination, and racism. *American Journal of Public Health* 93(2): 277–284.

Nettleton S (1997) Governing the risky self: How to become healthy, wealthy and wise. In: Petersen A and Bunton R (eds) *Foucault, Health and Medicine*. London: Routledge, pp 371–398.

Newby L and Denison N (2012) *A better York for everyone: An independent report by the York Fairness Commission to the City of York.* Available at: https://equalitytrust.org.uk/sites/default/files/York%20Fairness.pdf

Nnakwe NE (2008) Dietary patterns and prevalence of food insecurity among low-income families participating in community food assistance programs in a Midwest town. *Family and Consumer Sciences Research Journal* 36(3): 229–242.

Nyman M (2019) Food, meaning-making and ontological uncertainty: Exploring 'urban foraging' and productive landscapes in London. *GeoForum* 99: 170—80.

O'Connor N, Farag K and Baines R (2016) What is food poverty? A conceptual framework. *British Food Journal* 118(2): 429–449.

O'Connell R and Brannen J (2021) *Families and Food in Hard Times: European Comparative Perspective.* London: UCL Press.

Olssen M (2000) Ethical liberalism, education and the 'New Right'. *Journal of Education Policy* 15(5): 481–508.

Olusoga D (2016) *Black and British.* London: Pan Books.

Omi M and Winant H (2014) *Racial Formation in the United States.* New York, NY: Routledge.

ONS (2011) 2011 Census: Key statistics. Nomis. Available at: https://www.nomisweb.co.uk/sources/census_2011_ks

ONS (2016) *Dataset: Towns and cities analysis.* Available at: https://www.ons.gov.uk/peoplepopulationandcommunity/housing/datasets/townsandcitiesanalysis

ONS (2019) *Household income inequality, UK: Financial year ending 2019.* Available at: https://www.ons.gov.uk/peoplepopulationandcommunity/personalandhouseholdfinances/incomeandwealth/bulletins/householdincomeinequalityfinancial/financialyearending2019

ONS (2020) *Births in England and Wales: 2020.* Available at: https://www.ons.gov.uk/peoplepopulationandcommunity/birthsdeathsandmarriages/livebirths/bulletins/birthsummarytablesenglandandwales/2020#live-births-and-fertility-rates

Orwell G ([1933] 2001) *Down and Out in Paris and London.* London: Penguin.

Osborne G (2010) *Our tough but fair approach to welfare.* Available at: https://conservative-speeches.sayit.mysociety.org/speech/601446

Oxford English Dictionary (2021) *Caritas.* Available at: https://www.lexico.com/definition/caritas

Paret M and Gleeson S (2016) Precarity and agency through a migration lens. *Citizenship Studies* 20(3–4): 277–294.

Parveen N (2021) Priti Patel hits out at 'dreadful' Black Lives Matter protests. *The Guardian*, 12 February. Available at: https://www.theguardian.com/politics/2021/feb/12/priti-patel-hits-out-at-dreadful-black-lives-matters-protests

Pascall G (1986) *Social Policy: A Feminist Analysis.* London: Tavistock.

Patel R (2009) Food sovereignty. *The Journal of Peasant Studies* 36(3): 663–706.

Patrick R (2012) Work as the primary 'duty' of the responsible citizen: A critique of this work-centric approach. *People, Place & Policy Online* 6(1): 5–15.

Peck J (2008) Remaking laissez-faire. *Progress in Human Geography* 32(1): 3–43.

Peck J (2010) *Constructions of Neoliberal Reason.* Oxford: Oxford University Press.

Peck J and Tickell A (2002) Neoliberalizing space. *Antipode* 34(3): 380–404.

Pemberton CR (2020) *Bread of Life in Broken Britain: Food Banks, Faith and Neoliberalism.* London: SCM Press.

Perry J, Sefton T, Williams M and Haddad M (2014) *Emergency use only: Understanding and reducing the use of food banks in the UK.* Available at: https://cpag.org.uk/sites/default/files/Foodbank%20Report_web.pdf

Popay J (1989) Poverty and plenty: Women's experiences across social classes. In: Graham H and Popay J (eds) *Women and Poverty: Exploring the Research and Policy Agenda.* London: Thomas Coram Research Institute Unit/Warwick: University of Warwick, pp 33–58.

Poppendieck J (1999) *Sweet Charity? Emergency Food and the End of Entitlement.* New York, NY: Penguin.

Poppendieck J (2014) Food assistance, hunger and the end of welfare in the USA. In: Riches G and Silvasti T (eds) *First World Hunger Revisited: Food Charity or the Right to Food?* 2nd edn. New York: Palgrave MacMillan, pp 176–190.

Power EM (2005) The unfreedom of being Other: Canadian lone mothers' experiences of poverty and 'life on the cheque'. *Sociology* 39(4): 643–660.

Power MS (2019) Seeking justice: *How to understand and end food poverty in York.* York Food Justice Alliance. Available at: https://yorkfoodpover ty.files.wordpress.com/2019/07/seeking-justice-how-to-understand-and-end-food-poverty-in-york-4.pdf

Power M and Small N (2022) Disciplinary and pastoral power, food and poverty in late-modernity. *Critical Social Policy* 42(1): 43–63. doi: 10.1177/0261018321999799.

Power M, Uphoff E, Kelly B and Pickett KE (2017a) Food insecurity and mental health: An analysis of routine primary care data of pregnant women in the Born in Bradford cohort. *Journal of Epidemiology and Community Health* 71(4): 324–328.

Power M, Doherty B, Small N, Teasdale S and Pickett KE (2017b) All in it together? Community food aid in a multi-ethnic context. *Journal of Social Policy* 46(3): 447–471.

Power M, Small N, Doherty B, Stewart-Knox B and Pickett KE (2017c) 'Bringing heaven down to earth': The purpose and place of religion in UK food aid. *Social Enterprise Journal* 13(3): 251–267.

Power M, Uphoff E, Stewart-Knox B, Small N, Doherty B and Pickett KE (2017d) Food insecurity and socio-demographic characteristics in two UK ethnic groups: An analysis of women in the Born in Bradford cohort. *Journal of Public Health.* 40(1): 32–40. doi: 10.1093/pubmed/fdx029.

Power M, Small N, Doherty B and Pickett KE (2018a) Hidden hunger? Experiences of food insecurity amongst Pakistani and white British women. *British Food Journal* 120(11): 2716–2732.

Power MS, Small N, Doherty B, Stewart-Knox, B and Pickett KE (2018b) Is food insecurity associated with maternal health among UK ethnic groups? An exploration of women in the BiB cohort. *European Journal of Public Health* 28(4): 661–663.

Power M, Page G, Garthwaite K and Patrick, R (2020a) COVID realities – Experiences of social security for families on a low income during the pandemic. Available at: https://covidrealities.org/learnings/write-ups/socialsecurity

Power M, Patrick R, Garthwaite K and Page, G (2020b) COVID realities – Everyday life for families on a low income during the pandemic. Available at: https://covidrealities.org/learnings/write-ups/exploratory-study

Power M, Small N, Doherty B and Pickett KE (2020c) The incompatibility of system and lifeworld understandings of food insecurity and the provision of food aid in an English city. *VOLUNTAS: International Journal of Voluntary and Nonprofit Organizations* 31: 907–922.

Power M, Pybus K, Doherty B and Pickett KE (2021a) 'The reality is that on Universal Credit I cannot provide the recommended amount of fresh fruit and vegetables per day for my children': Moving from a behavioural to a systemic understanding of food practices. *Emerald Open Research* 3(3): 14062.

Power M, Goodwin S, Marshall M, Woods D, Babbs S, McIntosh K and Beck D (2021b) *Structural inequalities and the growing need for food aid.* Independent Food Aid Network. Available at: https://uploads.strikinglycdn.com/files/5b30e122-d1e5-47b7-8259-2001fdba20ec/IFANYORK%20Webinar%20Briefing%20-%20Final%20Version%2016.02.21.pdf

Poynter JR (1969) *Society and Pauperism: English Ideas on Poor Relief, 1795–1834.* London: Routledge & Kegan Paul.

Prayogo E, Chater A, Chapman S, Barker M, Rahmawati N, Waterfall T et al (2017) Who uses foodbanks and why? Exploring the impact of financial strain and adverse life events on food insecurity. *Journal of Public Health* 40(4): 676–683.

Prest AR and Adams AA (1954) *Consumers' Expenditure in the United Kingdom, 1900–1919.* Cambridge: Cambridge University Press.

Priestley JB (1934) *English Journey*. London: Heinemann.

Purdam K, Esmail A and Garratt E (2019) Food insecurity amongst older people in the UK. *British Food Journal* 121(3): 658–674.

Pybus K, Power M and Pickett KE (2021) 'We are constantly overdrawn, despite not spending money on anything other than bills and food': A mixed-methods, participatory study of food and insecurity in the context of income inequality. *Journal of Poverty and Social Justice* 29(1): 21–45.

Radandt NE, Corbridge T, Johnson DB, Kim AS, Scott JM, and Coldwell SE (2018) Validation of a two-item food security screening tool in a dental setting. *Journal of Dentistry for Children* 85(3): 114–119.

Ray L, Smith D (2004) Racist offending, policing and community conflict. *Sociology* 38(4): 681–699. doi:10.1177/0038038504045859.

Reed H and Portes J (2014) Cumulative impact assessment: A research report by Landman Economics and the National Institute of Economic and Social Research (NIESR) for the Equality and Human Rights Commission. Available at: https://www.equalityhumanrights.com/sites/default/files/research-report-94-cumulative-impact-assessment.pdf

Reeves A and Loopstra R (2020) The continuing effects of welfare reform on food bank use in the UK: The roll-out of Universal Credit. *Journal of Social Policy*. Epub ahead of print 2020/09/11. doi:10.1017/S0047279420000513, pp 1–21.

Rhodes J (2013) Remaking whiteness in the 'postracial' UK. In: Kapoor N, Kalra VS and Rhodes J (eds) *The State of Race*. London: Palgrave Macmillan, pp 49–71.

Riches G (2011) Thinking and acting outside the charitable food box: Hunger and the right to food in rich societies. *Development in Practice* 21(4–5): 768–775.

Riches G (2018) *Food Bank Nations: Poverty, Corporate Charity and the Right to Food*. Oxon: Routledge.

Riches G and Silvasti (2014a) *First World Hunger Revisited: Food Charity or the Right to Food?* London: Palgrave Macmillan.

Riches G and Silvasti T (2014b) Hunger in the rich world: Food aid and right to food perspectives. In: Riches G and Silvasti T (eds) *First World Hunger Revisited: Food Charity or the Right to Food?* 2nd edn. London: Palgrave Macmillan, pp 1–14

Riches G and Tarasuk V (2014) Canada: Thirty years of food charity and public policy neglect. In: Riches G and Silvasti T (eds) *First World Hunger Revisited: Food Charity or the Right to Food?* 2nd edn. London: Palgrave Macmillan, pp 42–56.

Riggins SH (1997) The rhetoric of othering. In: Riggins SH (ed) *The Language and Politics of Exclusion*. Thousand Oaks, CA: Sage, pp 1–30.

Ritchie D (2001) *Oldham Independent Review Panel Report*. Available at: http://image.guardian.co.uk/sys-files/Guardian/documents/2001/12/11/Oldhamindependentreview.pdf

Rose N (1992) Governing the enterprising self. In: Heelas P and Morris P (eds) *The Values of the Enterprise Culture*. London: Routledge, pp 141–164.

Sacks J (1991) *The Persistence of Faith: Religion, Morality and Society in a Secular Age*. Frome and London: Butler and Tanner Ltd.

Saher R and Stephens LS (2005) Serving up sermons: Clients' reactions to religious elements at congregation-run feeding establishments. *Nonprofit and Voluntary Sector Quarterly* 34(3): 297–315.

Saldanha A (2006) Reontologising race: The machinic geography of phenotype. *Environment and Planning D: Society and Space* 24(1): 9–24.

Salonen AS (2016a) Lifelong emergency? The food bank in an era of institutionalized food charity in Toronto. *Diaconia* 7(1): 27–42.

Salonen AS (2016b) Locating religion in the context of charitable food assistance: An ethnographic study of food banks in a Finnish city. *Journal of Contemporary Religion* 31(1): 35–50.

Salonen AS (2016c) 'You can vote with your feet if you want': Users' responses to religious services in the context of food charity in a Finnish city. *Social Compass* 63(1): 109–124.

Salvation Army (2021) *Emergency assistance*. Available at: https://www.salvationarmy.org.uk/budget-and-debt-advice/emergency-assistance.

Sayer A (2005) *The Moral Significance of Class*. Cambridge: Cambridge University Press.

Sbicca J and Myers JS (2017) Food justice racial projects: Fighting racial neoliberalism from the Bay to the Big Apple. *Environmental Sociology* 3(1): 30–41.

Senior PA and Bhopal R (1994) Ethnicity as a variable in epidemiological research. *British Medical Journal (Clinical research edition)* 309(6950): 327–330.

Shah S (2004) The researcher/interviewer in intercultural context: A social intruder! *British Educational Research Journal* 30(4): 549–575.

Shilliam R (2018) *Race and the Undeserving Poor: From Abolition to Brexit*. Newcastle upon Tyne: Agenda Publishing.

Shipman T (2014) Food bank charity 'is misleading the public': Claim that 1m need food parcels 'just self promotion'. *Daily Mail*, 17 April. Available at: https://www.dailymail.co.uk/news/article-2606573/Food-bank-charity-misleading-public-Claim-1m-need-food-parcels-just-self-promotion.html

Siddiqui M (2015) *Hospitality and Islam: Welcoming in God's Name*. New Haven, CT: Yale University Press.

Silvasti T and Karjalainen J (2014) Hunger in a Nordic welfare state: Finland. In: Riches G and Silvasti T (eds) *First World Hunger Revisited: Food Charity or the Right to Food?* 2nd edn. London: Palgrave Macmillan, pp 72–86.

Sime D (2008) Ethical and methodological issues in engaging young people living in poverty with participatory research methods. *Children's Geographies* 6(1): 63–78.

Singh J (2015) From the temple to the street: How Sikh kitchens are becoming the new food banks. *The Conversation*, 22 July. Available at: https://theconversation.com/from-the-temple-to-the-street-how-sikh-kitchens-are-becoming-the-new-food-banks-44611

Sitrin M and Sembrar C (2020) *Pandemic Solidarity: Mutual Aid during the Covid-19 Crisis.* London: Pluto Press.

Skeggs B (1997) *Formations of Class & Gender: Becoming Respectable.* Thousand Oaks, CA: Sage.

Skeggs B (2019) The forces that shape us: The entangled vine of gender, race and class. *The Sociological Review* 67(1): 28–35.

Slocum R (2006) Anti-racist practice and the work of community food organizations. *Antipode* 38(2): 327–349.

Slocum R (2007) Whiteness, space and alternative food practice. *Geoforum* 38(3): 520–533.

Slocum R (2010) Race in the study of food. *Progress in Human Geography* 35(3): 303–327.

Small N (2012) Infant mortality and migrant health in babies of Pakistani origin born in Bradford, UK. *Journal of Intercultural Studies* 33(5): 549–564.

Smith D (2020) 'America v socialism': Conservatives rage against the left and plot new red scare. *The Guardian*, 1 March. Available at: https://www.theguardian.com/us-news/2020/mar/01/trump-conservatives-socialism-bernie-sanders-politics

Smith D, Thompson C, Harland K, Parker, S and Shelton N (2018) Identifying populations and areas at greatest risk of household food insecurity in England. *Applied Geography* 91: 21–31.

Social Metrics Commission (2020) *Measuring Poverty 2020: A report of the Social Metrics Commission.* Available at: https://socialmetricscommission.org.uk/measuring-poverty-2020/

Sosenko F, Littlewood M, Bramley G, Fitzpatrick S, Blenkinsopp J and Wood J (2019) *State of Hunger: A study of poverty and food insecurity in the UK.* The Trussell Trust. Available at: https://www.stateofhunger.org/wp-content/uploads/2019/11/State-of-Hunger-Report-November2019-Digital. pdf

Spade D (2020) *Mutual Aid: Building Solidarity during the Crisis.* New York, NY: Verso.

Standing G (2011) *The Precariat: The New Dangerous Class.* London: Bloomsbury Academic.

StataCorp (2019) *Stata statistical software: Release 16.* College Station, TX: StataCorp LLC.

Stewart K and Reader M (no date) *The impact of the Health in Pregnancy Grant.* Available at: https://sticerd.lse.ac.uk/case/_new/research/ HPG/

Strong S (2019) The vital politics of foodbanking: Hunger, austerity, biopower. *Political Geography* 75: 102053.

Sue DW, Capodilupo CM, Torino GC, Bucceri JM, Holder AMB, Nadal KL and Esquilin M (2007) Racial microaggressions in everyday life: implications for clinical practice. *American Psychologist* 62(4): 271–286.

Sustain (2021) *Types of Community Food Projects.* Available at: https://www.sustainweb.org/sauce/types_of_community_food_projects/

Syal R (2021) Equalities minister Kemi Badenoch must apologise or be sacked, says peer. *The Guardian*, 5 February. Available at: https://www.theguardian.com/politics/2021/feb/05/equalities-minister-kemi-badenoch-must-apologise-or-be-sacked-says-peer

Tait C (2015) *Hungry for Change: The final report of the Fabian Commission on Food and Poverty.* Available at: https://fabians.org.uk/publication/hungry-for-change/

Tarasuk V and Eakin JM (2003) Charitable food assistance as symbolic gesture: An ethnographic study of food banks in Ontario. *Social Science & Medicine* 56(7): 1505–1515.

Taylor-Gooby P and Stoker G (2011) The Coalition Programme: A new vision for Britain or politics as usual? *The Political Quarterly* 82(1): 4–15.

Teddlie C and Tashakkori A (2009) *Foundations of Mixed Methods Research: Integrating Quantitative and Qualitative Approaches in the Behavioural Sciences.* London: Sage.

The Care Collective (2020) *The Care Manifesto: The Politics of Interdependence.* New York, NY: Verso.

Thompson E, Jitendra A and Rabindrakumar S (2019) *Five weeks too long: Why we need to end the wait for Universal Credit.* The Trussell Trust. Available at: https://www.trusselltrust.org/wp-content/uploads/sites/2/2019/09/PolicyReport_Final_ForWeb.pdf

Truss L (2020) *'Fight For Fairness' speech to set out government's new approach to equality.* Government Equalities Office. Available at: https://www.gov.uk/government/news/fight-for-fairness-speech-to-set-out-governments-new-approach-to-equality

Trussell Trust (2015) *Eleven foodbank myths you must not fall for.* Available at: https://www.trusselltrust.org/2015/04/24/eleven-foodbank-myths-you-must-not-fall-for/

Trussell Trust (2019) *Head of Church Engagement: Applicant information pack.* Available at: https://www.trusselltrust.org/wp-content/uploads/sites/2/2019/02/Head-of-Church-Engagement.pdf

Trussell Trust (2020a) *End of Year Stats.* Available at: https://www.trusselltrust.org/news-and-blog/latest-stats/end-year-stats/

Trussell Trust (2020b) *Preparing a Network for Change: Annual Report and Accounts 31 March 2020.* Available at: https://www.trusselltrust.org/wp-content/uploads/sites/2/2020/12/Annual_Report_and_Accounts_2020_web.pdf

Trussell Trust (2021a) *Food Vouchers*. Available at: https://www.trusselltrust.org/get-help/emergency-food/food-vouchers/#:~:text=Referral%20process.%20Each%20food%20bank%20works%20with%20different,offer%20practical%20guidance%20and%20prepare%20suitable%20emergency%20food

Trussell Trust (2021b) *Cisco*. Available at: https://www.trusselltrust.org/get-involved/partner-with-us/strategic-partners/cisco/

Trussell Trust (2021c) *Emergency food*. Available at: https://www.trusselltrust.org/get-help/emergency-food/

Trussell Trust (2021d) *If you need emergency food or support*. Available at: https://www.trusselltrust.org/coronavirus-food-banks/emergency-support/

Tyler I (2013) *Revolting Subjects: Social Abjection and Resistance in Neoliberal Britain*. London: Zed Books.

Tyler I and Slater T (2018) Rethinking the sociology of stigma. *The Sociological Review* 66(4): 721–743.

Ulmer M (2014) *Righteous Giving to the Poor: Tzedakah ('Charity') in Classical Rabbinic Judaism*. Piscataway, NJ: Gorgias Press.

UN General Assembly (1974) Universal Declaration on the Eradication of Hunger and Malnutrition (16 November). Available at: https://www.ohchr.org/en/professionalinterest/pages/eradicationofhungerandmalnutrition.aspx

Valluvan S and Kapoor N (2016) Notes on theorizing racism and other things. *Ethnic and Racial Studies* 39(3): 375–382.

van der Horst H, Pascucci S and Bol W (2014) The 'dark side' of food banks? Exploring emotional responses of food bank receivers in the Netherlands. *British Food Journal* 116(9): 1506–1520.

Vernon J (2007) *Hunger: A Modern History*. Cambridge, MA: Harvard University Press.

Wacquant LJD (2009) *Punishing the Poor: The Neoliberal Government of Social Insecurity*. Durham, NC; London: Duke University Press.

Walker R (2005) *Social Security and Welfare: Concepts and Comparisons*. Milton Keynes: Open University Press.

Ward R (1978) Race relations in Britain. *The British Journal of Sociology* 29(4): 464–480.

Washington H (2006) *Medical Apartheid: The Dark History of Medical Experimentation on Black Americans from Colonial Times to the Present*. New York, NY: Harlem Moon.

Weber M ([1905] 2002) *The Protestant Ethic and the Spirit of Capitalism*. New York, NY; London: Penguin Books.

Wells R and Caraher M (2014) UK print media coverage of the food bank phenomenon: From food welfare to food charity? *British Food Journal* 116(9): 1426–1445.

Whitworth A (2016) Neoliberal paternalism and paradoxical subjects: Confusion and contradiction in UK activation policy. *Critical Social Policy* 36(3): 412–431.

Wilkinson S (2004) Focus group research. In: Silverman D (ed) *Qualitative Research: Theory, Method, and Practice*. Thousand Oaks, CA: Sage, pp 177–199.

Williams A, Cloke P and Thomas S (2012) Co-constituting neoliberalism: Faith-based organisations, co-option, and resistance in the UK. *Environment and Planning A: Economy and Space* 44(6): 1479–1501.

Williams A, Cloke P, May J and Cherry L (2016) Contested space: The contradictory political dynamics of food banking in the UK. *Environment and Planning A: Economy and Space* 48(11): 2291–2316.

Wilson AD (2013) Beyond alternative: Exploring the potential for autonomous food spaces. *Antipode* 45(3): 719–737.

Wilson WJ (2009) Foreword: The Moynihan Report and research on the Black community. *The Annals of the American Academy of Political and Social Science* 621: 34–46.

Wolton S (2006) Immigration policy and the 'crisis of British values'. *Citizenship Studies* 10(4): 453–467.

Women's Budget Group (2017) *Intersecting inequalities: The impact of austerity on Black and Minority Ethnic women in the UK*. Available at: https://wbg.org.uk/wp-content/uploads/2018/08/Intersecting-Inequalities-October-2017-Full-Report.pdf

Women's Budget Group (2020) *Health inequalities and Covid-19: Policy briefings on coronavirus and inequalities*. Available at: https://wbg.org.uk/analysis/uk-policy-briefings/health-inequalities-and-covid-19/

Wood V (2020) Teachers presenting white privilege as fact are breaking the law, minister warns. *The Independent*, 21 October. Available at: https://www.independent.co.uk/news/uk/politics/kemi-badenoch-black-history-month-white-privilege-black-lives-matter-b1189547.html

Wright J, Small N, Raynor P, Tuffnell D, Bhopal R, Cameron N et al (2012) Cohort profile: The Born in Bradford multi-ethnic family cohort study. *International Journal of Epidemiology* 42(4): 978–991.

Wright S, Fletcher DR and Stewart ABR (2020) Punitive benefit sanctions, welfare conditionality, and the social abuse of unemployed people in Britain: Transforming claimants into offenders? *Social Policy & Administration* 54(2): 278–294.

York Food Justice Alliance (2021) *About Us*. Available at: https://yorkfoodpoverty.org/about-us/

Young J (2003) Merton with energy, Katz with structure: The sociology of vindictiveness and the criminology of transgression. *Theoretical Criminology* 7(3): 389–414.

Index

References to endnotes show both the page number
and the note number (231n3).

L

Labour Party 138 *see also* New Labour
landlords 137, 149
langar 61–62
language 16n3, 98, 122, 138, 147, 164–165
law 26, 55, 63, 77, 89, 103, 108, 139, 142, 149, 151
laziness 50–51
leadership 41, 64–65, 90, 131, 151
Leeds 10, 86, 156, 158
LGBTQ+ 135
liberalism 19–20, 24, 110n1
libertarian paternalism 39
life expectancy 9, 11, 89
Lions Club 67–68
living costs 11, 16, 45, 98, 100
local authority 9, 12, 13, 40, 50–52, 59n16, 66, 67, 145, 167
local government 30, 40–45, 47, 57, 58, 74
Local Housing Allowance 11
lockdown 46
Long, Edward 94
low wages 2, 27, 100, 103, 115, 139

M

making ends meet 121
manufacturing 10, 117
Martin, Trayvon 35
Marxism 23, 35n1, 64
maternal health 13
maternity leave 58n8, 111n3
Maximus 102
means-tested benefits 38, 59n11, 95, 98, 110n3, 115, 158–160
mental health 43, 69, 71, 111n7, 149
Mexico 35n7
micro aggression 88
Middle Ages 10
Midland Langar Seva Society 61
migration 7–9, 13, 117, 122–126
minimum wage 38, 58n5, 140
minority ethnic group (community) 65, 82–86, 90, 113–116, 128, 129, 135n1, n3, 136n7, 143–144
moralism 39, 52, 54, 56, 58
morality 25, 32, 33, 78
Morrison, Toni 28
mosque 9, 12, 25, 40, 66, 67, 74
motherhood 127, 134, 145, 156–160
motivation 12, 55, 61, 67, 70, 73–77, 81, 87–89, 139, 171
multiculturalism 26
Mumford, Catherine 69
Muslim 2, 9–10, 14, 26, 28, 34, 35n5, 39, 61–63, 66–68, 71, 84–87, 94, 107, 118,

124–125, 128, 136n5, 142–143, 162 *see also* Islam
mutual aid 3, 16, 18, 31–33, 54, 112, 125, 128–129, 132–135, 138, 140, 142

N

National Health Service (NHS) 137, 153, 156, 158–161
National Insurance Act 55
nationality 29, 94
Native American 113, 151
Neighbors Together 148–150
neoconservative 27, 35n3
neoliberalism 15, 16n3, n4, n5, 17n8, 18–20, 26–28, 33, 47, 49, 64, 92, 94, 100, 103, 132–133, 140, 144, 154
roll-out 20
Newcastle 10
New Labour 38, 58n5
New Testament 63
New York City 148–149
NGO 30, 150, 152
no recourse to public funds (NRPF) 91n4, 147
North Africa 10, 26
Northern Ireland 46, 59n9
nutrition 3, 7, 30, 52, 87, 97, 145, 155n5, 161, 164
Nvivo 10 162, 166

O

obedience 20–23, 52, 107, 109, 142
Old Testament 63
Olusoga, David 10
Orwell, George 77
Osborne, George 37, 56, 57, 83
Othering 21, 22, 94
outgoings 43, 97, 98, 144

P

Pakistani 75, 107, 110, 112–118, 120–128, 134, 135n2, n3, 145, 156, 160, 165, 172n1
women 110, 112, 114, 120, 134, 156, 158, 172n1
pandemic *see* COVID-19
panopticism 20
parents 10, 13, 18, 89, 95–98, 101–107, 112, 188, 121, 127, 137, 168, 169
lone 1, 44, 97, 98, 101, 115, 130–132, 137, 146
paternalism 23, 39, 52, 93, 99, 146
pastoral power 21, 23, 104, 109, 147 *see also* pastorship
pastorship 21, 109, 110
pauperisation 107
Pay-as-you-feel (PAYF) 5, 12, 37, 52–55
payday 32, 118
Pearson chi-square test 156, 158, 160

Printed and bound by CPI Group (UK) Ltd, Croydon, CR0 4YY

09/06/2025

14685899-0002